AQA Certificate in Physics (iGCSE) Level 1/2

SCIENCE

Jim Breithaupt

Editor
Lawrie Ryan

REVISION GUIDE

C901488889

7 Day Loan

D0178988

Nelson Thornes

Text © Jim Breithaupt and Pauline Anning 2013
Original illustrations © Nelson Thornes Ltd 2013

The right of Jim Breithaupt and Pauline Anning to be identified as authors
of this work has been asserted by them in accordance with the Copyright,
Designs and Patents Act 1988.

All rights reserved. No part of this publication may be reproduced or
transmitted in any form or by any means, electronic or mechanical,
including photocopy, recording or any information storage and retrieval
system, without permission in writing from the publisher or under licence
from the Copyright Licensing Agency Limited, of Saffron House,
6–10 Kirby Street, London, EC1N 8TS.

Any person who commits any unauthorised act in relation to this
publication may be liable to criminal prosecution and civil claims for
damages.

This edition published in 2013 by:
Nelson Thornes Ltd
Delta Place
27 Bath Road
CHELTENHAM
GL53 7TH
United Kingdom

13 14 15 16 17 / 10 9 8 7 6 5 4 3 2

A catalogue record for this book is available from the British Library

ISBN 978 1 4085 2117 5

Cover photograph: iStockphoto
Page make-up by Wearset Ltd. Boldon, Tyne and Wear

Printed and bound in Spain by GraphyCems

Photo acknowledgements
P3.2.1 AFP/Getty Images; P6.6.2 Cordelia Molloy/Science Photo Library;
P7.5.2 Berenice Abbott/Science Photo Library; P8.5.1 Czardases/
iStockphoto; P10.2.2 Pasieka/Science Photo Library; P12.2.1 Mark
Garlick/Science Photo Library; P12.2.2 NASA/Science Photo Library;
P14.6.1 Jack F/iStockphoto.

iGCSE Physics — Contents

Welcome to AQA Level 1/2 Certificate in Physics

Key points

At the start of each topic are the important points that you must remember.

Maths skills

This feature highlights the maths skills that you will need for your Science exams with short, visual explanations.

⬤⬤ links

Links will tell you where you can find more information about what you are learning and how different topics link up.

This book has been written for you by very experienced teachers and subject experts. It covers everything you need to revise for your exams and is packed full of features to help you achieve the very best that you can.

Key words are highlighted in the text. You can look them up in the glossary at the back of the book if you are not sure what they mean.

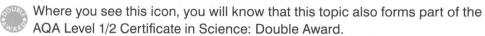 Where you see this icon, you will know that this topic also forms part of the AQA Level 1/2 Certificate in Science: Double Award.

⟫ *These questions check that you understand what you're learning as you go along. The answers are all at the back of the book.*

Many diagrams are as important for you to learn as the text, so make sure you revise them carefully.

Study tip

Study tips give you important advice on things to remember and what to watch out for.

Practical

This feature helps you become familiar with key practicals. It may be a simple introduction, a reminder or the basis for a practical in the classroom.

At the end of each chapter you will find:

End of chapter questions

These questions will test you on what you have learned throughout the whole chapter, helping you to work out what you have understood and what you need to go back and revise.

And at the end of each unit you will find:

Examination-style questions

These questions are examples of the types of questions you will answer in your actual examination, so you can get lots of practice during your course.

You can find answers to the End of chapter and Examination-style questions at the back of the book.

Student's book
pages 2–3

P1.1

Distance–time graphs

Key points

- The gradient of a distance–time graph for an object represents the object's speed.
- Speed, m/s, = $\dfrac{\text{distance travelled in metres, m}}{\text{time taken seconds, s}}$

Key words: speed, gradient

We can use graphs to help us describe the motion of a body.

A distance–time graph shows the distance of a body from a starting point (*y*-axis) against time taken (*x*-axis).

- The **speed** of a body is the distance travelled each second. The **gradient** of the line on a distance–time graph represents speed. The steeper the gradient, the greater the speed.

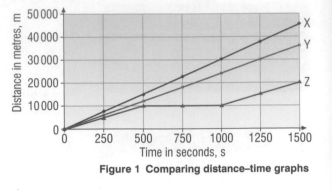

Figure 1 Comparing distance–time graphs

- If an object is stationary, the line on a distance–time graph is horizontal.
- If a body is moving at a constant speed, the line on a distance–time graph is a straight line that slopes upwards.
- Figure 1 shows the speed of three vehicles X, Y and Z.

> 1 a *What can you say about the speed of X compared with the speed of Y?*
>   b *What can you say about the speed of Z compared with the speed of Y?*

> 2 a *Calculate the speed of Y in Figure 1.*
>   b *Calculate the average speed of Z in Figure 1 over 1500 s.*

We can calculate the speed of a body using the equation:

speed in metres per second, m/s = $\dfrac{\text{distance travelled in metres, m}}{\text{time taken in seconds, s}}$

This can be written as speed $v = \dfrac{s}{t}$ where s is the distance travelled in time t.

Rearranging this equation gives $s = vt$ or $t = \dfrac{s}{v}$

Student's book
pages 4–5

P1.2

Velocity and acceleration

Key points

- Velocity is speed in a given direction.
- A vector is a physical quantity that has a direction as well as a magnitude.
- A scalar is a physical quantity that has a magnitude only and does not have a direction.
- Displacement is distance in a given direction.
- Acceleration is change of velocity per second. The unit of acceleration is the metre per second squared (m/s²).
- Deceleration is the change of velocity per second when an object slows down.

Key words: velocity, acceleration, deceleration

- The **velocity** of an object is its speed in a given direction. If the object changes direction it changes velocity, even if its speed stays the same.
- If the velocity of a body changes, we say that it accelerates.
- Velocity is a vector because it has direction as well as magnitude. Speed is a scalar because it is non-directional. See topic P2.3 for more about vectors.

> 1 *What is the difference between speed and velocity?*

We can calculate **acceleration** using the equation

acceleration = $\dfrac{\text{change in velocity}}{\text{time taken for the change}}$ or $a = \dfrac{v - u}{t}$

where a is the acceleration in metres per second squared, m/s²
  v is the final velocity in metres per second, m/s
  u is the initial velocity in metres per second, m/s
  t is the time taken for the change in seconds, s.

The above equation can be rearranged to give $v = u + at$

> 2 *A passenger jet taking off accelerated from rest to a velocity of 120 m/s in 50 seconds. Calculate its acceleration.*

Study tip

Be sure to learn the units here carefully. Don't confuse m/s (unit of speed and velocity) and m/s² (unit of acceleration).

If the value calculated for acceleration is negative, the body is decelerating (slowing down). A **deceleration** is the same as a negative acceleration.

P1.3

More about velocity–time graphs

A velocity–time graph shows the velocity of an object (*y*-axis) against time taken (*x*-axis).

- The gradient of the line on a velocity–time graph represents acceleration.
- The steeper the gradient, the greater the acceleration.
- If the line on a velocity–time graph is horizontal, the acceleration is zero. Therefore the object is travelling at a steady speed.
- If the gradient of the line is negative, the object is decelerating.
- The area under the line on a velocity–time graph represents the distance travelled in a given time. The bigger the area, the greater the distance travelled.

Key points

- If the line on a velocity–time graph is horizontal, the acceleration is zero.
- The gradient of a velocity–time graph represents acceleration.
- The area under the line on a velocity–time graph represents distance travelled.

> 1 *What would the velocity–time graph look like for* **a** *a steadily accelerating object?* **b** *a steadily decelerating object?*
>
> 2 *What would the velocity–time graph for an object moving at constant velocity look like?*

P1.4

Using graphs

- The gradient of a distance–time graph gives the speed of an object.
- To find the gradient at a point on a curved graph, draw the tangent to the curve at that point and calculate the gradient of the tangent.

Key points

- The speed of an object is given by the gradient of the line on its distance–time graph.
- The acceleration of an object is given by the gradient of the line on its velocity–time graph.
- The distance travelled by an object is given by the area under the line of its velocity–time graph.

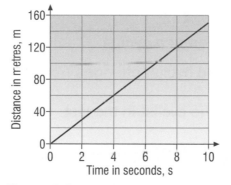

Figure 1 A distance–time graph for constant speed

- The gradient of a velocity–time graph gives the acceleration of an object.
- The area under the line on a velocity–time graph between two times gives the distance travelled between those times.

Acceleration = gradient of graph = $\dfrac{12\,\text{m/s} - 4\,\text{m/s}}{10\,\text{s}} = 0.8\,\text{m/s}^2$

Distance travelled = area under line = area of rectangle + area of triangle
$= (4\,\text{m/s} \times 10\,\text{s}) + \tfrac{1}{2} \times (12\,\text{m/s} - 4\,\text{m/s}) \times 10\,\text{s} = 80\,\text{m}$

> 1 *What does an upwardly curving line represent on a* **a** *distance–time graph?* **b** *velocity–time graph?*
>
> 2 *In Figure 2, how far did the object travel when it was accelerating?*

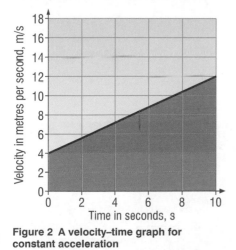

Figure 2 A velocity–time graph for constant acceleration

1 What is the average speed, in m/s, of a car that completes a distance of 1.2 km in 1 minute?

2 What does the distance–time graph for a stationary object look like?

3 What quantity has the unit m/s^2?

4 What does a negative value for acceleration mean?

5 What happens to the gradient of the line on a distance–time graph if the speed increases?

6 How can an object travelling at a steady speed be accelerating?

7 A car accelerates from rest to a speed of 40 m/s in 10 s.
   a What is its acceleration?
   b Explain why its average speed over this time is 20 m/s.
   c How far does it travel in this time?

8 What part of a velocity–time graph represents distance travelled?

9 Figure 1 shows a graph of the motion of a car.
   a What is the acceleration of the car?
   b What is the distance travelled by the car?

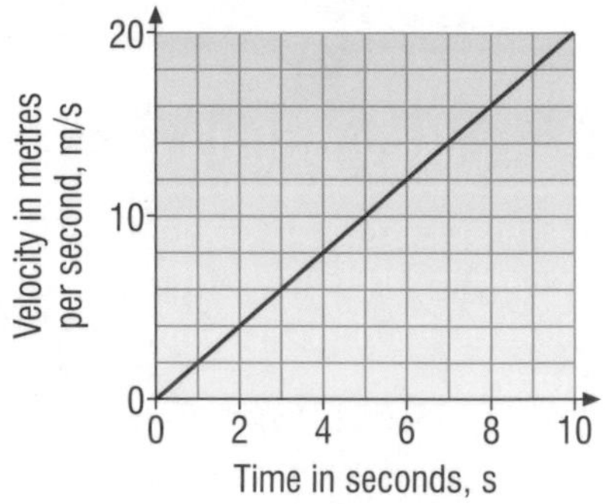

The graph in Figure 2 shows the motion of a cyclist.

10 a Describe how the speed of the cyclist changes from start to finish.
   b Calculate the acceleration of the cyclist in the last 10 seconds.

11 a Describe how the acceleration of the cyclist changes from start to finish.
   b Calculate the acceleration of the cyclist:
      i at the start
      ii 5.0 s after starting.

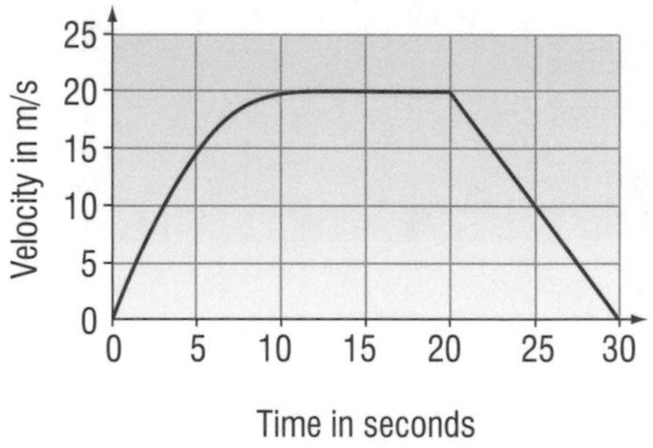

12 a Estimate the total distance travelled.
   b Calculate the average speed of the cyclist.

Figure 1

Figure 2

Chapter checklist ✓ ✓ ✓

Tick when you have:

reviewed it after your lesson	✓ ☐ ☐
revised once – some questions right	✓ ✓ ☐
revised twice – all questions right	✓ ✓ ✓

Move on to another topic when you have all three ticks

Distance–time graphs ☐ ☐ ☐

Velocity and acceleration ☐ ☐ ☐

More about velocity–time graphs ☐ ☐ ☐

Using graphs ☐ ☐ ☐

Student's book
pages 12–13 **P2.1**

Forces between objects

Forces are measured in **newtons**, abbreviated to N.

Objects always exert **equal** and **opposite** forces on each other when they interact. If object A exerts a force on object B, object B exerts an equal and opposite force on object A.

These are sometimes called 'action and reaction' forces.

- If a car hits a barrier, it exerts a force on the barrier. The barrier exerts a force on the car that is equal in size and in the opposite direction.
- If you place a book on a table the weight of the book will act vertically downwards on the table. The table will exert an equal and opposite reaction force upwards on the book.
- When a car is being driven forwards there is a force from the tyre on the ground pushing backwards. There is an equal and opposite force from the ground on the tyre which pushes the car forwards.

> 1 *In what direction does the weight of an object act?*
>
> 2 *When a sprinter starts running, the action force is the force of each running shoe on the starting blocks. What is the reaction force and in which direction does it act?*

Study tip

It is important to understand that action and reaction forces act on different objects. (See Q2!)

Key points

- A force can change the shape of an object or change its motion or state of rest.
- The unit of force is the newton (N).
- When two objects interact they always exert equal and opposite forces on each other.

Direction of car

Force of tyre on road   Force of road on tyre

Figure 1 Driving force

Key words: force, newton, equal, opposite

Student's book
pages 14–15 **P2.2**

Resultant force

Most objects have more than one force acting on them. The **resultant force** is the single force that would have the same effect on the object as all the original forces acting together.

When the resultant force on an object is zero:

- if the object is at rest, it will stay at rest
- if the object is moving, it will carry on moving at the same speed and in the same direction.

When the resultant force on an object is not zero, there will be an acceleration in the direction of the force. This means that:

- if the object is at rest, it will accelerate in the direction of the resultant force
- if the object is moving in the same direction as the resultant force, it will accelerate in that direction
- if the object is moving in the opposite direction to the resultant force, it will decelerate.

> 1 *An object slides across ice at constant velocity. What can you say about the resultant force on it?*

Suppose an object is acted on by two forces only, A and B, acting along the same line:

- in the same direction, the resultant force = A + B
- in opposite directions, the resultant force = A – B if A is greater than B (or B – A if B is greater than A).

> 2 *What is the resultant of a 4N force and a 3N force acting **a** in the same direction? **b** in opposite directions?*

Key points

- The resultant force is a single force that has the same effect as all the forces acting on an object.
- If two forces act on an object along the same line, the resultant force is:
  - their sum, if the forces act in the same direction
  - their difference, if the forces act in opposite directions.

Study tip

Remember that if an object is accelerating there must be a resultant force acting on it.

Key words: resultant force

P2.3

Force as a vector

Key points

- On a diagram, a force as a vector is shown as an arrow.
- The parallelogram of forces is used to find the resultant of two forces that do not act along the same line.

When an object is acted on by more than one force, we can draw a **force diagram** to work out the resultant force on the object. A force diagram shows the forces acting on the object.

To find the resultant of two forces that do not act along the same line, we use the **parallelogram of forces** rule as shown in Figure 1.

- We can represent each force accurately on the diagram by a **vector** which is an arrow of length proportional to the size (i.e. magnitude) of the force in the direction of the force.
- The two force vectors are drawn as adjacent sides of a parallelogram.
- The resultant force is the diagonal of the parallelogram from the origin of the two forces.

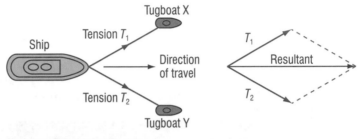

Figure 1 Combining forces

> 1 *Use a ruler to find the resultant force in Figure 1 if $T_1 = T_2 = 10.0\,kN$.*

> 2 *Show that the resultant force would be 14.1 kN if the two forces in Figure 1 acted at 90° to each other.*

Many physical quantities in addition to force are directional and are therefore vectors. Examples include displacement, velocity, acceleration, force, momentum, weight and gravitational field strength.

Physical quantities that are not directional are called **scalars.** Examples include speed, distance, time, mass, energy and power.

Maths skills

Worked example

A tow rope is attached to a car at two points 0.80 m apart. The two sections of rope joined to the car are of the same length and are at 30° to each other (see Figure 2). The pull on each attachment should not exceed 3000 N. Use the parallelogram of forces to determine the maximum tension in the main tow rope.

Solution

The maximum tension T in the main tow rope is the resultant of the two 3000 N forces at 30° to each other.

Drawing the parallelogram of forces as shown in Figure 2 gives:
$$T = 5800\,N$$

Figure 2 Investigating the link between force and motion

Key words: force diagram, parallelogram of forces, vector, scalar

P2.4 Force and acceleration

Key points

- The bigger the resultant force on an object is, the greater its acceleration is.
- The greater the mass of an object is, the smaller its acceleration is for a given force.
- Resultant force = mass × acceleration.

🔗 links

In questions where you need to use F = ma, you may have to calculate the acceleration first. See 1.2 'Velocity and acceleration'.

Study tip

If an object is accelerating or decelerating, there must be a resultant force acting on it.

- A **resultant force** always causes an **acceleration**. Remember that a deceleration is a negative acceleration. If there is no acceleration in a particular situation, the resultant force must be zero.
- Acceleration is a change in velocity. An object can accelerate by changing its direction even if it is going at a constant speed. So a resultant force is needed to make an object change direction.
- We can find the resultant force on an object using the equation:

$$F = m \times a$$

where F is the resultant force in newtons, N
m is the mass in kilograms, kg
a is the acceleration in m/s².

- The greater the resultant force on an object, the greater its acceleration. The bigger the **mass** of an object, the bigger the force needed to give it a particular acceleration.

▶ **1** *What is the resultant force on a car of mass 1000 kg if its acceleration is 2 m/s²?*

Practical

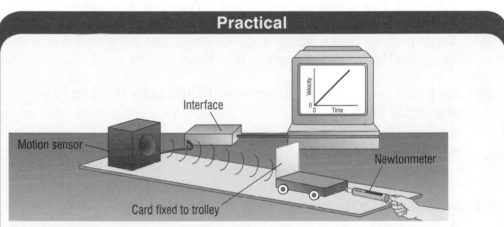

Figure 1 Investigating the link between force and motion

Test a newtonmeter

Measure the acceleration of a trolley of known mass along a level runway with a motion sensor connected to a computer.

Use a newtonmeter to pull the trolley along with a measured force.

Use the equation $F = m \times a$ to calculate the force F needed to accelerate the trolley.

▶ **2** *Outline one way the measurements could be made more accurate.*

▶ **3** *In Figure 2, what force applied to an object of mass 1.5 kg would give the same acceleration as the red line gives?*

Key word: mass

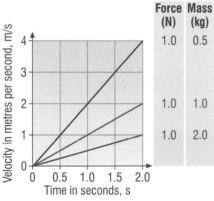

	Force (N)	Mass (kg)
	1.0	0.5
	1.0	1.0
	1.0	2.0

Figure 2 Velocity–time graph for different combinations of force and mass

1 When two objects interact, what can you say about the forces they exert on each other?

2 What can you say about the velocity of a moving object if no resultant force acts on it?

3 What is the difference between a vector quantity and a scalar quantity?

4 An object is acted on by a 4.0 N force and a 6.0 N force.
   a What is the least value of the resultant of these two forces?
   b What is the greatest value of the resultant?

5 Use the parallelogram of forces to show that the resultant of a 4.0 N and a 6.0 N force acting at 90° to each other is 7.2 N.

6 What is the acceleration of a truck of mass 4000 kg if the resultant force acting in the direction of motion is 1800 N?

7 If the mass of the truck in Q6 was 6000 kg, what resultant force would be needed to give the truck the same acceleration as the truck in Q6?

8 A sprinter of mass 60 kg accelerates from zero to 9.6 m/s in 1.2 s. Calculate the resultant force on the sprinter during this time.

9 A cyclist moving at a velocity of 16 m/s on a level road stops pedalling and comes to a standstill in 20 s.
   a Calculate the deceleration of the cyclist.
   b The total mass of the cyclist and the cycle is 75 kg. Calculate the average value of the resultant force on the cyclist.

10 What force is needed to give an object of mass 1.0 kg an acceleration of:
   a 1.0 m/s²?
   b 2.0 m/s²?

11 A constant force acts on an object of mass 180 kg and reduces its speed from 20 m/s to 12 m/s in 16 s. Calculate:
   a the deceleration of the object
   b the resultant force on the object.

12 How much longer would the same force need to act on the object in Q11 to reduce its velocity to zero?

Chapter checklist		✓	✓	✓
Tick when you have:		Forces between objects	☐ ☐ ☐	
reviewed it after your lesson	☑ ☐ ☐	Resultant force	☐ ☐ ☐	
revised once – some questions right	☑ ☑ ☐	Force as a vector	☐ ☐ ☐	
revised twice – all questions right	☑ ☑ ☑	Force and acceleration	☐ ☐ ☐	
Move on to another topic when you have all three ticks				

P3.1

Momentum

Key points

- Momentum = mass × velocity
- The unit of momentum is kg m/s
- Momentum is conserved whenever objects interact, provided the objects are in a closed system so that no external forces act on them.

- All moving objects have **momentum**. The greater the mass and the greater the velocity of an object, the greater its momentum.
- Momentum can be calculated using the equation:

$$p = m \times v$$

where p is the momentum in kilogram metres per second , kg m/s

m is the mass in kilograms, kg

v is the velocity in metres per second, m/s.

➡ **1** *What is the momentum of a 1000 kg car travelling at 30 m/s?*

- The **law of conservation of momentum** states that whenever objects interact, the total momentum before the interaction is equal to the total momentum afterwards, provided no external forces act on them.
- Another way to say this is that the total momentum is unchanged or the change in the total momentum is zero.
- The interaction could be a collision or an explosion. After a collision the objects may move off together, or they may move apart.

➡ **2** *A rail truck of mass 2500 kg moving at a velocity of 2.0 m/s collides with a stationary truck of the same mass. The two trucks couple together and move at the same velocity after the collision.*
 a What is the total momentum before the collision?
 b Calculate the velocity of the two trucks after the collision.

Practical

Investigating collisions

Use a computer and a motion sensor to investigate a collision between two trolleys.

Trolley A is given a push so it collides with a stationary trolley B. The two trolleys stick together after the collision. The computer gives the velocity of A before the collision and the velocity of both trolleys afterwards.

Measure the mass of the trolleys.

➡ **3** *How would you use your results to show that momentum is conserved in the collision?*

Study tip

Remember that momentum has a size and a direction.
The units of momentum are kg m/s. They can also be written as written as newton seconds (N s).

Key words: momentum, law of conservation of momentum

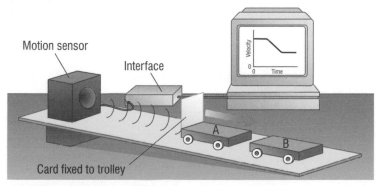

Figure 1 Investigating collisions

P3.2 | # Explosions

Key points

- Momentum = mass × velocity; and velocity is speed in a certain direction.
- When two objects push each other apart, they move apart:
  - with equal and opposite momentum so their total momentum is zero
  - with different speeds if they have unequal masses.

Figure 1 An artillery gun in action

Study tip

Be careful in calculations – momentum is a vector quantity, so if two objects are travelling in opposite directions, one has positive momentum, and the other has negative momentum.

- Like velocity, momentum has both size and direction. In calculations, one direction must be defined as positive, so momentum in the opposite direction is negative.
- When two objects are at rest their momentum is zero. In an **explosion** the objects move apart with equal and opposite momentum. One momentum is positive and the other negative, so the total momentum after the explosion is zero.
- Firing a bullet from a gun is an example of an explosion. The bullet moves off with a momentum in one direction and the gun 'recoils' with equal momentum in the opposite direction.

⫸ 1 *What can you say about the total momentum of an object after an explosion if it was initially at rest then explodes?*

⫸ 2 *Student X and student Y are on roller skates holding each other in the playground. They push each other away and X moves away faster than Y. What can you say about*
   a *the force they exert on each other?*
   b *the mass of X compared with the mass of Y?*

Practical

Investigating a controlled explosion

Set up the arrangement shown in Figure 2. Make sure the trolleys are in contact and at rest at the start. When the trigger rod is tapped, a bolt springs out and the trolleys recoil (spring back) from each other.

Using trial and error, place blocks on the runway so the trolleys reach them at the same time. The ratio of the distances they move is equal to the ratio of their speeds. Because they move away with equal (and opposite) amounts of momentum, their speed ratio is the inverse of their mass ratio.

⫸ 3 *How would you find out if your measurements are* **a** *precise?*
   b *accurate?*

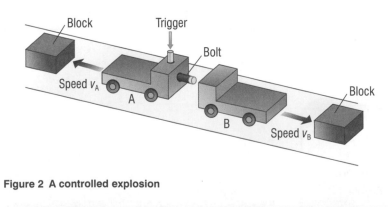

Figure 2 A controlled explosion

Key word: explosion

Student's book
pages 26–27

P3.3

Impact forces

- When a force acts on an object that is able to move, or is moving, its momentum changes.
- For a particular change in momentum the longer the time taken for the change, the smaller the force that acts.
- In a collision, the momentum of an object changes as a result of a force acting on the object.
- If the **impact time** is short, the force on the object is large. Making the impact time longer makes the force smaller.
- For a change of momentum Δp in time t, the force F acting is given by the equation:

$$F = \frac{\Delta p}{t}$$

Key points

- When vehicles collide, the force of the impact depends on mass, change of velocity and the duration of the impact.
- When two vehicles collide:
  – they exert equal and opposite forces on each other
  – their total momentum is unchanged.

1 *A car of mass 800 kg moving at 10 m/s collides with a wall in an impact that lasts 0.1 s. Calculate the force of the impact.*

- **Crumple zones** in cars are designed to fold in a collision. This increases the impact time and so reduces the force on the car and the people in it.
- **Seat belts** in cars reduce the force of an impact by increasing the time over which the wearer's momentum changes.

Study tip

Make sure that you can explain how crumple zones in cars reduce the forces acting by increasing the time taken to change the momentum of a car.

2 *Why do cars have crumple zones at both the front and the rear?*

Key words: impact time, crumple zone, seat belt

Student's book
pages 28–29

P3.4

Car safety

- Modern cars contain a number of safety features designed to reduce the forces on the occupants of the car in a collision.
- Side impact bars and crumple zones fold up in a collision to increase the impact time and reduce the forces acting.
- Seat belts and **air bags** spread the forces on the body across a larger area. If a driver's head hits an air bag it changes momentum slowly, so the force on the head is less than it would be if it changed momentum quickly by hitting the steering wheel.
- A seat belt stops the wearer being flung forward if the car stops suddenly. The seatbelt stretches, slightly increasing the impact time and reducing the force.
- A collapsible steering wheel in a car is designed to collapse if it is pushed onto the driver's chest in a car crash that squashes the front end of the car.

Key points

- Seat belts and air bags spread the force across the chest and they also increase the impact time.
- Side impact bars and crumple zones 'give way' in an impact so increasing the impact time.
- We can use the conservation of momentum to find the speed of a car before an impact.

1 a *What happens to a passenger in a head-on collision if they are not wearing a seat belt?*
  b *What would happen to a passenger in a head-on collision if they were wearing a very narrow seat belt?*

2 *What difference does a collapsible steering wheel make to the impact time and the impact force when the driver and the steering wheel make contact in a car crash?*

Study tip

Make sure that you can explain how different vehicle safety features work in terms of spreading out and reducing the forces on the occupants of the vehicle.

Key word: air bag

1. What is the unit of momentum?

2. What is the momentum of a 2500 kg truck travelling at 16 m/s?

3. A 1000 kg car moves with the same momentum as the truck in Q2. What is the velocity of the car?

4. A car and a truck have equal and opposite momentum just before they collide. What is the total momentum:

   a before the collision?

   b after the collision?

5. A trolley of mass 0.20 kg travelling at 1.5 m/s to the right collides with a stationary trolley of mass 0.30 kg. After the collision, they move off together. Calculate the velocity of the trolleys after the collision.

6. A trolley of mass 0.20 kg travelling at 1.5 m/s to the right collides with a trolley of mass 0.30 kg moving in the opposite direction at 0.5 m/s. Calculate the total momentum before the collision.

7. Calculate the velocity of the trolleys in Q6 after the impact if they move off together.

8. Two skaters standing next to each other push on each other and move away at equal and opposite velocities. What is their total momentum just after they separate?

9. In a simulated explosion, a 2.0 kg trolley and a 1.0 kg trolley are initially at rest in contact with each other before they repel each other. The 1.0 kg trolley moves away at a velocity of 0.12 m/s. What is the velocity of the 2.0 kg trolley?

10. In the equation $F = \dfrac{\Delta p}{t}$, what does Δp represent?

11. An object initially at rest is acted on by a force of 12 N for 6 s. What is its momentum after this time?

12. Why does wearing a seat belt in a moving car reduce the risk of injury if the car suddenly stops?

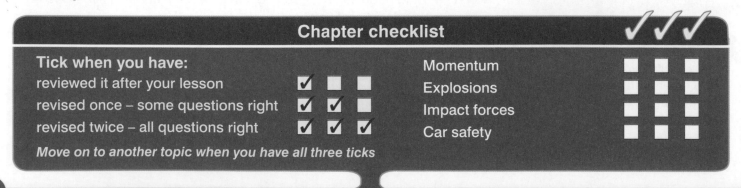

Chapter checklist

Tick when you have:				Momentum			
reviewed it after your lesson	✔	☐	☐	Explosions	☐	☐	☐
revised once – some questions right	✔	✔	☐	Impact forces	☐	☐	☐
revised twice – all questions right	✔	✔	✔	Car safety	☐	☐	☐

Move on to another topic when you have all three ticks

1 A student used a motion sensor connected to a computer to record the motion of a trolley rolling down a slope, as shown in Figure 1. The trolley was released from rest near the top of the slope.

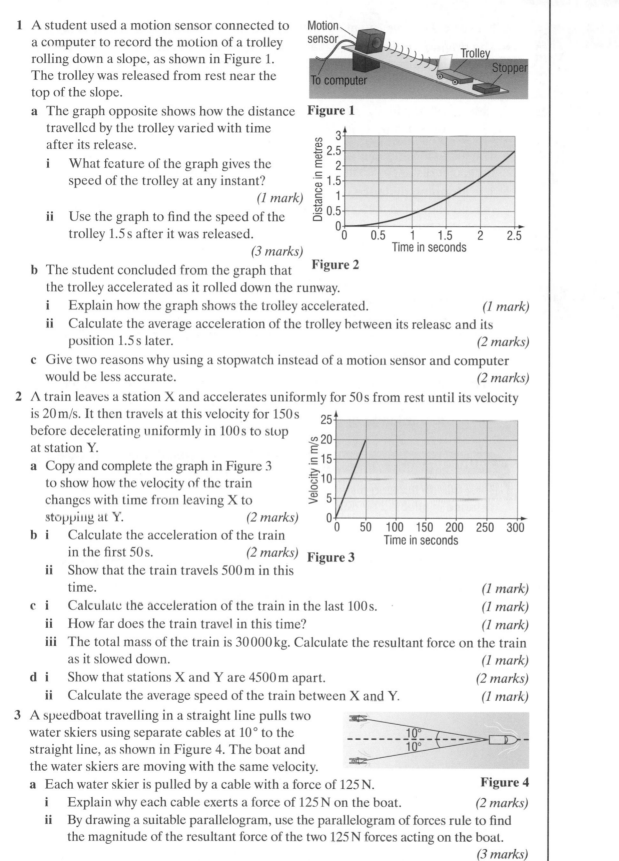

Figure 1

Figure 2

  a The graph opposite shows how the distance travelled by the trolley varied with time after its release.

   i What feature of the graph gives the speed of the trolley at any instant?
        (1 mark)

   ii Use the graph to find the speed of the trolley 1.5 s after it was released.
        (3 marks)

  b The student concluded from the graph that the trolley accelerated as it rolled down the runway.

   i Explain how the graph shows the trolley accelerated.   *(1 mark)*

   ii Calculate the average acceleration of the trolley between its release and its position 1.5 s later.   *(2 marks)*

  c Give two reasons why using a stopwatch instead of a motion sensor and computer would be less accurate.   *(2 marks)*

2 A train leaves a station X and accelerates uniformly for 50 s from rest until its velocity is 20 m/s. It then travels at this velocity for 150 s before decelerating uniformly in 100 s to stop at station Y.

  a Copy and complete the graph in Figure 3 to show how the velocity of the train changes with time from leaving X to stopping at Y.   *(2 marks)*

  Figure 3

  b i Calculate the acceleration of the train in the first 50 s.   *(2 marks)*

   ii Show that the train travels 500 m in this time.   *(1 mark)*

  c i Calculate the acceleration of the train in the last 100 s.   *(1 mark)*

   ii How far does the train travel in this time?   *(1 mark)*

   iii The total mass of the train is 30 000 kg. Calculate the resultant force on the train as it slowed down.   *(1 mark)*

  d i Show that stations X and Y are 4500 m apart.   *(2 marks)*

   ii Calculate the average speed of the train between X and Y.   *(1 mark)*

3 A speedboat travelling in a straight line pulls two water skiers using separate cables at 10° to the straight line, as shown in Figure 4. The boat and the water skiers are moving with the same velocity.

  Figure 4

  a Each water skier is pulled by a cable with a force of 125 N.

   i Explain why each cable exerts a force of 125 N on the boat.   *(2 marks)*

   ii By drawing a suitable parallelogram, use the parallelogram of forces rule to find the magnitude of the resultant force of the two 125 N forces acting on the boat.   *(3 marks)*

  b The force of the engine pushing the boat forward at constant velocity is 320 N. Explain why this force is greater than the resultant force of the cables acting on the boat.   *(2 marks)*

P4.1 # Forces and braking 🌀

Student's book
pages 32–33

Key points

- Friction and air resistance oppose the driving force of a car.
- The stopping distance of a car depends on the thinking distance and the braking distance.
- High speed, poor weather conditions and poor maintenance of the vehicle all increase the braking distance. Poor reaction time and high speed both increase the thinking distance.

- If a vehicle is travelling at a steady speed, the resultant force on it is zero.
- The **driving forces** are equal and opposite to the **resistive forces**. The resistive forces are caused by air resistance and by friction between the parts that move against each other.

▌▌▌➡ **1** *What can you say about the resultant force on a vehicle when the brakes are applied?*

- The faster the speed of a vehicle, the bigger the deceleration needed to stop it in a particular distance. So the bigger the braking force needed.
- The **stopping distance** of a vehicle is the distance it travels during the driver's reaction time (the thinking distance) plus the distance it travels under the braking force (the braking distance).
- The **thinking distance** is increased if the driver is tired or under the influence of alcohol or drugs.
- The **braking distance** can be increased by:
  – poorly maintained roads
  – bad weather conditions
  – the condition of the car. For example, worn tyres or worn brakes will increase braking distance.

▌▌▌➡ **2 a** *What is the relationship between stopping distance, thinking distance and braking distance?*
  b *Why does tiredness cause the thinking distance to increase?*

Study tip

Don't mix up thinking distance and braking distance. Make sure you know which distance is affected by reaction time.

Key words: driving force, resistive force, stopping distance, thinking distance, braking distance

P4.2

Forces and terminal velocity

Key points

- The weight of an object is the force of gravity on it. Its mass is the quantity of matter in it.
- An object falling freely accelerates at about 10 m/s².
- The terminal velocity of an object is the velocity it eventually reaches when it is falling in a fluid. The weight of the object is then equal to the frictional force on the object.

If an object falls freely, the resultant force acting on it is the force of gravity. It will make the object accelerate at about 10 m/s² close to the Earth's surface. We call the force of gravity **weight**, and the acceleration the **acceleration due to gravity** (symbol g).

Applying the equation $F = m \times a$ to an object of mass m falling freely therefore gives:

$$W = m \times g$$

where W is the weight in N
g is the acceleration due to gravity in m/s².
g is also called the **gravitational field strength** and may be written in newtons per kilogram, N/kg.

> **1** *Calculate the weight in newtons of a person of mass 60 kg on the surface of the earth.*

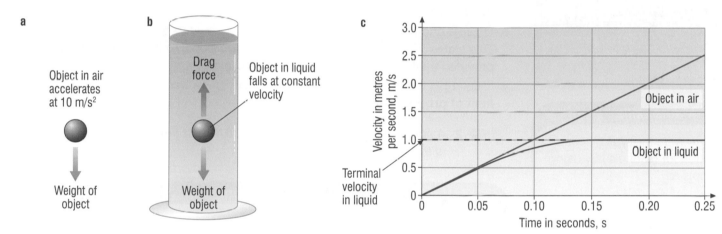

Figure 1 Falling objects

a — Object in air accelerates at 10 m/s² — Weight of object

b — Drag force — Object in liquid falls at constant velocity — Weight of object

c — Velocity in metres per second, m/s — Terminal velocity in liquid — Object in air — Object in liquid — Time in seconds, s

When an object falls through a fluid, the fluid exerts a **drag force** on the object, resisting its motion. The faster the object falls, the bigger the drag force becomes. The resultant force therefore decreases and so the acceleration decreases. Eventually the drag force becomes equal to the weight of the object, so the resultant force becomes zero and the body stops accelerating. It moves at a constant velocity called the **terminal velocity**.

> **2 a** *When an object at rest in a fluid is released, what can we say about the drag force initially?*
> **b** *Why is the initial acceleration equal to g?*

> **3** *What eventually happens to the velocity of an object falling in a fluid?*

Study tip

Do not confuse mass and weight. Mass is the amount of matter in an object, weight is the force of gravity acting on it.
The drag force may also be called air resistance or fluid resistance.

Key words: weight, acceleration due to gravity, gravitational field strength, drag force, terminal velocity

P4.3 Forces and elasticity

Key points

- An object is called **elastic** if it returns to its original shape after removing the force deforming it.
- The extension is the difference between the length of the spring and its original length.
- The extension of a spring is directly proportional to the force applied to it, provided the limit of proportionality is not exceeded.
- The spring constant of a spring is the force per unit extension needed to stretch it.

Maths skills

We can write the word equation for Hooke's law using symbols as:

$$F = k \times e$$

where:

F = force in newtons, N

k = the **spring constant** in newtons per metre, N/m

e = extension in metres, m.

k is the spring constant of the spring in newtons per metre, N/m. The stiffer a spring is the greater its spring constant.

Rearranging the above equation gives:

$$k = \frac{F}{e} \text{ or } e = \frac{F}{k}$$

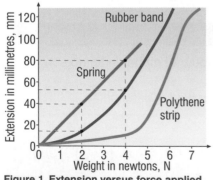

Figure 1 Extension versus force applied for different materials

- If we hang small weights from a spring it will stretch. The increase in length from the original is called the **extension**. When we remove the weights the spring will return to its original length.
- Objects and materials that behave in this way are called **elastic**.
- An elastic object is one that regains its original shape when the forces deforming it are removed.
- When an elastic object is stretched work is done. This is stored as elastic potential energy in the object. When the stretching force is removed, this stored energy is released.

> 1 *Which of the following objects – a rubber band, a strip of polythene and a spring – behave elastically?*

- If we plot a graph of extension against force applied for a spring, we obtain a straight line that passes though the origin. This tells us that the extension is **directly proportional** to the force applied.
- Objects and materials that behave like this are said to obey **Hooke's law**. This states that the extension is directly proportional to the force applied, provided the limit of proportionality is not exceeded.
- If we apply too big a force, the line begins to curve because we have exceeded the **limit of proportionality**.

> 2 *A spring has a spring constant of 30 N/m. If the extension is 0.30 m what is the force applied?*

Practical

Test a spring

Hang a spring from a stand with a metre ruler fixed vertically next to it.

Place different weights W on the lower end of the spring. Use a set square to measure the position of the lower end of the spring for each weight.

Calculate the extension of the spring for each weight W and record the measurements in a table.

Plot a graph of extension on the y-axis against weight W to find the spring constant of the spring.

> 3 *How could you tell if the spring has exceeded its limit of proportionality?*

> 4 *Calculate the spring constant of the spring that gave the results shown in Figure 1.*

Study tip

Two quantities are directly proportional to each other only if plotting them on a graph gives a straight line through the origin.

Key words: extension, elastic, directly proportional, Hooke's law, limit of proportionality, spring constant

1 What can we say about the driving force and the resistive forces on a car travelling at constant velocity on a level road?

2 What is meant by thinking distance?

3 What can you say about the braking distance of a vehicle on a wet road compared with when it is on a dry road?

4 What is the effect of the speed of a vehicle on its stopping distance?

5 What is terminal velocity?

6 What is the weight of a person of mass 70 kg?

7 After an object is released in water, why does the drag force on it increase?

8 What can we say about the acceleration of a falling object which is acted on only by the force of gravity?

9 What is meant by the extension of a stretched spring?

10 What is an elastic object?

11 What does Hooke's law state?

12 When a force of 10 N is applied to a spring it extends by 2.0 cm. What is the spring constant of the spring?

Chapter checklist ✓✓✓

Tick when you have:

reviewed it after your lesson ☑ ☐ ☐

revised once – some questions right ☑ ☑ ☐

revised twice – all questions right ☑ ☑ ☑

Move on to another topic when you have all three ticks

Forces and braking ☐ ☐ ☐

Forces and terminal velocity ☐ ☐ ☐

Forces and elasticity ☐ ☐ ☐

Student's book
pages 40–41

P5.1 Energy and work

- Whenever an object starts to move, a force must have been applied to it.
- When a force moves an object, energy is transferred and **work** is done.
- When work is done moving the object, the supplied energy is transferred to the object so the work done is equal to the energy transferred.
- Both work and energy have the unit joule, J.

The work done on an object is calculated using the equation:

$$W = F \times d$$

Where W is the work done in joules, J
F is the force in newtons, N
d is the distance moved in the direction of the force in metres, m.

Note that if the distance moved is zero, no work is done on the object.

We can rearrange the above equation to give $F = \dfrac{W}{d}$ or $d = \dfrac{W}{F}$

- Work done to overcome **friction** is mainly transferred into energy by heating. When the brakes are applied to a vehicle, friction between the brake pads and the wheel discs opposes the motion of the wheel. The kinetic energy of the vehicle is transferred into energy that heats the brake pads and the wheel discs as well as the surrounding air.

> **1** What is the work done on an object if a force of 300 N moves it a distance of 8 m in the direction of the force?
>
> **2 a** What is the force if the work done is 50 J in a distance of 5.0 m in the direction of the force?
> **b** What is the distance moved in the direction of the force if the work done is 60 J when the force is 15 N?

Key points

- Work is done on an object when a force makes the object move.
- Energy transferred = work done.
- Work done (joules) = force (newtons) × distance moved in the direction of the force (metres).
- Work done to overcome friction is transferred as energy that heats the objects that rub together and the surroundings.

Study tip

Remember that work done is equal to energy transferred.

Key words: work, friction

Student's book
pages 42–43

P5.2 Power

- When you use a lift to go up, a powerful electric motor pulls you and the lift up. The work done by the lift motor transfers energy from electricity to gravitational potential energy. Sound and energy that heats the motor are also produced.
- The work done per second by the motor is the output **power** of the motor.
- We measure the power of an appliance in watts (W) or kilowatts (kW) or megawatts (millions of watts, MW). One watt is a rate of transfer of energy of 1 joule per second (J/s).
- Machines are labour-saving devices that do work for us. The faster a machine can do work, the more powerful it is.
- Whenever a machine does work on an object, energy is transferred to the object. The **useful energy** transferred is equal to the work done by the machine. This is the energy in the required form that is transferred to the object.

> **1** A machine has an output power of 2000 W. How much useful energy does it transfer in 100 s?

The output power of a machine is the rate at which it does work. This is the same as the rate at which it transfers useful energy.

$$\text{Power } P \text{ (watts)} = \frac{\text{work done (joules)}}{\text{time taken (seconds)}} = \frac{\text{useful energy transferred (joules)}}{\text{time taken (seconds)}}$$

If energy E is transferred in time t, power $P = \dfrac{E}{t}$

> **2 a** What is the output power of a crane that does 10 000 J of work in 10.0 s?
> **b** What is the output power of a weightlifter who transfers 300 J of energy to a weight in 0.4 seconds?

Key points

- Power is the rate at which energy is transferred.
- The unit of power is the watt (W) equal to 1 J/s.
- Power (in watts) = $\dfrac{\text{energy transferred (in joules)}}{\text{time taken (in seconds)}}$

links

Revise more on work and energy in 5.1 'Energy and work'.

Key words: power, useful energy

Gravitational potential energy ⬤

Key points

- The gravitational potential energy of an object increases when it moves up and decreases when the object moves down.
- An object gains gravitational potential energy when it is lifted up because work is done on it to overcome the gravitational force.
- The change of gravitational potential energy of an object is equal to its mass × the gravitational field strength × its change of height.

Key words: gravitational potential energy

- **Gravitational potential energy** is energy stored in an object because of its position in the Earth's gravitational field. Whenever an object is moved vertically upwards it gains gravitational potential energy equal to the work done on it by the lifting force.
- The change in gravitational potential energy can be calculated using the equation:

$$E_p = m \times g \times h$$

where E_p is the change in gravitational potential energy in joules, J

m is the mass in kilograms, kg

g is the gravitational field strength in newtons per kilogram, N/kg

h is the change in height in metres, m.

The value of g on the Earth's surface is approximately 10 N/kg.

▶ **1 a** *What is the increase in gravitational potential energy when an object of mass 40 kg is lifted through a height of 8 m?*

   b *It takes 2 seconds to lift the object in Q1. What is the power developed?*

▶ **2** *An object gains 500 J of gravitational potential when it is raised through a height of 4.0 m. Calculate **a** the mass of the object, **b** the weight of the object.*

Study tip

Watch out for objects going up a slope. To calculate a gain in gravitational potential energy, you need the vertical height gained, not the distance up the slope.

P5.4 Kinetic energy ⬤

Key points

- The kinetic energy of a moving object depends on its mass and its speed.
- Kinetic energy (J) = ½ × mass (kg) × speed² (m/s)²
- Elastic potential energy is the energy stored in an elastic object when work is done on the object.

Study tip

If an elastic band is stretched and released elastic potential energy is transferred to kinetic energy.

- All moving objects have **kinetic energy**. The greater the mass and the faster the speed of an object, the more kinetic energy it has.
- Kinetic energy can be calculated using the equation:

$$E_k = ½ \, mv^2$$

where E_k is the kinetic energy in joules, J

m is the mass in kilograms, kg

v is the speed in metres per second, m/s.

▶ **1 a** *A boy of mass 40 kg runs at a speed of 5 m/s. What is his kinetic energy?*

   b *A ball of mass 0.40 kg has 20 J of kinetic energy. Calculate its speed.*

- An object is described as being elastic if it regains its shape after being stretched or squashed. When work is done on an elastic object to stretch or squash it, the energy transferred to it is stored as **elastic potential energy**. When the object returns to its original shape this energy is released.

▶ **2** *When a spring is squashed and released it warms up. Why?*

Key words: kinetic energy, elastic potential energy

1 When is work done by a force?

2 What is the relationship between work and energy?

3 What is the unit of power?

4 What is the change in gravitational potential energy when an object of mass 6 kg is lowered through a distance of 9 m?

5 What is elastic potential energy?

6 What is the kinetic energy of a car of mass 1200 kg travelling at 30 m/s?

7 A ball of mass 0.50 kg is released from rest at a height of 1.6 m above the floor. How much gravitational potential energy does the ball lose before it hits the floor?

8 Assuming the gain of kinetic energy of the ball in Q7 is equal to its loss of gravitational potential energy, calculate the speed of the ball just before it hits the floor.

9 What energy transfers take place when a steel ball falls at terminal velocity in a liquid?

10 An electric motor is used to raise a 0.1 kg mass vertically upwards. If the mass gains 2 J of gravitational potential energy, calculate the height it is raised through.

11 The motor in Q10 has a power of 1.5 W. Calculate the time taken to raise the load.

12 A vehicle has a velocity of 40 m/s on a level road when the output power of its engine is 20 kW. Calculate the resistive force of the vehicle at this speed.

Chapter checklist

Tick when you have:

reviewed it after your lesson	✓	☐	☐	
revised once – some questions right	✓	✓	☐	
revised twice – all questions right	✓	✓	✓	

Move on to another topic when you have all three ticks

Energy and work	☐	☐	☐
Power	☐	☐	☐
Gravitational potential energy	☐	☐	☐
Kinetic energy	☐	☐	☐

P6.1 # Centre of mass

- The centre of mass of an object is that point where its mass can be thought to be concentrated.
- When a suspended object is in equilibrium, its centre of mass is directly beneath the point of suspension.
- The centre of mass of a symmetrical object is along the axis of symmetry.

⬭ **links**

Revise more on centre of mass in 6.4 'Moments in balance'.

- Although any object is made up of many particles, its mass can be thought of as being concentrated at one single point. This point is called the **centre of mass**.
- Any object that is freely suspended will come to rest with its centre of mass directly below the point of suspension. The object is then in **equilibrium**.

⫸ **1** *What is the centre of mass of an object?*

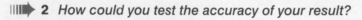

Practical

You can find the centre of mass of a thin irregular sheet of a material as follows:
- Suspend the thin sheet from a pin held in a clamp stand.
- Because it is freely suspended, it is able to turn.
- When it comes to rest, hang a plumbline from the same pin.
- Mark the position of the plumbline against the sheet.
- Hang the sheet with the pin at another point and repeat the procedure.
- The centre of mass is where the lines that marked the position of the plumbline cross.

⫸ **2** *How could you test the accuracy of your result?*

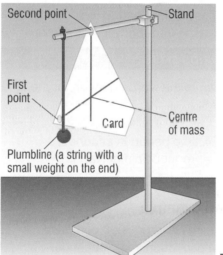

Figure 1 Finding the centre of mass of a card

- For a symmetrical object, its centre of mass is along the axis of symmetry. If the object has more than one axis of symmetry, the centre of mass is where the axes of symmetry meet.

⫸ **3** *Where is the centre of mass of **a** a circular plate? **b** a rectangular board of even thickness? **c** a ladder with an odd number of identical rungs?*

Key words: centre of mass, equilibrium

Make sure that you can describe the experiment to find the centre of mass of a thin sheet of a material, including sketching a labelled diagram.

P6.2 # The pendulum

Key points

- The time period of a simple pendulum depends only on its length.
- To measure the time period of a pendulum, we can measure the average time for 20 oscillations and divide the timing by 20.
- Friction at the top of a playground swing and air resistance will stop it oscillating if it is not pushed repeatedly.

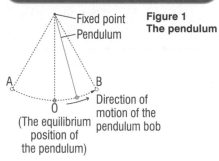

**Figure 1
The pendulum**

Fixed point
Pendulum

A   B
O   Direction of motion of the pendulum bob
(The equilibrium position of the pendulum)

⚭ links

Revise more on frequency in 7.2 'Measuring waves'.

Study tip

Make sure that you can describe what one complete oscillation is.

▐▶ **2** *What is the independent variable in the practical?*

▐▶ **3 a** *What is the time period of a pendulum of frequency 10 Hz?*
   b *A simple pendulum undergoes 20 complete cycles of oscillation in 6.0 s. Calculate its time period.*

Key words: simple pendulum, oscillating motion, amplitude, time period

A **simple pendulum** consists of a mass, called a bob, suspended on the end of a string. When the bob is displaced to one side and let go, the pendulum oscillates back and forth, through the equilibrium position. This is an example of **oscillating motion**.

- The **amplitude** of the oscillation is the distance from the equilibrium position to the highest position on either side.
- The **time period** of the oscillation is the time taken for one complete cycle, (the time taken from the highest position on one side to the highest position on the other side and back to the start position).

▐▶ **1** *A simple pendulum has a time period of 1.6 s. How long does it take for the bob to move from the highest position on one side to the highest position on the other side?*

To measure the time period of a pendulum, we can measure the average time for 20 oscillations and divide the timing by 20.

- The time period depends only on the length of the pendulum and increases as its length increases.
- The frequency of the oscillations is the number of complete cycles of oscillation per second.
- The time period and frequency are related by the equation:

$$T = \frac{1}{f}$$

where T is the time period in seconds, s
f is the frequency in hertz, Hz.

Maths skills

We can write the word equation for the time period of a pendulum using symbols, as follows:

$$T = \frac{1}{f}$$

where T = time period in seconds, s
f = frequency in hertz, Hz.

Note: Rearranging $T = \frac{1}{f}$ to make f the subject gives $f = \frac{1}{T}$

Worked example

A pendulum undergoes 20 complete cycles of oscillation in 4.0 seconds. Calculate **a** the frequency of the oscillations, **b** the time period.

Solution

a For 20 complete cycles in 4 seconds, there must be 5 cycles each second (20 ÷ 4 = 5). The frequency is therefore **5 Hz**.

b $T = \frac{1}{f}$ so the time period is $\frac{1}{5}$
= **0.2 seconds**.

Practical

Investigate the time period of a simple pendulum

Hang a simple pendulum from a fixed point. Use a metre ruler to measure the length L of the pendulum from the point of suspension to the centre of the pendulum bob.

To measure the time period, use a stopwatch to measure the average time for 20 oscillations and divide by 20. Repeat the measurements for different lengths L.

Record your measurements in a table and use them to plot a suitable graph.

P6.3 Moments at work

Key points

- The moment of a force is a measure of the turning effect of the force on an object.
- $M = F \times d$
- To increase the moment of a force F, increase F or increase d.

- The turning effect of a force is called its **moment**. The moment of a force is given by the equation

$$M = F \times d$$

where M is the moment of the force in newton metres, Nm
F is the force in newtons, N
d is the perpendicular distance from the **line of action** of the force to the **pivot** in metres, m.

- The above equation can be rearranged to give $F = \dfrac{M}{d}$ or $d = \dfrac{M}{F}$

> **1** *A door opens when you apply a force of 20N at right angles to it, 0.6m from the hinge. What is the moment of the force about the hinge?*

> **2** *What force would be needed to open the door if it were applied 0.3m from the hinge?*

- To increase the moment:
  - either the force must increase
  - or the distance to the pivot must increase.
- It is easier to undo a wheel nut by pushing on the end of a long spanner than a short one. That is because the long spanner increases the distance between the line of action of the force and the pivot.
- We make use of a lever to make a job easier. When using a lever the force we are trying to move is called the **load** and the force applied to the lever is the **effort**. A lever acts as a force multiplier, so the effort we apply can be much less than the load.

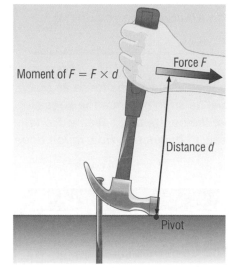

Moment of $F = F \times d$

Force F

Distance d

Pivot

Figure 1 Using a claw hammer

Maths skills

Worked example

A force of 50N is exerted on a claw hammer of length 0.30m, as shown in Figure 1. Calculate the moment of the force.

Solution

Force $= 50N \times 0.30m = $ **15Nm**

Figure 2 A turning effect

> **3** *A spanner is used to tighten a wheel nut as shown in Figure 2. What is the maximum force that can be applied to a spanner of length 0.25m if the torque exerted on a wheel nut is not to exceed 30Nm?*

Study tip

Remember when calculating moments, it is the perpendicular distance from the pivot that is needed.
Be careful with units: you need to be consistent – Nm or Ncm.

🔗 **links**

Revise more on moments in 6.5 'Stability'.

Key words: moment, line of action, pivot, load, effort

P6.4 # Moments in balance

Key points

- For an object in equilibrium, the sum of the anticlockwise moments about any point = the sum of the clockwise moments about that point.

- To calculate the force needed to stop an object turning, we use the equation above. We need to know all the forces that don't act through the pivot and their perpendicular distances from the line of action to that point.

Maths skills

Worked example

Calculate W_1 in Figure 1, if
$W_2 = 4.0\,N$
$d_1 = 0.25\,m$ and d_2
$\quad = 0.20\,m$

Solution

Rearranging $W_1d_1 = W_2d_2$ gives

$$W_1 = \frac{W_2d_2}{d_1}$$

$$= 4.0\,N \times \frac{0.20\,m}{0.25\,m}$$

$$= 3.2\,N$$

⬭ links

Revise more on moments in 6.5 'Stability'.

- The **principle of moments** states that for an object that is not turning, the sum of the anticlockwise moments about any point = the sum of the clockwise moments about that point.

- There are lots of everyday examples of the principle of moments, such as seesaws and balance scales.

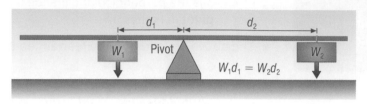

Figure 1 The principle of moments

▐▶ **1** *If someone sits in the centre of a seesaw, the moment about the pivot is zero. Why?*

Study tip

Be sure to add together all the clockwise moments and all the anticlockwise moments. It may help to tick them off if they are on a diagram, so you do not miss any out.

▐▶ **2 a** *Aimie sits 2 m from the centre of a seesaw. Leo weighs twice as much as Aimie. How far from the centre must he sit to balance the seesaw?*
   b *Luke weighs 600 N and sits 1.5 m from the centre of a seesaw. Fiona sits 2.0 m from the centre of the seesaw to balance it. How much does she weigh?*

Practical

Measuring the weight of a beam

Measure the weight of a beam by balancing it off-centre using a known weight W_1. The weight of the beam acts at its centre of mass, which is at distance d_0 from the pivot.

- The moment of the beam about the pivot = W_0d_0 clockwise, where W_0 is the weight of the beam.
- The moment of W_1 about the pivot = W_1d_1 anticlockwise, where d_1 is the perpendicular distance from the pivot to the line of action of W_1.
- Measure the distances d_0 and d_1.

The principle of moments gives $W_1d_1 = W_0d_0$. Use this equation and your measurements to calculate W_0.

▐▶ **3** *What could you do to improve the accuracy of your measurements?*

Key words: principle of moments

P6.5 Stability

Key points

- The stability of an object is increased by making its base as wide as possible and its centre of mass as low as possible.
- An object will tend to topple over if the line of action of its weight is outside its base.
- An object topples over if the resultant moment about its point of turning is **not** zero.

- The line of action of the weight of an object acts through its centre of mass.
- If the line of action of the weight lies outside the base of an object, there will be a **resultant moment** and the object will tend to topple over.

▸ 1 *Why does hanging heavy bags from the handle of a pushchair make it more likely to topple over?*

- The wider the base of an object, and the lower its centre of mass, the further it has to tilt before the line of action of the weight moves outside the base. So the stability of an object is increased by making its base wider and its centre of mass lower.

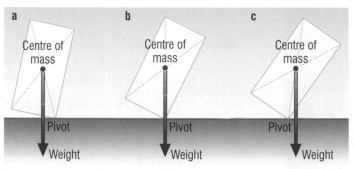

Figure 1 Tilting and toppling a tilted, b at balance, c toppled over

Study tip

Stability is important in the design of lots of different objects, including double-decker buses, racing cars, high chairs, prams, vases and filing cabinets. The stability of any object is increased by making its centre of mass lower and its base wider.

Practical

Tilting and toppling tests

Test how far you can tilt a brick or a tall box before it topples over. Figure 1 shows how you can do this.

- Tilt the brick until it just about balances on one edge. Its centre of mass is then directly above the edge on which it balances. Its weight has no turning effect in this position.
- Tilt it a little more and it will topple over if it is released.

▸ 2 *Explain why the box topples over.*

▸ 3 a *Why do ten-pin bowling pins have a narrow base and a high centre of gravity?*

 b *Why is a tall stool designed with the base wider than the seat?*

Key words: resultant moment

P6.6 # Circular motion

Key points

- The velocity of an object moving in a circle at constant speed is continually changing as the object's direction is continually changing.
- Centripetal acceleration is the acceleration towards the centre of the circle of an object that is moving round the circle.
- Centripetal force is the resultant force that causes the centripetal acceleration of an object moving round a circle.
- The centripetal force on an object depends on its mass, its speed and the radius of the circle.

∞ ∞ links

Revise more on velocity and acceleration in 1.2 'Velocity and acceleration'.

Figure 1 Whirling an object round

Key words: centripetal acceleration, centripetal force

- When an object moves in a circle it is continuously changing direction, so it is continuously changing velocity. In other words, it is accelerating. This acceleration is called the **centripetal acceleration**.
- An object only accelerates when a resultant force acts on it. This force is called the **centripetal force** and always acts towards the centre of the circle.
- If the centripetal force stops acting, the object will continue to move in a straight line at a tangent to the circle.
- The centripetal force needed to make an object perform circular motion increases as:
  - the mass of the object increases
  - the speed of the object increases
  - the radius of the circle decreases.

▷ **1 a** *A student is whirling a nut around on a piece of string, in a horizontal circle. What force provides the centripetal force?*
   b *What will happen to the nut if the string breaks?*

▷ **2 a** *What force provides the centripetal force when a vehicle travels round a roundabout?*
   b *What happens to a car on a roundabout if the centripetal force on it is too small?*

Study tip

Centripetal force is not a force in its own right. It is always provided by another force, for example gravitational force, electric force or tension.

In questions on circular motion, you may need to identify the force that provides the centripetal force.

Practical

Testing circular motion

An object whirled round on the end of a string moves in a circle, as shown in Figure 1. The pull force on the object from the string changes the object's direction of motion. Find out if the pull force increases or decreases if the object is rotated faster at the same radius.

▷ **3** *What can you say about the centripetal force if the object is rotated faster at the same radius?*

▷ **4** *Look at the fairground gravity wheel in Figure 2.*
   a *Why don't the riders fall out as they pass through the highest position?*
   b *Why do the riders need to be strapped in?*

Figure 2 A fairground gravity wheel

Student's book
pages 62–63

P6.7 Hydraulics

Key points

- Pressure is force divided by the area that the force acts on.
- The pressure in a fluid acts equally in all directions.
- A hydraulic system uses the pressure in a fluid to exert a force.
- When the cross-sectional areas on the load side and the effort side of a hydraulic system are different, the system can be used as a force multiplier.

Maths skills

Worked example

A caterpillar vehicle of weight 12000 N is fitted with tracks that have an area of 3.0 m² in contact with the ground. Calculate the pressure of the vehicle on the ground.

Solution

$$\text{Pressure} = \frac{\text{force}}{\text{cross-sectional area}}$$

$$= \frac{12000\,\text{N}}{3.0\,\text{m}^2} = 4000\,\text{Pa}$$

∞ links

Revise more on liquids in 13.1 'States of matter'.

Study tip

Remember that a hydraulic pressure system is usually used as a force multiplier. So if you calculate that the force produced by such a system is less than the effort applied to the system you have made a mistake.

Maths skills

Pressure is given by the equation:

$$p = \frac{F}{A}$$

where p is the pressure in pascals, Pa (or N/m²)
    F is the force in newtons, N
    A is the cross-sectional area in square metres (m²) at right angles to the direction of the force.
We can rearrange the above equation to give $F = pA$ or $A = \frac{F}{p}$.

1 a **What is the pressure exerted on the ground by a person of weight 300 N if the area of their feet in contact with the ground is 0.04 m²?**
  b **The pressure on the base of a submarine at a certain depth under water is 120 million pascals (MPa). Calculate the force due to this pressure on an area of 1.5 square metres.**

- Liquids are virtually incompressible and the pressure in a liquid is transmitted equally in all directions. This means that a force exerted at one point on a liquid will be transmitted to other points in the liquid. This is made use of in **hydraulic pressure** systems.
- The force exerted by a hydraulic pressure system depends on:
  - the force exerted on the system
  - the area of the cylinder which this force acts on
  - the area of the cylinder that exerts the force.
- The use of different cross-sectional areas on the effort and load sides of a hydraulic system means that the system can be used as a **force multiplier**. Therefore, a small effort can be used to move a large load.

2 **In a hydraulic pressure system, a force of 25 N is applied to a piston of area 0.50 m². The area of the other piston is 1.5 m². Calculate the pressure transmitted through the system and the force exerted on the other piston.**

3 a **What properties of a liquid make it useful in a hydraulic system?**
  b **Why is a hydraulic system less effective if air leaks into it?**

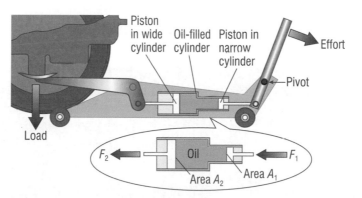

Figure 1 A hydraulic car jack

Key words: pressure, hydraulic pressure, force multiplier

1 Where is the position of the centre of mass of each of the shapes on the right?

2 An object that is freely suspended is displaced slightly then let go. Where will its centre of mass be when it comes to rest?

3 A simple pendulum performs 30 cycles of oscillation in 10 seconds.
  a Calculate:
    i its frequency
    ii its time period.
  b State if the frequency would be smaller or larger or unchanged if the pendulum were shortened.

4 **a** Why will an oscillating simple pendulum eventually come to rest?
  b What is the amplitude of an oscillation?

5 **a** What is the moment of a force?
  b What is the unit of the moment of a force?

6 A force of 15 N is applied at right angles to the end of a spanner 0.5 m long.
  a What is the moment of this force?
  b What force would be necessary to achieve this moment if it were applied at a distance of 0.3 m from the nut?

7 Why is it easier to move a big rock with a crowbar than with your hands?

8 The crowbar is applied such that the fulcrum is 0.05 m from the end of the crowbar in contact with the rock. A force of 150 N is applied to the crowbar at a distance of 0.50 m from the fulcrum.

How much force must be exerted on the rock by the crowbar to move the rock?

9 Why is a long rectangular box more likely to topple over when knocked if it stands 'end on' on the floor?

10 A small stone on the end of a string is whirled round in a circle. What is the angle between the direction of the centripetal force acting on the object and the direction of its velocity?

11 How does the centripetal force change if the object is whirled round at the same speed in a larger circle?

12 A force of 30 N acts on a surface of area 0.0006 square metres. Calculate the pressure on the surface.

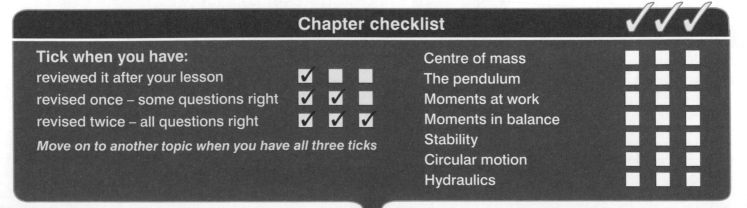

Chapter checklist ✓ ✓ ✓

Tick when you have:

reviewed it after your lesson	✓	☐	☐
revised once – some questions right	✓	✓	☐
revised twice – all questions right	✓	✓	✓

Move on to another topic when you have all three ticks

Centre of mass	☐	☐	☐
The pendulum	☐	☐	☐
Moments at work	☐	☐	☐
Moments in balance	☐	☐	☐
Stability	☐	☐	☐
Circular motion	☐	☐	☐
Hydraulics	☐	☐	☐

1 a i What is meant by the stopping distance of a car? *(1 mark)*

ii Explain why the stopping distance of a car travelling at a certain speed is greater if the road is wet. *(2 marks)*

b Figure 1 shows how the velocity of a car on a dry level road decreases with time after the driver sees an obstruction in the road ahead.

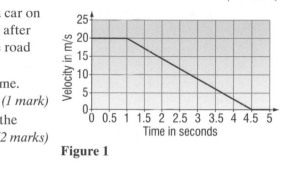

i Estimate the driver's reaction time. *(1 mark)*

ii How far did the car travel after the driver applied the brakes? *(2 marks)*

Figure 1

c The mass of the car was 910 kg.
Calculate

i the deceleration of the car when the brakes were applied, *(2 marks)*

ii the resultant force on the car when it was decelerating. *(1 mark)*

d The shortest safe braking distance on a dry level road at this speed is 31 m. Use the graph to estimate the deceleration of the car if its braking distance had been 31 m. *(3 marks)*

2 Figure 2 shows a hydraulic lift which is used to raise a car above the ground so the underside can be inspected.

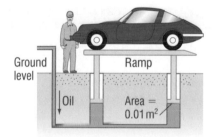

Figure 2

a i Explain why forcing oil into the hydraulic system raises the car. *(2 marks)*

ii Explain why the lift would not operate effectively if air was trapped in the hydraulic system. *(1 mark)*

b The lift has a ramp of weight 1800 N that is lifted by four pistons, each of area 0.010 m². The pressure in the hydraulic system must not exceed 600 kPa.

i Calculate the force exerted on each piston when the pressure in the system is 600 kPa. *(2 marks)*

ii Calculate the maximum weight of a vehicle on the ramp that can be lifted by the platform. *(2 marks)*

c A vehicle of weight 12 000 N is raised by 0.80 m.

i Show that the pressure in the system needed to raise this vehicle is 290 kPa. *(3 marks)*

ii Calculate the gain of gravitational potential energy of the vehicle. *(2 marks)*

iii Give two reasons why the work done to raise the vehicle is greater than its gain of gravitational potential energy. *(2 marks)*

P7.1

The nature of waves

DOUBLE AWARD

Key points

- We use waves to transfer energy and transfer information.
- Transverse waves oscillate perpendicular to the direction of energy transfer of the waves.
- Longitudinal waves oscillate parallel to the direction of energy transfer of the waves.

⚲ links

Revise more on electromagnetic waves in 8.1 'The electromagnetic spectrum'.

Waves transfer energy and information. The direction of travel of the wave is the direction in which the wave transfers energy. There are different types of waves:

- **Mechanical waves** are vibrations that travel through a medium (substance). Examples include waves on springs, on stretched strings and wires, and sound waves. Mechanical waves may be transverse or longitudinal.
- **Electromagnetic waves** are electric and magnetic disturbances that can travel through a vacuum, e.g. light waves and radio waves. No medium is needed. Electromagnetic waves all travel through a vacuum at the same speed of 300 000 km/s. All electromagnetic waves are transverse waves.

➠ **1** *What type of waves are produced when a piano is played?*

- For a **transverse wave** the **oscillation** (vibration) of the particles is **perpendicular** (at right angles) to the direction in which the wave travels.
- For a **longitudinal wave** the oscillation of the particles is parallel to the direction of travel of the wave.
- A longitudinal wave is made up of **compressions** (where the particles are closest together) and **rarefactions** (where the particles become furthest apart).

➠ **2** *When a longitudinal wave passes through air, what happens to the air particles during a compression then during a rarefaction?*

Study tip

Make sure you understand the difference between longitudinal and transverse waves.

Remember that electromagnetic waves are transverse and sound waves are longitudinal.

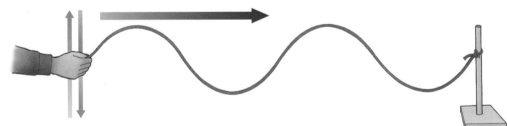

Figure 1 Transverse waves

Figure 2 Longitudinal waves on a slinky

Key words: mechanical wave, electromagnetic wave, transverse wave, oscillation, perpendicular, longitudinal wave, compression, rarefaction

P7.2 Measuring waves

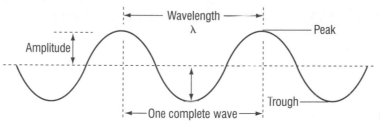

Figure 1 Waves on a rope

Key points

- For any wave, its **amplitude** is the height of the wave crest or the depth of the wave trough from the position at rest.
- For any wave, its **frequency** is the number of wave crests passing a point in one second.
- For any wave, its **wavelength** is the distance from one wave crest to the next wave crest.

  Wave speed = frequency × wavelength: $v = f\lambda$

Maths skills

The wave speed equation can be written as $v = f \times \lambda$
where v = speed,
f = frequency, λ = wavelength.
The equation above can be rearranged to work out

- the wavelength if we know the frequency and the wave speed.

To do this, we rearrange the equation into $\lambda = \dfrac{v}{f}$

- the frequency if we know the wavelength and the wave speed.

To do this, we rearrange the equation into $f = \dfrac{v}{\lambda}$

Note: The Greek letter λ is pronounced 'lambda'.

links

Revise more on the speed of waves in 8.1 'The electromagnetic spectrum'.

Study tip

Make sure that you know what the wave terms mean and can mark them on a diagram.

Key words: wavelength, frequency

Look at Figure 1 and Table 1 to see the meaning of the terms **amplitude**, **wavelength** and **frequency** as applied to a transverse wave and to a longitudinal wave.

Figure 1 shows a transverse wave but all of the same terms apply to a longitudinal wave.

▶ **1** *The diagram above can be used to represent the displacement of the particles of a longitudinal wave (that is, how far they are from their position at rest). Explain why the compressions and rarefactions are at zero displacement.*

Table 1

	Transverse waves	**Longitudinal waves**
Amplitude	The height of the wave crest or the depth of the wave trough from the position at rest.	The maximum distance of a vibrating particle from its position at rest.
Wavelength	The distance from a crest to the next crest, or from a trough to the next trough.	The distance between the centres of adjacent compressions (or between the centres of adjacent rarefactions).
Frequency	The number of wave crests passing a point in one second.	The number of compressions passing a point in one second.

- The greater the amplitude, the more energy the wave transfers.
- The unit of frequency is the hertz (Hz). This unit is equivalent to 'per second' (/s).
- The unit of wavelength is the metre (m).
- The **speed** of a wave is the distance travelled per second by a crest or a trough. The unit of speed is the metre/second (m/s).
- The speed of a wave is given by the equation:

  wave speed = frequency × wavelength

▶ **2 a** *What is the speed of waves with a frequency of 600 Hz and a wavelength of 3.0 m?*

b *The speed of sound in air is 340 m/s. What is the wavelength of sound waves in air that have a frequency of 1700 Hz?*

Practical

Measure the speed of water waves in a ripple tank

A **stopwatch** is used to time how long a wave takes to travel across the tank and back 5 times (= 10 crossings).

This timing is repeated two more times to obtain an average value and to calculate the time t for the wave to travel across the tank once.

A **metre ruler** is used to measure the distance D across the tank. The speed of the wave = $\dfrac{D}{t}$

▶ **3** *What is the advantage of repeating the timing two more times?*

P7.3 Reflection and refraction

Key points

- Plane waves that reflect from a straight barrier reflect at the same angle to the barrier as the incident waves.
- Refraction is the change of direction of waves when they cross a boundary, due to a change of the speed of waves when they cross a boundary.

∞ links

Revise more on refraction in 10.2 'Refraction of light'.

∞ links

Revise more on reflection in 10.1 'Reflection of light'.

Reflection of plane waves

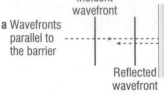

Figure 1 Reflection of plane waves

- In Figure 1a, the incident wavefront is parallel to the barrier as it approaches the barrier. It is still parallel to the barrier after **reflection** as it travels away from the barrier.
- In Figure 1b, the reflected wavefront moves away from the barrier at the same angle to the barrier as the incident wavefront.
- All parts of both wavefronts move at the same speed. This means that the reflected wavefront is at the same angle to the barrier as the incident wavefront.

➡ **1** *Plane waves are directed at a straight barrier at an angle of 30° to the barrier. What is the angle between each reflected wave and **a** the barrier? **b** the incident waves?*

➡ **2** *The frequency of the waves does not change on reflection. What can you say about the wavelength before and after reflection?*

Practical

A reflection test

Use a ruler in a ripple tank to create and direct plane waves at a straight barrier, as shown in Figure 1. Find out if the reflected waves are always at the same angle to the barrier as the incident waves. You could align a second ruler with the reflected waves and measure the angle of each ruler to the barrier. Repeat the test for different angles.

➡ **3** *How would you improve the accuracy of your measurements?*

Refraction of waves

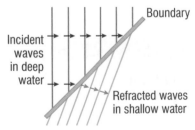

Figure 2 Refraction of plane waves

- **Refraction** is the change of direction of waves when they cross a boundary at a non-zero angle to a boundary and their speed changes at the boundary.
- Figure 2 shows what happens when water waves cross a boundary between 'deep' and 'shallow' water. The wavefronts are at a smaller angle to the boundary than the incident wavefronts. This is because they travel more slowly in shallow water than in deep water. So the direction in which they are moving changes.
- If the waves had moved faster after crossing the boundary (e.g. if they had travelled from shallow to deep water), the refracted wavefronts would be at a larger angle to the boundary than the incident wavefronts.

➡ **4** *Planes waves are directed at a straight boundary at an angle of 30° to the boundary. The waves travel faster after crossing the boundary. State and explain whether the angle between the boundary and each wave after it crosses the boundary is smaller than or greater than 30°.*

Key words: reflection, refraction

P7.4 Diffraction

- Diffraction is the spreading out of waves when they pass through a gap or round the edge of an obstacle.
- The narrower a gap is, the greater the diffraction is.
- If radio waves do not diffract enough when they go over hills, radio and TV reception will be poor.

∞ links

Revise more on diffraction in 9.1 'Sound'.

Study tip

Remember that diffraction can be through a hole or round an obstacle.
The smaller the hole, the greater the diffraction.
Diffraction is most noticeable when the hole is the same size as the wavelength of the wave.

Key word: diffraction

2 a *High frequency ultrasound and low frequency ultrasound are diffracted by the same obstacle. State and explain which is diffracted least.*

b *The wavelengths of radio waves that carry TV mobile phone signals are shorter than the wavelengths that carry local radio channels. Which are diffracted most when they both pass through a gap between two buildings?*

Diffraction is the spreading of waves when they pass through a gap or move past an obstacle. The waves that pass through the gap or past the edges of the obstacle spread out.

Figure 1 shows waves in a ripple tank spreading out after they pass through two gaps. The effect is most noticeable if the wavelength of the waves is similar to the width of the gap. Note that:

- The narrower the gap, the more the waves spread out.
- The wider the gap, the less the waves spread out.

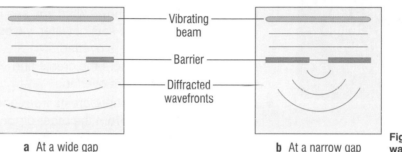

a At a wide gap   **b** At a narrow gap   **Figure 1 Diffraction of waves by a gap**

Diffraction examples

- **Light** is diffracted when it enters an optical instrument. This can reduce the detail seen in an image. The Hubble Space Telescope provides detailed images of objects far away in space because it is so wide. Therefore little diffraction occurs when light passes through it.
- **Ultrasound waves** are used in medicine to scan organs in the body. Ultrasound waves are sound waves at frequencies above the range of the human ear. When an ultrasound scan is made of a baby in the womb, the waves spread out from a hand-held transmitter and then reflect from tissue boundaries inside the womb. If the transmitter is too narrow, the waves diffract and spread out too much and the image is not very clear.
- **Radio waves** are used to carry TV signals. People in hilly areas often have poor TV reception. If there are hills between a TV receiver and the mast, the signal may not reach the receiver. The radio waves passing the top of a hill are diffracted by the hill but they do not spread enough behind the hill.

1 *The three examples of diffraction above show that both transverse and longitudinal waves can be diffracted. Which example(s) shows the diffraction of **a** longitudinal waves? **b** transverse waves?*

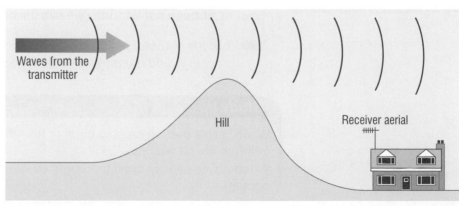

Figure 2 Poor reception

P7.5 Interference

Key points

- Interference is the reinforcement or cancellation of waves when two identical sets of waves overlap.
- When a crest meets a trough, the two waves cancel each other out.
- When a crest meets a crest, or a trough meets a trough, they reinforce each other.
- Interference is a property of all types of wave.

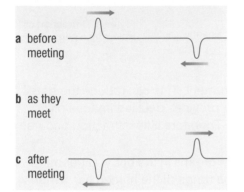

Figure 1 A crest meets a trough

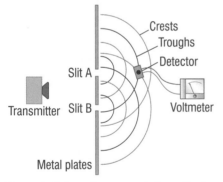

Figure 3 Using microwaves to investigate interference

- Figure 1 shows two waves travelling along a rope towards each other. One wave is a **crest** and the other is a **trough**. They meet and pass through each other. When they meet, they **cancel** each other out at that instant. This **cancellation** is an example of **interference**.

> 1 *If the amplitude of the crest is less than that of the trough, what would be observed where the crest meets the trough?*

- All types of waves can be made to interfere regardless of whether they are transverse or longitudinal. Figure 2 shows what you see in a ripple tank where two sets of water waves produced by two dippers overlap. Interference occurs where the crests and troughs from the dippers overlap.
- **Cancellation** occurs where crests from one dipper cancel troughs from the other dipper. Gaps in the waves are seen where this happens.
- **Reinforcement** occurs where crests from each dipper meet or where troughs meet. This happens between the gaps.

Notice that if the dippers are moved closer together, the gaps move further apart.

Figure 2 Interference of water waves

> 2 *In Figure 2, what is observed if **a** one of the dippers is removed? **b** the frequency of vibration of the dippers is reduced?*

- Interference can be demonstrated by directing waves from a single source at two close slits or gaps. The waves diffract as they pass through each slit and interfere where they overlap. Figure 3 shows how an interference pattern is produced using microwaves. By moving a detector connected to a voltmeter, the points of cancellation and reinforcement can be located from the detector signal.

In general, at any point **P**:

- Reinforcement occurs wherever the difference in the distances to each slit is a whole number of wavelengths. This is because whenever a crest or a trough arrives from one slit, the same arrives from the other slit.
- Cancellation occurs wherever the difference in the distances to each slit is a whole number of wavelengths + *an extra half wavelength*. This is because whenever a crest or a trough arrives from one slit, the opposite arrives from the other slit.

> 3 *If the detector in Figure 3 is at a point of cancellation, state and explain what would happen if one of the two slits was covered?*

Study tip

When waves overlap crest to crest or trough to trough, constructive interference (reinforcement) occurs.
When waves overlap crest to trough, destructive interference (cancellation) occurs.

Key words: cancellation, interference, reinforcement

1 State the difference between a transverse wave and a longitudinal wave.

2 Give one example of:

   a a longitudinal wave

   b a transverse wave.

3 What is a rarefaction?

4 A loudspeaker produces sound waves in air of wavelength 0.10 m. What is the distance between a compression and the nearest rarefaction?

5 What do we mean by the amplitude of:

   a a transverse wave?

   b a longitudinal wave?

6 Waves on a canal move on the water surface at a speed of 0.4 m/s with a wavelength of 0.5 m. Calculate the frequency of the waves.

7 In terms of waves, what is refraction?

8 A plane wave crosses a straight boundary at a non-zero angle to the boundary. What happens to the wave if it slows down when it crosses the boundary?

9 What is the difference between diffraction and interference?

10 Why is TV reception often poor in hilly areas?

11 Sound waves of a certain wavelength from a loudspeaker pass through two closely spaced slits in a large board. Explain why someone on the other side of the board would be unable to hear the loudspeaker at certain positions.

12 What difference would the observer in Q11 find if one of the slits is covered?

Chapter checklist

Tick when you have:

reviewed it after your lesson	☑ ☐ ☐	
revised once – some questions right	☑ ☑ ☐	
revised twice – all questions right	☑ ☑ ☑	

Move on to another topic when you have all three ticks

	✓ ✓ ✓
The nature of waves	☐ ☐ ☐
Measuring waves	☐ ☐ ☐
Reflection and refraction	☐ ☐ ☐
Diffraction	☐ ☐ ☐
Interference	☐ ☐ ☐

P8.1 # The electromagnetic spectrum

Key points

- The electromagnetic spectrum (in order of **increasing** frequency and energy) is: radio waves, microwaves, infrared, visible, ultraviolet, X-rays, gamma rays.
- $v = f\lambda$ can be used to calculate the frequency or wavelength of electromagnetic waves.

- Electromagnetic radiations are electric and magnetic disturbances. They travel as waves and move energy from place to place.
- All electromagnetic waves travel through space (a vacuum) at the same speed and their wavelengths and frequencies cover a very wide range.
- The full range of wavelengths is called the **electromagnetic spectrum**. We group the waves according to their **wavelength** and **frequency**.
- Gamma rays have the shortest wavelength and highest frequency.
- Radio waves have the longest wavelength and lowest frequency.
- The wavelengths are from about a millionth of a millionth of a millimetre to about 10 kilometres.

The spectrum is continuous. The frequencies and wavelengths at the boundaries are approximate as the different parts of the spectrum are not precisely defined.

- All electromagnetic waves travel through space at a **wave speed** of 300 million m/s. We can link the speed of the waves to their wavelength and frequency using the equation:

$$v = f\lambda$$

where v is the wave speed in m/s
f is the frequency in hertz, Hz
λ is the wavelength in metres, m.

🖩 Maths skills

Worked example
A mobile phone gives out electromagnetic waves of frequency 900 million Hz. Calculate the wavelength of these waves.
The speed of electromagnetic waves in air = 300 million m/s.

Solution
Rearrange the equation $v = f\lambda$ to give

$$\lambda = \frac{v}{f} = \frac{300\,000\,000\,\text{m/s}}{900\,000\,000\,\text{Hz}} = \textbf{0.33\,m}$$

🔗 links
Revise more on the speed of waves in 7.2 'Measuring waves'.

- Different wavelengths of electromagnetic radiation are reflected, absorbed or transmitted differently by different substances and types of surface.
- The higher the frequency of an electromagnetic wave the shorter its wavelength is and the more energy it transfers.

⫸ 1 *What is the frequency of microwaves of wavelength 3.0 cm?*

⫸ 2 *Which part of the electromagnetic spectrum **a** transfers the most energy? **b** has the longest wavelength?*

⫸ 3 *Write down the main parts of the electromagnetic spectrum in order of increasing wavelength.*

Study tip
Make sure that you can put the different parts of the spectrum in the correct order – which may be either increasing or decreasing in wavelength, frequency or energy.

Key words: electromagnetic spectrum, wavelength, frequency, wave speed

Student's book pages 80–81 **P8.2**

Light, infrared, microwaves and radio waves

Key points

- White light contains all the colours of the spectrum.
- Visible light, infrared radiation, microwaves and radiation are all used for communication.
- Microwaves and radio waves can heat the internal parts of the body. Infrared radiation can cause skin burns.

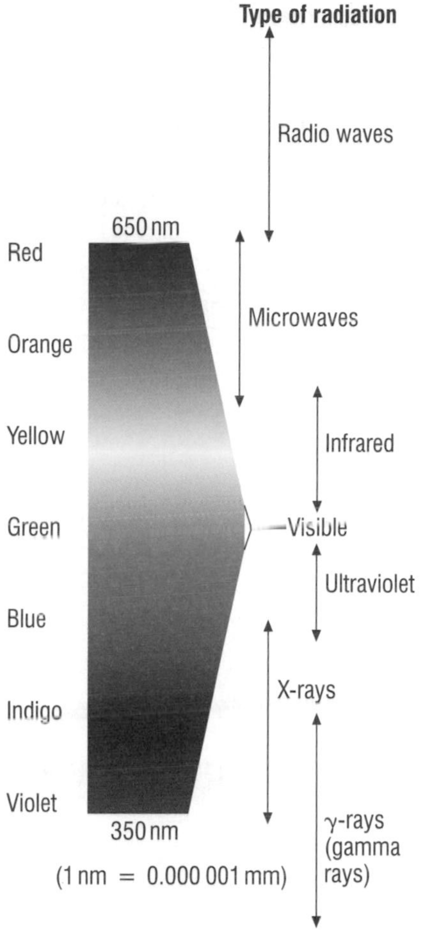

Figure 1 The electromagnetic spectrum with an expanded view of the visible range

links

Revise more on infrared radiation in 14.4 'Infrared radiation'.

- **Visible light** is the part of the electromagnetic spectrum that is detected by our eyes. We see the different wavelengths within it as different colours.
- The wavelength increases across the spectrum from violet to red. We see a mixture of all the colours as white light.
- Visible light can be used for photography and can be transmitted along optical fibres.

1 ***In order of increasing wavelength, write down the types of electromagnetic waves which are used for communication.***

Study tip

The spectrum of visible light covers just a very small part of the electromagnetic spectrum.

- **Infrared radiation** is given out by all objects. The hotter the object, the more infrared radiation it emits. Remote controls for devices such as TVs, videos and CD players use infrared radiation. It can be transmitted along optical fibres.
- **Microwaves** are used in communications. Microwave transmitters produce wavelengths that are able to pass through the atmosphere. They are used to send signals to and from satellites and within mobile phone networks.
- **Radio waves** are used to transmit radio and TV programs and carry mobile phone signals.

2 ***Why is it not possible to use light to carry signals to and from satellites?***

- Microwaves and radio waves penetrate your skin and are absorbed by body tissue. This can heat internal organs and may damage them.
- Infrared radiation is absorbed by skin; too much will burn your skin.

Key words: visible light, infrared radiation, microwaves, radio waves

P8.3

Communications

Key points

- Radio waves of different frequencies are used for different purposes because their wavelength (and therefore their frequency) affects
  - how far they travel
  - how much they spread
  - how much information they can carry.
- Microwaves are used for satellite TV signals.
- Further research is needed to evaluate whether or not mobile phones are safe to use.
- Optical fibres are very thin fibres that are used to transmit signals using light and infrared radiation.

∞ links

Revise more on optical fibres in 10.4 'Total internal reflection'.

Study tip

Make sure that you can sketch a diagram to show light travelling down an optical fibre by total internal reflection.

- When an alternating voltage is applied to an aerial, it emits radio waves with the same frequency as the alternating voltage. When the waves are received they produce an alternating current in the aerial with the same frequency as the radiation received.
- The radio and microwave spectrum is divided into different **bands**. The different bands are used for different communications purposes.
- The shorter the wavelength of the waves:
  - the more information they carry
  - the shorter their range
  - the less they spread out.

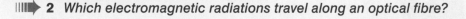 **1** *Which can carry more information, light or radio waves? Give a reason for your answer.*

- Mobile phones communicate with a local mobile phone mast using radio waves of wavelengths not quite in the microwave range. They are usually referred to as microwaves because they have a similar heating effect.
- Some scientists think that the radiation from mobile phones may affect the brain, especially in children.
- **Optical fibres** are very thin glass fibres. We use them to transmit signals carried by light or infrared radiation. The signals travel down the fibre by repeated total internal reflection.
- Optical fibres carrying visible light or infrared are useful in communications because they carry much more information and are more secure than radio wave and microwave transmissions.

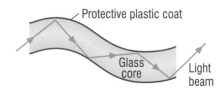

Protective plastic coat

Glass core

Light beam

Figure 1 Optical fibres

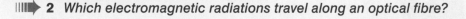 **2** *Which electromagnetic radiations travel along an optical fibre?*

Practical

Investigate the absorption of light by glass

A **light meter** is placed at a fixed distance from a light bulb in a darkened room.

Different numbers of glass slides (or blocks) are placed together between the meter and the bulb. The number of slides (including with no slides) is recorded together with the reading of the light meter each time.

A graph of the meter reading is plotted against the number of glass slides.

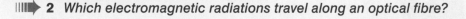 **3** *Why is it important to keep the distance between the meter and the bulb fixed?*

Key words: band, optical fibre

Student's book
pages 84–85

P8.4

Ultraviolet rays, X-rays and gamma rays

Student's book pages 84–85

Key points

- Ultraviolet radiation is shorter in wavelength than light and harms the skin and the eyes.
- X-rays are used in hospitals to make X-ray pictures.
- Gamma rays are used to kill harmful bacteria in food, to sterilise surgical equipment and to kill cancer cells.
- X-rays and gamma radiation damage living tissue when they pass through it.

links

Revise more on X-rays in 8.5 'X-rays in medicine'.

links

Revise more on gamma radiation in 19.3 'More about alpha, beta and gamma radiation'.

- **Ultraviolet (UV) radiation** is between violet light and X-rays in the electromagnetic spectrum. It makes some chemicals emit light. The chemicals **absorb** ultraviolet radiation and emit light as a result.
- Ultraviolet radiation is harmful to human eyes and can cause blindness. UV rays carry more energy than light rays. Too much UV radiation causes sunburn and can cause skin cancer. Special 'goggles' must be worn by sun-bed users to protect their eyes.

▥➡ **1** *Suncream is designed to protect the skin from sunburn. What does suncream do to ultraviolet radiation?*

X-rays and gamma rays both travel straight into substances and may pass through them if the substances are not too dense or not too thick. A thick lead plate will stop them. Gamma rays penetrate substances more than X-rays can.

X-rays are produced by X-ray tubes. Gamma rays are produced by radioactive substances when unstable nuclei release energy.

X-rays are used:
- in hospitals to make X-ray pictures of broken limbs
- to detect internal cracks in metal objects.

▥➡ **2** *Which is the better absorber of X-rays, an aluminium plate or a lead plate of the same thickness?*

Gamma rays are used:
- to kill harmful bacteria in food
- to sterilise surgical instruments
- to kill cancer cells.

▥➡ **3** *Why are X-rays more suitable than gamma rays for making radiographs?*

Study tip

Make sure that you know the dangers, as well as the uses, of electromagnetic waves.

Key word: absorb

P8.5 X-rays in medicine

Key points

- X-rays are used in hospitals:
  - to make images and CT scans
  - to destroy tumours at or near the body surface.
- X-rays can damage living tissue when they pass through it.
- X-rays are absorbed more by bones and teeth than by soft tissue.
- CT scans distinguish between different types of soft tissue as well as between bone (or teeth) and soft tissue.

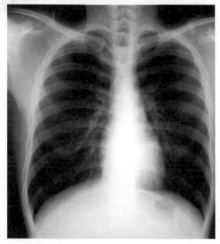

Figure 1 Taking a chest X-ray

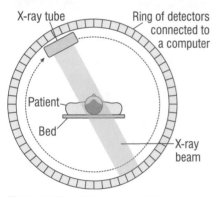

Figure 2 The CT scanner – it can distinguish between different types of soft tissue, as well as bone

∞ links

Revise more on ionisation in 19.3 'More about alpha, beta and gamma radiation'.

- **X-rays** are produced in an X-ray tube when fast-moving electrons hit a target. To make a radiograph or X-ray photograph, X-rays from the tube are directed at the patient.
- X-rays pass through soft tissue but they are absorbed by bones and teeth.
- An organ that consists of soft tissue can be filled with a **contrast medium** which is a substance that absorbs X-rays easily. This enables the internal surfaces in the organ to be seen on the radiograph.
- Lead 'absorber' plates between the tube and the patient stop X-rays reaching other parts of the body. The X-rays reaching the patient pass through a gap between the plates.
- A light-proof cassette containing a photographic film or a **flat-panel detector** is placed on the other side of the patient. A flat-panel detector containing a **charge-coupled device** (CCD) may be used to display a digital X-ray image.

> 1 *Why is a contrast medium necessary to obtain a radiograph of the stomach?*

X-rays and gamma rays **ionise** substances they pass through.
- Ionisation in a living cell can damage or kill the cell.
- High doses of **ionising radiation** kill living cells and low doses cause cell mutation and cancerous growth.

Workers who use X-ray equipment or radioactive substances must wear a film badge. If the badge is overexposed to such radiation, its wearer is stopped from working with the equipment.

> 2 a *What is an ion?*
> b *Why is it harmful for a person with a broken bone to have too many radiographs?*

Doctors use X-ray therapy to destroy cancerous tumours in the body. X-rays for therapy are shorter in wavelength than X-rays used for imaging.

> 3 *What can you say about the energy of short wavelength X-rays compared with long-wavelength X-rays?*

- In a **computerised tomography** scanner (**CT scanner**), the patient lies stationary on a bed that is in a ring of detectors, as shown in Figure 2.
- The X-ray tube automatically moves round the inside of the ring in small steps.
- X-rays from the tube pass through the patient and reach the detector ring.
- Electronic signals from the detectors are recorded by a computer until the tube has moved round the ring.

The detector signal depends on:
- the different types of tissue along the X-ray path
- how far the X-rays pass through each type of tissue.

Compared with an ordinary X-ray machine, a CT scanner distinguishes between different types of soft tissue and gives a three-dimensional image. However, it gives a greater radiation dose and is much more expensive.

Key words: X-ray, charge-coupled device, ionise, ionising radiation, CT scanner

1 Write down the main parts of the electromagnetic spectrum in order of increasing frequency.

2 Which part of the electromagnetic spectrum has most energy?

3 Why is exposure to intense infrared radiation harmful?

4 What part of the electromagnetic spectrum is used for:

   a satellite communications?

   b mobile phone signals?

5 How does light travel along an optical fibre?

6 State one advantage and one disadvantage of optical fibre communications compared with radio communications.

7 Why is it not possible to use infrared radiation to send signals to or from a satellite?

8 **a** What is ionisation?

   b Why is ionisation in living tissue harmful?

9 State two parts of the electromagnetic spectrum that are non-ionising?

10 Why do bones show up against soft tissue on a radiograph?

11 State two uses of gamma radiation.

12 State one medical advantage and one medical disadvantage of using a CT scanner compared with an ordinary X-ray system.

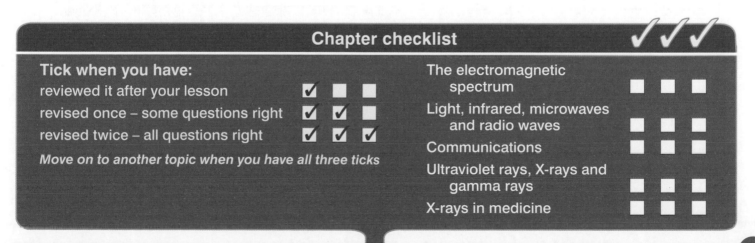

Chapter checklist	✓ ✓ ✓
Tick when you have:	The electromagnetic spectrum ▢ ▢ ▢
reviewed it after your lesson ✓ ▢ ▢	Light, infrared, microwaves and radio waves ▢ ▢ ▢
revised once – some questions right ✓ ✓ ▢	Communications ▢ ▢ ▢
revised twice – all questions right ✓ ✓ ✓	Ultraviolet rays, X-rays and gamma rays ▢ ▢ ▢
Move on to another topic when you have all three ticks	X-rays in medicine ▢ ▢ ▢

Student's book
pages 90–91 **P9.1** | # Sound 🔵

Key points

- The frequency range of the normal human ear is from about 20 Hz to about 20 kHz.
- Sound waves are vibrations that travel through a substance.
- Sound waves cannot travel through a vacuum.
- Echoes are caused by sound waves reflected from a smooth, hard surface.

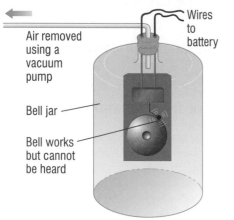

Figure 1 A sound test

🔗 links

Revise more on longitudinal waves in 7.1 'The nature of waves'.

Study tip

Remember that sound waves are longitudinal and need a medium to compress.

Key words: sound, echo

- **Sound** is caused by mechanical vibrations in a substance, and travels as a wave.
- It can travel through liquids, solids and gases. Sound waves generally travel fastest in solids and slowest in gases.
- They cannot travel through a vacuum (like space). This can be tested by listening to a ringing bell in a 'bell jar'. As the air is pumped out of the jar, the ringing sound fades away.

Sound waves are **longitudinal waves**. Tthe vibrations are parallel to the direction in which the wave travels.

The range of frequencies that can be heard by the human ear is from 20 Hz to 20 000 Hz. The ability to hear the higher frequencies declines with age.

Sound waves can be reflected to produce **echoes**.

- Only hard, flat surfaces such as flat walls and floors reflect sound.
- Soft objects like carpets, curtains and furniture absorb sounds.

Sound waves can be refracted. Refraction takes place at the boundaries between layers of air at different temperatures.

Sound waves can also be diffracted. For significant diffraction, the wavelength of the sound waves should be of the same order as the size of the obstacle or gap that diffracts the waves.

▷ 1 *Why does an empty room sound different once carpets, curtains and furniture are put into it?*

▷ 2 *Sound in air travels at a speed of about 340 m/s. If a person hears an echo 0.4 s after shouting, how far away is the reflecting surface?*

Practical

Investigating sound waves

Use a loudspeaker to produce sound waves by passing alternating current through it. Figure 2 shows how to do this using a signal generator. This is an alternating current supply unit with a variable frequency dial.

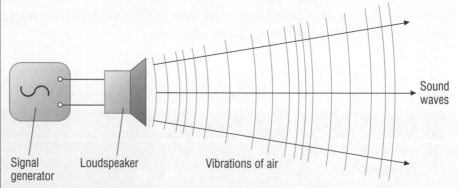

Figure 2 Using a loudspeaker

Find out the highest frequency different people can hear.

Estimate from the variable frequency dial how precise the measurements are.

▷ 3 *What conclusion can you draw from your measurements?*

P9.2

Musical sounds

- The **pitch** of a note depends on the frequency of the sound waves. The higher the frequency of the wave, the higher the pitch of the sound.
- The **loudness** of a sound depends on the amplitude of the sound waves. The greater the amplitude, the more energy the wave carries and the louder the sound.
- The **waveform** of a sound can be shown on an oscilloscope.

> **1** *A siren on an ambulance produces sound waves with a pitch that repeatedly increases sharply then decreases more slowly. Describe how the frequency of the waves varies.*

The quality of a note depends on the waveform.

- Tuning forks and signal generators produce 'pure' waveforms as shown in Figure 2.
- When a musical instrument is played, vibrations created in it produce sound waves in the surrounding air. Different instruments produce different waveforms.
- In wind instruments a column of air vibrates. In string instruments, a string vibrates. Percussion instruments vibrate when they are struck.

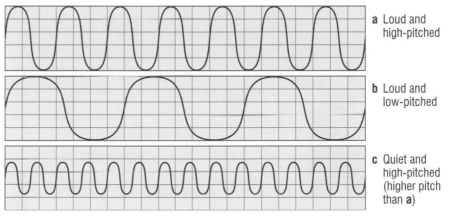

a Loud and high-pitched

b Loud and low-pitched

c Quiet and high-pitched (higher pitch than a)

Figure 2 A pure sound a loud and high-pitched, b quiet and higher pitch than in a

> **2 a** *Figure 2a shows the waveform of the sound from a signal generator. Describe how the waveform would differ if the sound had been louder and lower in pitch.*
> **b** *If the frequency of the waveform in Figure 2a is 2000 Hz, what is the frequency of the waveform in Figure 2b? Assume the time scale in b is the same as in a.*

Key points

- The pitch of a note increases if the frequency of the sound waves increases.
- The loudness of a note increases if the amplitude of the sound waves increases.
- Vibrations created in an instrument when it is played produce sound waves.

Figure 1 Investigating different sounds

⊂⊃ links

Revise more on the oscilloscope in 17.1 'Alternating current'.

Study tip

Practise sketching waveforms, e.g. sketch a wave with twice the frequency and half the amplitude of the original.

> **3** *With several cycles on the screen, why not just measure across just one cycle?*

Key words: pitch, loudness, waveform

Practical

Measure the frequency of sound waves

A signal generator is connected to a loudspeaker to produce sound waves at a constant frequency.

A microphone is connected to an **oscilloscope**. The oscilloscope is adjusted to display the waveform of the sound waves on its screen. Several cycles can be displayed on the oscilloscope screen.

The time taken across several complete cycles is measured. This time measurement is divided by the number of cycles to give the time period T of the waveform.

The frequency of the sound waves = $\frac{1}{T}$.

Ultrasound

Key points

- Ultrasound waves are sound waves of frequency above 20 000 Hz.
- Ultrasound is used in medicine for ultrasound scanning and for destroying kidney stones.
- Ultrasound waves are partly reflected at a boundary between two different types of body tissue.
- An ultrasound scan is non-ionising so it is safer than an X-ray.

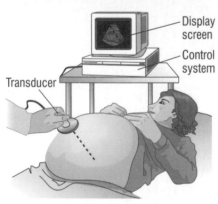

Figure 1 An ultrasound scanner system

∞ links

Revise more on speed calculations in 1.1 'Distance–time graphs'.

Maths skills

The distance equation in symbols:

$$s = v \times t$$

where s is the distance in metres, m
v is the wave speed in metres per second, m/s
t is the time taken in seconds, s.

Key words: ultrasound wave

- The human ear can detect sound waves with frequencies between 20 Hz and 20 000 Hz. Sound waves of a higher frequency than this are called **ultrasound waves**.
- Ultrasound is non-ionising so is safer than X-rays. It can be used for scanning unborn babies and soft tissue such as the eye.
- Ultrasound may also be used in therapy, for example to shatter kidney stones into small pieces.

▶ **1** *Ultrasound frequencies used for scanning have wavelengths of about 0.8 mm in the body. Why would ultrasound of a much lower frequency be unsuitable for scanning?*

In an **ultrasound scanner**, a **transducer** is used to produce and detect ultrasound waves.

- Pulses of ultrasound from a transducer are directed into the body.
- The pulses partially reflect from tissue boundaries in the body.
- The transducer detects the reflected pulses.

The electronic signals from the transducer due to the reflected pulses are processed by a computer to give a visual image.

The signals may also be used to measure the time each pulse takes to travel to and from a boundary and so calculate how far away the boundary is.

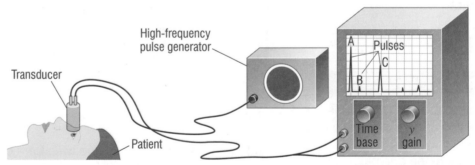

Figure 2 Ultrasound used to measure the length of an eyeball. Partial reflection occurs for pulse A at the cornea, for pulse B at the eye lens and for pulse C at the back of the eye. The oscilloscope is used to measure the time t taken for pulse C to travel from the front to the back of the eye. The length of the eyeball is calculated by multiplying $0.5t$ by the speed of ultrasound waves in the eye.

▶ **2** *What is meant by partial reflection?*

▶ **3** *The speed of ultrasound waves in body tissue is about 1500 m/s. In an ultrasound scanner, an ultrasound pulse is emitted from a transducer and a reflected pulse is received 0.00012 s later. Calculate **a** the distance travelled by the pulse in this time, **b** the distance from the transducer to the reflecting boundary.*

Study tip

When ultrasound is reflected, it goes there and back, so be careful, in calculations, about distance.

1 Describe the movement of the particles of air when sound waves pass through the air.

2 How does a buzzing bee create sound?

3 A loudspeaker is connected to a variable frequency generator. Describe how the sound from the loudspeaker changes as the frequency is increased from about 5000 Hz.

4 Why can outdoor sounds sometimes be heard over a long distance at night?

5 Why do sound waves from a loudspeaker diffract more than ultrasonic waves from the same loudspeaker?

6 What type of surface best causes echoes?

7 A loudspeaker connected to a signal generator produces sound waves of constant amplitude and frequency. What adjustment to the amplitude and frequency of the sound waves from the loudspeaker needs to be made:

a to make the pitch higher?

b to reduce the loudness?

8 How does a flute produce sound waves?

9 Why is ultrasound used rather than X-rays for pre-natal scans?

10 What is a transducer used for in an ultrasound scanner?

11 Why is partial reflection an essential feature of an ultrasound scanner?

12 In an ultrasound scanner, ultrasound pulses are received at the transducer 0.00010 s and 0.00020 s after each pulse is generated. The speed of ultrasound in the body is 1500 m/s. Calculate the distance between the two tissue boundaries responsible for the pulses.

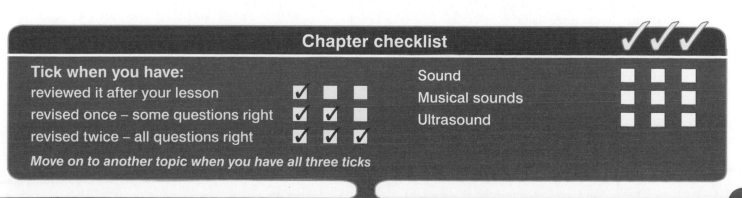

Chapter checklist	✓ ✓ ✓
Tick when you have:	
reviewed it after your lesson ✓ ☐ ☐	Sound ☐ ☐ ☐
revised once – some questions right ✓ ✓ ☐	Musical sounds ☐ ☐ ☐
revised twice – all questions right ✓ ✓ ✓	Ultrasound ☐ ☐ ☐
Move on to another topic when you have all three ticks	

1 In an experiment to measure the speed of water waves in a ripple tank, a student obtained the following measurements of the time taken by a water wave to travel the length of the tank ten times.

26.2 s, 25.8 s, 26.8 s, 27.2 s, 26.4 s

    a Calculate the mean value of the time taken for the wave to travel the length of the tank. *(1 mark)*

    b The length of the tank was 0.440 m. Calculate the speed of the waves in the tank. *(2 marks)*

    c The precision of the stopwatch used by the student was 0.01 s. Give one reason why the measurements above are not the same. *(1 mark)*

2 Electromagnetic waves are transverse waves. Sound waves are longitudinal waves.

    a What is the difference between a transverse wave and a longitudinal wave? *(2 marks)*

    b Microwaves are used in communications to send signals to and from satellites.

       i State two other parts of the electromagnetic spectrum other than radio waves and microwaves that are used for communications. *(2 marks)*

       ii Explain why the two parts named in **b i** are not used to send signals to or from satellites. *(2 marks)*

    c The signals from a television satellite reach a wide area of the Earth's surface. Homes in a certain valley can receive the TV signals from such a satellite but not from a terrestrial TV transmitter on the other side of a hill. Why is it possible to receive signals from the satellite but not from the TV transmitter? *(2 marks)*

    d A TV satellite dish is a metal bowl that focuses the microwaves from a satellite onto an aerial at the centre of the dish, as shown in Figure 1.

       i Explain why the dish needs to be metallic. *(2 marks)*

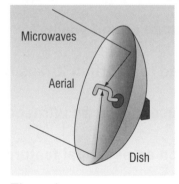

Figure 1

       ii The dish needs to be aligned so it points towards the satellite. The larger the dish is, the more difficult it can be to align in areas at the edge of the satellite's reception area. State the property of waves that causes this effect and explain why a larger dish at the edge of such an area can be more difficult to align. *(2 marks)*

3 Ultrasound waves are used in hospitals to obtain a scan of an unborn baby. When an ultrasound scan is taken, a transducer placed on the body surface sends pulses of ultrasound into the body.

    a What is ultrasound? *(1 mark)*

    b i Explain why each pulse directed into the body can cause several weaker pulses to return to the transducer.
       In this question, you will be assessed on using good English, organising information clearly and using specialist terms where appropriate. *(6 marks)*

       ii A pulse directed into the body caused a reflected pulse to return to the transducer 0.12 milliseconds later. The speed of ultrasound waves in the body is 1550 m/s. What can be deduced about the body from this data? *(2 marks)*

    c Why is ultrasound used to scan an unborn baby rather than X-rays? *(2 marks)*

P10.1 | Reflection of light

Key points

- The normal at a point on a mirror is a line drawn perpendicular to the mirror.
- For a light ray reflected by a plane mirror
  - the angle of incidence is the angle between the incident ray and the normal
  - the angle of reflection is the angle between the reflected ray and the normal.
- The law of reflection states that the angle of incidence equals the angle of reflection.

The image seen in a mirror is due to the **reflection** of light. The diagram shows how an image is formed by a **plane** (flat) **mirror**. Reflection is a property of all waves including light waves.

- A **ray** of light is a thin beam of light and gives the direction the light waves travel in.
- The **normal** is the line perpendicular to the mirror at the point where the incident ray hits the mirror.
- The **angle of incidence** is the angle between the incident ray and the normal.
- The **angle of reflection** is the angle between the reflected ray and the normal.

The law of reflection states that, for any reflected ray, the angle of incidence is equal to the angle of reflection.

▐▶ 1 *If the angle between the incident ray and the reflected ray is 120°, what is the angle of incidence?*

Study tip

Remember that angles of incidence and angles of reflection are measured between the ray and the normal.

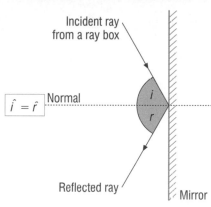

$\hat{i} = \hat{r}$

Figure 1 The law of reflection

Figure 2 shows how an image is formed by a plane mirror. The light rays from the object reflect off the mirror and appear to come from the image. The image in a plane mirror is:

- the same size as the object
- upright
- the same distance behind the mirror as the object is in front
- virtual.

A **real image** is one that can be formed on a screen, because the rays of light that produce the image actually pass through it.

A **virtual image** cannot be formed on a screen, because the rays of light that produce the image only appear to pass through it.

▐▶ 2 *An object is placed 1.5 m in front of a plane mirror. What is the distance from the object to the image?*

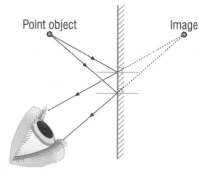

Figure 2 Image formation by a plane mirror

Practical

A reflection test

Test the law of reflection by using a ray box to direct a light ray at a plane mirror as shown in Figure 1. Repeat the test for different angles of incidence.

▐▶ 3 *Describe how you set up this experiment and how you made the necessary measurements.*

⚭ links

Revise more on reflection of light in 10.4 'Total internal reflection'.

Key words: plane mirror, normal, angle of incidence, angle of reflection, real image, virtual image

Student's book
pages 100–101

P10.2 Refraction of light

Key points

- Refraction of light is the change of direction of a light ray when it crosses a boundary between two transparent substances.

- When a light ray refracts as it travels from air into glass, the angle of refraction is less than the angle of incidence.

- When a light ray refracts as it travels from glass into air, the angle of refraction is more than the angle of incidence.

∞ **links**

Revise more on refraction of waves in 7.3 'Reflection and refraction'.

- **Refraction** is the change of direction of waves when they cross a **boundary**. It is a property of all waves. It is due to the change of speed of the waves at the boundary. The wavelength of the waves also changes, but the frequency stays the same.

- A light ray refracts when it crosses a boundary between two substances, such as air and glass or air and water.

- When light enters a more dense substance, such as going from air to glass, it slows down and the ray changes direction towards the normal.

- When light enters a less dense substance, such as going from glass to air, it speeds up and the ray changes direction away from the normal.

However, if the ray is travelling along a normal, then it will not change direction.

▷ **1** *When a light ray travels from water to glass, it bends towards the normal. What does this tell you about the speed of light in water compared with the speed in glass?*

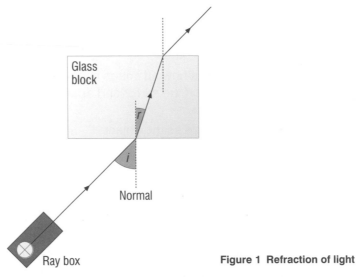

Figure 1 Refraction of light

- Different colours of light have different wavelengths, and are refracted by slightly different amounts. When a ray of white light is shone onto a triangular glass prism we can see this because a spectrum is produced. This is called **dispersion**.

- Violet light is refracted the most.

- Red light is refracted the least.

▷ **2** *Which travels faster in glass, violet light or red light?*

Study tip

Remember that angles of incidence and angles of refraction are measured between the ray and the normal.

Figure 2 Refraction by a prism

Key words: refraction, boundary, dispersion

Refractive index

Student's book
pages 102–103

Key points

- Refractive index, n, is a measure of how much a substance can refract a light ray.

- $n = \dfrac{\text{speed of light in a vacuum (air)}}{\text{speed of light in the substance}}$

- $n = \dfrac{\sin i}{\sin r}$

Study tip

When calculating the refractive index, remember it is the sine of the angle not the angle itself that is needed.

⬭ links

Revise more on refractive index in 11.5 'More about the eye'.

Maths skills

Using a calculator

Make sure your calculator is in degree mode.

To find the value of the sine of a given angle in degrees, key the angle in degrees into your calculator then press the button marked 'sin' (or on some calculators press 'sin' first).

To find the angle for a given sine value, key the sine value into your calculator and press the button marked 'inv sin' (or 'sin⁻¹' on some calculators).

Key words: refraction, refractive index

- **Refraction** of light is the change of direction of light as it passes from one transparent substance into another.

- The **refractive index** of a substance is a measure of how much the substance can refract a light ray.
  It is given by the equation:

  $$n = \frac{\text{speed of light in a vacuum}}{\text{speed of light in the substance}}$$

- The speed of light in air is almost the same as the speed of light in a vacuum which is 300 000 km/s.

> ⮕ **1** *A certain type of glass has a refractive index of 1.50. Calculate the speed of light in this glass.*

- For a light ray that passes from air into a substance of refractive index n

  $$n = \frac{\sin i}{\sin r}$$

  where $\sin i$ is the sine of the angle of incidence, i
  and $\sin r$ is the sine of the angle of refraction, r.

- We can write the above equation as
  $\sin a = n \sin g$
  where a = the angle between the normal and the light ray in air,
  and g = the angle between the normal and the light ray in the glass.

- This equation can be used for a ray travelling from air to glass or from glass to air.

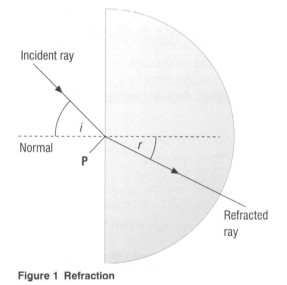

Figure 1 Refraction

> ⮕ **2** *A light ray in air enters a glass block of refractive index 1.57 at an angle of incidence of 45°. Calculate the angle of refraction of the light ray.*

> ⮕ **3** *A light ray in glass of refractive index 1.53 enters the surrounding air at an angle of incidence of 30°. Calculate the angle of refraction of the light ray.*

Practical

Measuring the refractive index of glass

Look at Figure 1.

A **protractor** is used to measure the angle of refraction r for different angles of incidence i.

For each measurement, the refractive index n is calculated and then used to work out the average value of n.

> ⮕ **4** *What type of error, random or systematic, would result in Figure 1 if the normal was not exactly at right angles to the block?*

Student's book
pages 104–105

P10.4 Total internal reflection

Key points

- The critical angle, *c*, is the angle of incidence of a light ray in a transparent substance which produces refraction along the boundary.

- Refractive index $= \dfrac{1}{\sin c}$

- Total internal reflection occurs when the angle of incidence of a light ray in a transparent substance is greater than the critical angle.

- An endoscope uses total internal reflection to see inside the body directly.

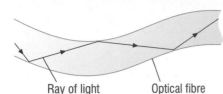

Figure 1 Light rays in an optical fibre

Maths skills

Worked example

Calculate the critical angle for glass of refractive index 1.59.

Solution

$\sin c = \dfrac{1}{n} = \dfrac{1}{1.59} = 0.629$

Therefore *c* = 39.0°

Study tip

Remember that total internal reflection only takes place for a ray travelling from a more dense to a less dense material, **e.g. from glass into air**.

Key words: critical angle, total internal reflection, endoscope, optical fibre

- A light ray will refract away from the normal when it crosses from glass to air. A partially reflected ray is also seen.
- If the angle of incidence in the glass is gradually increased, the angle of refraction increases until the refracted ray emerges along the boundary. This angle of incidence is called the **critical angle**.
- If the angle of incidence is increased beyond the critical angle, the light ray undergoes **total internal reflection**. When total internal reflection occurs, the angle of reflection is equal to the angle of incidence.

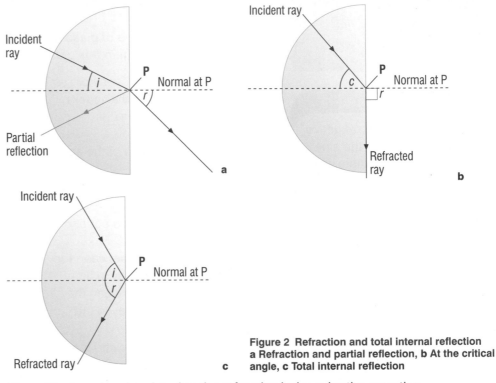

**Figure 2 Refraction and total internal reflection
a Refraction and partial reflection, b At the critical angle, c Total internal reflection**

The critical angle *c* is related to the refractive index *n* by the equation

$$n = \frac{1}{\sin c}$$

⟫ **1 a** *What is the critical angle for glass of refractive index 1.50?*
   b *What is the refractive index of a substance that has a critical angle of 46°?*

- An **endoscope** is used to look inside a patient's body without cutting it open or when performing keyhole surgery. The endoscope contains bundles of **optical fibres**. These are very thin, flexible glass fibres.
- Light can be sent along the fibres by total internal reflection. Each light ray in the fibre undergoes total internal reflection whenever it is incident on the fibre-air boundary.
- Laser light may be used with an endoscope to carry out some surgical procedures such cutting, cauterising and burning. The colour of the laser light is matched to the type of tissue to produce maximum absorption. Eye surgery on the retina of the eye can be carried out by using laser light that passes straight through the cornea and lens at the front of the eye and is absorbed by the retina at the back.

⟫ **2 a** *Optical fibre X has a refractive index of 1.50 and optical fibre Y has a refractive index of 1.55. Which fibre, X or Y, has the bigger critical angle?*
   b *State and explain which fibre, X or Y, retains more light?*

1 A ray diagram shows the reflection of a light ray by a plane mirror. What is the normal in such a diagram?

2 A light ray is directed at a plane mirror at an angle of incidence of 40°. What is the angle between the reflected ray and:

a the normal?

b the incident ray?

3 In the above example, if the angle of incidence is increased by 1° to 41°, what is the change in the angle between the incident ray and the reflected ray?

4 A person stands facing a plane mirror 0.50 m in front of the mirror. What is the distance from the person to the image he sees?

5 What type of image, a real image or a virtual image, is seen in a plane mirror?

6 Light travels at a speed of 300 000 km/s in air and 225 000 km/s in water. Calculate the refractive index of water.

7 A light ray enters a glass block of refractive index 1.52 at an angle of incidence of 20°. Calculate the angle of refraction of the light ray.

8 Calculate the critical angle of the glass block in Q7.

9 What is the angle of refraction of a light ray that is incident on a boundary between air and glass at an angle of incidence equal to the critical angle?

10 State the condition necessary for a light ray to undergo total internal reflection in a glass block surrounded by air.

11 A ray of blue light is refracted more than a ray of red light on entering a transparent substance. Which travels faster in the substance, blue light or red light?

12 The critical angle of glass is less than the critical angle of water. What does this tell you about the speed of light in glass compared with the speed in water?

Chapter checklist	✓ ✓ ✓

Tick when you have:				Reflection of light	■ ■ ■
reviewed it after your lesson	✓ ■ ■			Refraction of light	■ ■ ■
revised once – some questions right	✓ ✓ ■			Refractive index	■ ■ ■
revised twice – all questions right	✓ ✓ ✓			Total internal reflection	■ ■ ■
Move on to another topic when you have all three ticks					

P11.1 # Lenses

Key points

- A converging lens focuses parallel rays to a point called the principal focus.
- A diverging lens makes parallel rays spread out as if they came from a point called the principal focus.
- A real image is formed by a converging lens if the object is further away than the principal focus.
- A virtual image is formed by a diverging lens, and by a converging lens if the object is nearer to the lens than the principal focus.
- Magnification = $\dfrac{\text{image height}}{\text{object height}}$

Converging (convex) lenses

- Parallel rays of light that pass through a **converging (convex) lens** are refracted so that they converge to a point. This point is called the **principal focus** (focal point). The distance from the centre of the lens to the principal focus is the **focal length**.
- Because light can pass through the lens in either direction, there is a principal focus on either side of the lens. If the object is further away from the lens than the principal focus, an inverted, **real image** is formed. The size of the image depends on the position of the object. The nearer the object is to the lens, the larger the image.
- If the object is nearer to the lens than the principal focus, an upright, **virtual image** is formed behind the object. The image is magnified – the lens acts as a **magnifying glass**.
- The **magnification** can be calculated using: magnification = $\dfrac{\text{image height}}{\text{object height}}$

> 1 *A converging lens is used to form an image of a distant tree on a screen. State whether the image is **a** real or virtual, **b** upright or inverted, **c** magnified or diminished.*

Diverging (concave) lenses

Parallel rays of light that pass through a **diverging (concave) lens** are refracted so that they diverge away from a point. This point is called the principal focus.

- The distance from the centre of the lens to the principal focus is the focal length.
- Because light can pass through the lens in either direction, there is a principal focus on either side of the lens.
- The image produced by a diverging (concave) lens is always virtual.

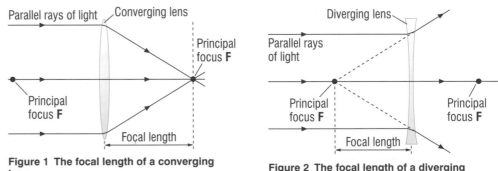

Figure 1 The focal length of a converging lens

Figure 2 The focal length of a diverging lens

> 2 *A diverging lens is used to observe a flower. State whether the image is **a** real or virtual, **b** upright or inverted, **c** magnified or diminished.*

> 3 *How can a converging lens be made to produce a magnified image of a postage stamp?*

Key words: converging lens, principal focus, focal length, magnifying glass, magnification, diverging lens

Study tip

Remember that a diverging lens makes light rays from a point object spread out (diverge) more.

Using lenses

Key points

- A ray diagram can be drawn to find the position and nature of an image formed by a lens.

- When an object is placed between a converging lens and its principal focus F, the image formed is virtual, upright, magnified and on the same side of the lens as the object.

- A camera contains a converging lens that is used to form a real image of an object.

- A magnifying glass is a converging lens that is used to form a virtual image of an object.

- We can draw ray diagrams to find the image that different lenses produce with objects in different positions.

- The line through the centre of the lens and at right angles to it is called the **principal axis**. This should be included in the diagram.

- **Converging lens ray diagrams** use three construction rays from a single point on the object to locate the corresponding point on the image: 1) A ray parallel to the principal axis is refracted through the principal focus. 2) A ray through the centre of the lens travels straight on. 3) A ray through the principal focus is refracted parallel to the principal axis.

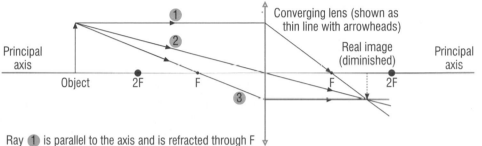

Ray ① is parallel to the axis and is refracted through F
Ray ② passes straight through the centre of the lens
Ray ③ passes through F and is refracted parallel to the axis

Figure 1 Formation of a real image by a converging lens

Table 1 shows the nature of the image formed by a converging lens for different object distances (that is, distances from the object to the lens).

Table 1

Object distance	Image position	Nature of the image	Application example
Beyond 2F	Between F and 2F on the other side	Real, inverted, smaller than object	Film or digital camera*
2F	2F on the other side	Real, inverted, same size as object	Inverter
Between F and 2F	Beyond 2F on the other side	Real, inverted, larger than object	Projector
Less than F	On the same side as the object	Virtual, upright, larger than object	Magnifying glass

* A camera uses a converging lens to form a real image of an object on a film or an array of pixels

➤ **1** Which row in Table 1 described the image in Figure 1?

➤ **2** An object is placed 0.40 m from a converging lens which has a focal length of 0.30 m. Describe the nature of the image formed.

- **Diverging lens ray diagrams** use two construction rays from a single point on the object to locate the corresponding point on the image: 1) A ray parallel to the principal axis is refracted as if it passes through the principal focus. 2) A ray through the centre of the lens travels straight on.

- The image formed by a diverging lens of an object is always virtual, upright and smaller than the object (diminished) and on the same side as the object.

➤ **3** An image of an object is formed by a diverging lens. Describe **a** the nature of the image, **b** its position relative to the object.

Study tip

Make sure you practise drawing ray diagrams. Only two of the construction rays are needed to find the image, but if you have time it is worth drawing all three to be sure that you have the correct position.

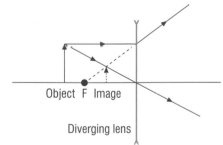

Figure 2 Image formation by a diverging lens

Key words: principal axis

Student's book
pages 112–114 **P11.3**

The lens formula

- The lens formula can be used instead of a ray diagram to find the distance from a lens to the image it forms, if the focal length *f* of the lens and the distance from the object to the lens are known.

$$\frac{1}{u} + \frac{1}{v} = \frac{1}{f}$$

where u = the distance from the object to the lens
v = the distance from the image to the lens.

When we use the lens formula, the following **sign convention** is used:

- Real images have positive values. Virtual images have negative values.
- Converging lenses are given positive values. Diverging lenses are given negative values.

> **1** *An object is placed 0.200 m from a converging lens of focal length 0.120 m. Calculate the distance from the lens to the image formed by the lens.*

> **2** *An object is placed 0.200 m from a converging lens of focal length 0.250 m.*
> **a** *Determine the position of the image formed by the lens.*
> **b** *State whether the image is **i** real or virtual, **ii** upright or inverted, **iii** smaller than or larger than the object.*

Key points

- The lens formula is $\frac{1}{u} + \frac{1}{v} + \frac{1}{f}$
- Real images have positive values. Virtual images have negative values.
- Converging lenses are given positive values. Diverging lenses are given negative values.

Maths skills

$\frac{1}{x}$ is called the reciprocal of *x*.

When you have calculated $\frac{1}{f}$, don't forget to use the reciprocal button on your calculator to calculate *f*.

You don't need to know the proof of the lens formula.

> **3** *Why is the measurement of v less accurate than the measurement of u?*

Key words: sign convention

Practical

Measuring the focal length of a converging lens

A lamp box, a converging lens and a screen are placed in a line so a real image of the crosswires of the lamp box is seen on the screen. A **metre ruler** is used to measure the object distance *u* and the image distance *v* for different object distances and recorded in a table. The lens formula is used to calculate a value of the focal length *f* of the lens for each set of measurements, from which we can get an average value of *f*.

Student's book
pages 114–115 **P11.4**

The eye

- Light enters the eye through the **cornea**. The cornea and the **eye lens** focus the light on to the **retina**. The **iris** adjusts the size of the **pupil** to control the amount of light entering the eye.
- The **ciliary muscles** alter the thickness of the lens to control the fine focusing of the eye. They are attached to the lens by the **suspensory ligaments**. The ciliary muscle fibres are parallel to the circular edge of the eye lens. When these muscle fibres 1) tighten, they become shorter, making the circumference of the lens shorter so the lens becomes thicker and more powerful; 2) relax, they become longer, making the circumference of the lens longer so the lens becomes thinner and less powerful.

> **1** *What is the purpose of **a** the iris? **b** the ciliary muscles?*

- The eye lens is:
  – thickest and at its most powerful when the eye is focused on a nearby object
  – thinnest and at its least powerful when the eye is focused on an object at infinity.
- The normal human eye has a **near point** of 25 cm and a **far point** of infinity so its **range of vision** is from 25 cm to infinity.

Key points

- Light is focused on to the retina by the cornea and the eye lens which is a variable focus lens.
- The normal human eye has a range of vision from 25 cm to infinity.
- An object is brought to focus:
  – on the retina in the eye by changing the shape of the eye lens
  – on the film in a camera by changing the distance between the film and the lens.

Lenses and the eye

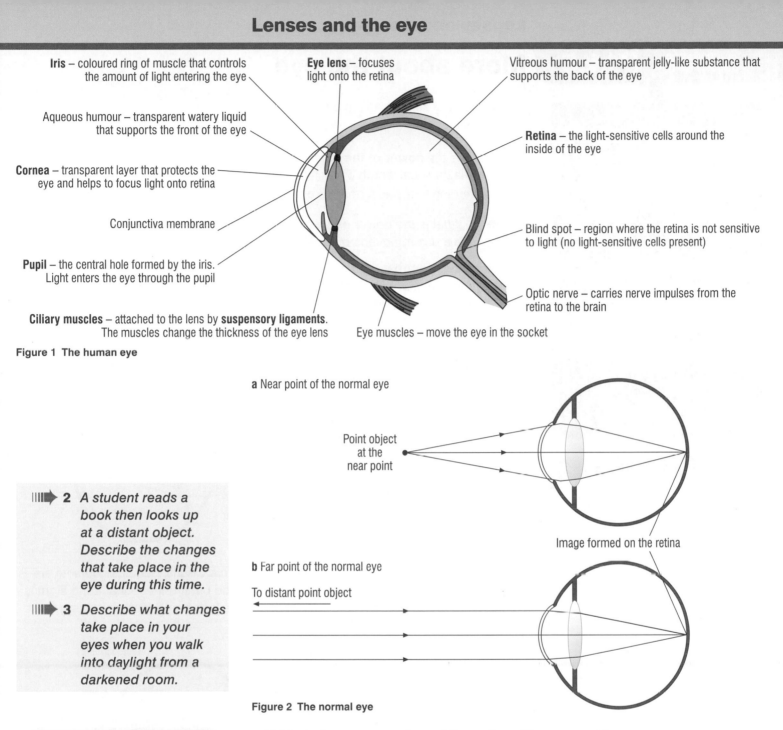

Iris – coloured ring of muscle that controls the amount of light entering the eye

Aqueous humour – transparent watery liquid that supports the front of the eye

Cornea – transparent layer that protects the eye and helps to focus light onto retina

Conjunctiva membrane

Pupil – the central hole formed by the iris. Light enters the eye through the pupil

Ciliary muscles – attached to the lens by **suspensory ligaments**. The muscles change the thickness of the eye lens

Eye lens – focuses light onto the retina

Vitreous humour – transparent jelly-like substance that supports the back of the eye

Retina – the light-sensitive cells around the inside of the eye

Blind spot – region where the retina is not sensitive to light (no light-sensitive cells present)

Optic nerve – carries nerve impulses from the retina to the brain

Eye muscles – move the eye in the socket

Figure 1 The human eye

a Near point of the normal eye

Point object at the near point

Image formed on the retina

b Far point of the normal eye

To distant point object

Figure 2 The normal eye

2 A student reads a book then looks up at a distant object. Describe the changes that take place in the eye during this time.

3 Describe what changes take place in your eyes when you walk into daylight from a darkened room.

Study tip

You may be asked to compare the structure of the eye and the camera. The camera has a lens of fixed shape but variable position. The eye has a lens of variable shape but fixed position.

Key words: cornea, eye lens, retina, iris, pupil, ciliary muscle, suspensory ligament, near point, far point, range of vision

● Table 1 gives a comparison of the optics of the eye and the camera.

Table 1

	Eye	Camera
Type of lens	Variable focus converging lens	Fixed focus converging lens
Focusing adjustment	Change of lens thickness	Adjustment of lens position
Image detection	Light-sensitive cells on the retina	Photographic film or CCD sensors
Brightness control	Iris controls width of eye pupil	Adjustment of aperture 'stop'
Nature of image	Real, inverted, smaller than object	

Student's book
pages 116–117 **P11.5**

More about the eye

Student's book
pages 116–117

Key points

- A short-sighted eye is an eye that can only see near objects clearly. We use a diverging (concave) lens to correct it.

- A long-sighted eye is an eye that can only see distant objects clearly. We use a converging (convex) lens to correct it.

- The higher the refractive index of the glass used to make a corrective lens, the flatter and thinner the lens can be.

- $P = \dfrac{1}{f}$

Study tip

When calculating the power of a lens, make sure that the focal length is in metres so that the power of the lens is in dioptres.

- The power of a lens is given by:

$$P = \frac{1}{f}$$

where P is the **power of the lens** in dioptres (symbol D)
f is the focal length of the lens in metres, m.

- A converging lens has a positive power; a diverging lens has a negative power.

 1 *What is the power of **a** a converging lens of focal length 0.25 m?*
   ***b** a diverging lens of focal length 0.20 m?*

- A person with normal sight can see objects from the near point 25 cm away from the eye to a far point at infinity. See Figure 2 in the previous topic.

- A person with **short sight** can see close objects clearly, but distant objects are blurred because the uncorrected image is formed in front of the retina. Short sight is caused by the eyeball being too long or the eye lens being too powerful. Short sight may be corrected using a diverging lens.

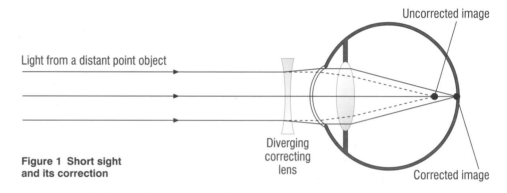

Figure 1 Short sight and its correction

- A person with **long sight** can see distance objects clearly, but close objects are blurred because the uncorrected image is formed behind the retina. Long sight is caused by the eyeball being too short or the eye lens being too weak. Long sight may be corrected using a converging lens.

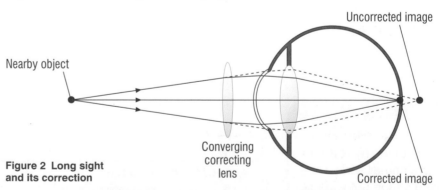

Figure 2 Long sight and its correction

∞ links

Revise more on refractive index in 10.3 'Refractive index'.

- The focal length of a lens is determined by: 1) the refractive index of the material from which the lens is made; 2) the curvature of the two surfaces of the lens.

- For a lens of a given focal length, the greater the refractive index of the lens material, the flatter and thinner the lens can be.

 2 a *Which type of lens may be used to correct long sight?*
   b *What defect of the eyeball may cause it to be short-sighted?*

- Lasers can be used for correcting short sight by making part of the cornea slightly thinner.

Key words: power of a lens, short sight, long sight

1　What is meant by the principal focus of a converging lens?

2　What is the difference between a converging lens and a diverging lens in terms of the effect of each type of lens on parallel rays of light?

3　A converging lens is used to form an image of a light bulb on a screen on the other side of the lens. The image is 24 mm in diameter and the light bulb is 6 mm in diameter. What is the magnification?

4　If the object in Q3 is moved away from the lens, state whether the image:
　a　moves further from or nearer to the lens
　b　becomes larger or smaller.

5　An object is placed 45 cm from a converging lens of focal length 15 cm, as shown in Figure 1.
　a　Copy and complete the ray diagram and find the distance from the lens to the image.
　b　Describe the nature of the image formed.

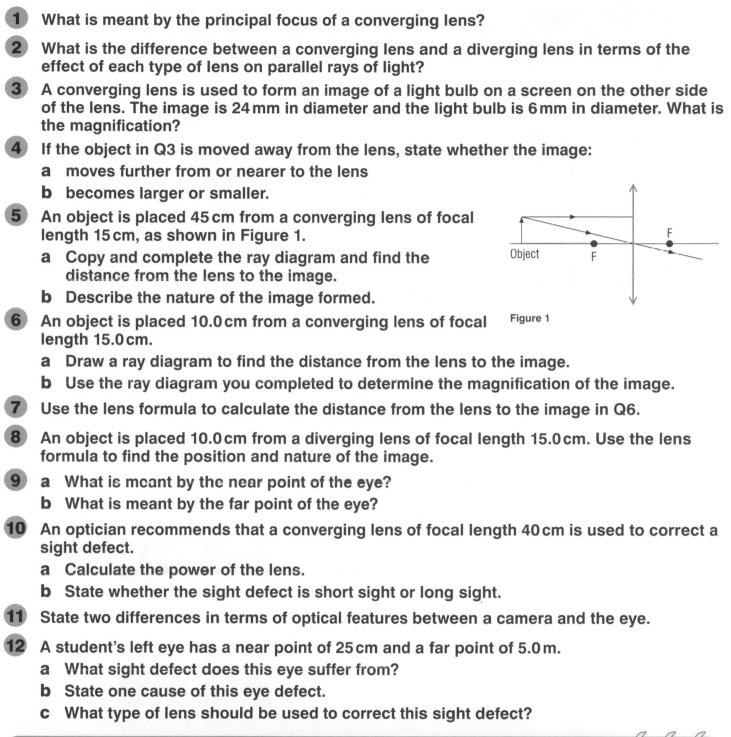

Figure 1

6　An object is placed 10.0 cm from a converging lens of focal length 15.0 cm.
　a　Draw a ray diagram to find the distance from the lens to the image.
　b　Use the ray diagram you completed to determine the magnification of the image.

7　Use the lens formula to calculate the distance from the lens to the image in Q6.

8　An object is placed 10.0 cm from a diverging lens of focal length 15.0 cm. Use the lens formula to find the position and nature of the image.

9　a　What is meant by the near point of the eye?
　b　What is meant by the far point of the eye?

10　An optician recommends that a converging lens of focal length 40 cm is used to correct a sight defect.
　a　Calculate the power of the lens.
　b　State whether the sight defect is short sight or long sight.

11　State two differences in terms of optical features between a camera and the eye.

12　A student's left eye has a near point of 25 cm and a far point of 5.0 m.
　a　What sight defect does this eye suffer from?
　b　State one cause of this eye defect.
　c　What type of lens should be used to correct this sight defect?

Chapter checklist			✓	✓	✓
Tick when you have:			Lenses		
reviewed it after your lesson	✓	☐	☐	Using lenses	
revised once – some questions right	✓	✓	☐	The lens formula	
revised twice – all questions right	✓	✓	✓	The eye	
Move on to another topic when you have all three ticks			More about the eye		

Student's book
pages 120–121

P12.1

The expanding universe

The **Doppler effect** is the change in the observed wavelength and frequency of the waves from a moving source due to the motion of the source relative to the observer. When the source moves:

- away from the observer, the waves are stretched out so the observed wavelength increases and the frequency decreases
- towards the observer, the waves are squashed together so the observed wavelength decreases and the frequency increases.

> **1 a** *If a wave source is moving away from you, what happens to its wavelength?*
>   **b** *If a wave source is moving towards you, what happens to its frequency?*

Galaxies are large collections of stars. Light observed from distant galaxies has been stretched in wavelength and has therefore undergone a **red-shift** (a 'shift' towards the red end of the spectrum).

We are able to see these effects by observing dark lines in the spectra from distant galaxies. These dark lines are due to absorption of light in the source.

For any distant galaxy:

- The position of the dark lines in the spectrum is shifted towards the red end of the spectrum.
- The greater its red-shift is, the faster the galaxy is moving away from us.

A **blue-shift** is a shift of towards the blue end of the spectrum. It would indicate that the galaxy is moving towards us.

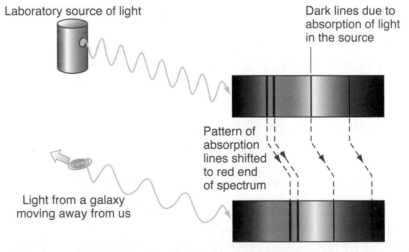

Laboratory source of light

Dark lines due to absorption of light in the source

Pattern of absorption lines shifted to red end of spectrum

Light from a galaxy moving away from us

Figure 1 Red-shift

- The further away a distant galaxy is, the bigger its red-shift is. This suggests that all distant galaxies are moving away from us, and the most distant galaxies are moving the fastest. This is true of galaxies no matter which direction you look.
- All the distant galaxies are moving away from each other, so the whole universe must be expanding.

> **2** *Galaxy X shows a red-shift, galaxy Y shows a blue-shift and galaxy Z shows a larger red-shift than X. Which galaxy is **a** nearest? **b** furthest?*

> **3** *How does red-shift show that the universe is expanding?*

Key points

- The red-shift of a distant galaxy is the shift to longer wavelengths of light from a galaxy moving away from us.
- The faster a distant galaxy is moving away from us, the greater its red-shift is.
- The further away a distant galaxy is from us, the greater its red-shift is.
- The distant galaxies are all moving away from us because the universe is expanding.

Study tip

Make sure you know the evidence for the expanding universe.

Key words: Doppler effect, red-shift, blue-shift

P12.2

The Big Bang

Key points

- The universe started with the Big Bang; a massive explosion from a very small point.
- The universe has been expanding ever since the Big Bang.
- Cosmic microwave background radiation (CMBR) is electromagnetic radiation created just after the Big Bang.
- CMBR can only be explained by the Big Bang theory.

⊂⊃ **links**

Revise more on electromagnetic radiation in 8.1 'The electromagnetic spectrum'.

- Red-shift gives us evidence that the universe is expanding outwards in all directions.
- We can imagine travelling backwards in time to see where the universe came from. If it is now expanding outwards, this suggests that it started with a massive explosion at a very small initial point. This is known as the **Big Bang** theory.

▷ **1** *What caused the initial expansion of the universe?*

- If the universe began with a Big Bang, then high energy gamma radiation would have been produced. As the universe expanded this would have become lower-energy radiation.
- Scientists discovered microwaves coming from every direction in space. This is **cosmic microwave background radiation (CMBR)**, the radiation produced by the Big Bang.
- The Big Bang theory is the only way at present to explain the existence of CMBR.

▷ **2 a** *What sort of electromagnetic radiation would have been produced in the Big Bang?*
   b *What sort of radiation is detected from all directions in space?*

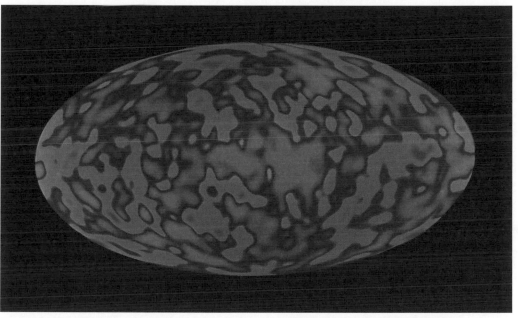

Figure 1 A microwave image of the universe from the Cosmic Background Explorer satellite

Study tip

Be sure that you can explain why red-shift is evidence for an expanding universe and the Big Bang.

Key words: Big Bang, cosmic microwave background radiation (CMBR)

1 What is the Doppler effect?

2 What is a red-shift?

3 What can you say about the red-shift of a distant galaxy and the motion of the galaxy?

4 A galaxy has a blue-shift. What does this tell you about the galaxy?

5 Galaxy P has a smaller red-shift than galaxy Q.

   a   Which galaxy is furthest from us?

   b   What else can we say about the two galaxies?

6 What can we say about the variation of red-shift with distance of distant galaxies?

7 How do we know the universe is expanding?

8 What is the Big Bang theory?

9 What is cosmic microwave background radiation (CMBR)?

10 What is the origin of CMBR?

11 Why is CMBR described as cosmic background radiation?

12 What was deduced from the discovery of CMBR?

Chapter checklist	✓	✓	✓
Tick when you have:			
reviewed it after your lesson	✓	☐	☐
revised once – some questions right	✓	✓	☐
revised twice – all questions right	✓	✓	✓
Move on to another topic when you have all three ticks			

The expanding universe	☐	☐	☐
The Big Bang	☐	☐	☐

1 Figure 1 shows a ray of light directed into a semi-circular glass block.

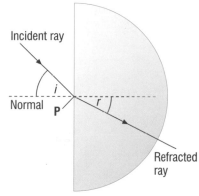

Figure 1

a Describe how you would use this arrangement and a protractor to measure the refractive index of the glass. In your description, you should

- state the measurements you would make
- describe the procedure you would follow to make the measurements
- describe how you would calculate the refractive index from your measurements.

In this question, you will be assessed on using good English, organising information clearly and using specialist terms where appropriate. *(6 marks)*

b A semi-circular glass block was found to have a refractive index of 1.52.

i Calculate the critical angle of the glass block in air. *(2 marks)*

ii A light ray was directed into the block through the curved side of the block towards the centre of the long flat side of the block, P. The angle of incidence of the light ray at P was such that the light ray underwent total internal reflection at P. Explain what is meant by total internal reflection. *(2 marks)*

iii Draw the arrangement described in **ii** and draw the path of the light ray into and out of the block. *(3 marks)*

2 A student's left eye has a near point 25 cm from the eye and a far point 5.0 m from it.

a i What sight defect does this eye suffer from? *(1 mark)*

ii State one possible cause of this sight defect. *(1 mark)*

b In a sight test of a different person, an optician found that a converging lens of focal length 0.40 m was needed to correct a sight defect.

i Calculate the power of this lens. *(1 mark)*

ii The optician recommends two possible lens, one thinner than the other and made of glass with a different refractive index. State which lens has the higher refractive index and explain why it would not be suitable if it was made of the same type of glass as the other lens. *(2 marks)*

3 By studying the spectra of light from a large number of different galaxies at known distances from Earth, Edwin Hubble deduced that the distant galaxies are all moving away from us.

a What further deduction did he make about the speed of the distant galaxies? *(1 mark)*

b What conclusion did astronomers draw from these deductions about the universe? *(1 mark)*

c What is cosmic microwave background radiation (CMBR)? *(2 marks)*

d What was the significance of the discovery of CMBR? *(1 mark)*

P13.1 States of matter

The three states of matter are **solid**, **liquid** and **gas**. We can make a substance change between these states by heating or cooling it. Figure 1 shows these changes.

Key points

- Flow, shape, volume and density are properties used to describe each state of matter.
- The particles in a solid are held next to each other, vibrating in their fixed positions.
- The particles in a liquid move about at random and are in contact with each other. The particles in a liquid are more energetic than in a solid.
- The particles in a gas move about randomly and are much farther apart, on average, than particles in a solid or liquid. The particles in a gas are more energetic than in a liquid.

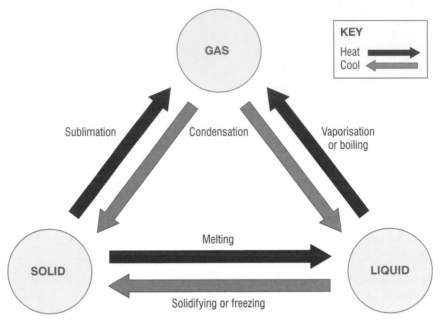

KEY
Heat →
Cool ←

Figure 1 Change of state

- In a solid the particles vibrate about fixed positions so the solid has a fixed shape.
- In a liquid the particles are in contact with each other but can move about at random, so a liquid does not have a fixed shape and can flow.

> **1** *State one difference between the arrangement of the particles in a liquid and in a solid.*

In a gas the particles are further apart on average than in a liquid or a solid and they move at random much faster. Therefore a gas does not have a fixed shape and can flow, and its **density** is much less than that of a solid or liquid.

The average energy of a particle in a gas is greater than that of a particle in a liquid, which is greater than that of a particle in a solid.

> **2** *Why is the density of a gas much less than that of a solid or a liquid?*

Figure 2 The arrangement of particles in **a** a solid, **b** a liquid, **c** a gas.

links

Revise more on changing state in 13.3 'Change of state'.

Key words: solid, liquid, gas, density

Study tip

Make sure that you can describe the arrangement and the motion of the particles in each of the three states of matter.

P13.2 # Specific heat capacity

Key points

- The greater the mass of an object, the more slowly its temperature increases when it is heated.
- Temperature change in a substance when heated depends on the energy transferred to or from it, its mass and its specific heat capacity.
- $E = m \times c \times \theta$

- The **specific heat capacity** of a substance is the amount of energy required to raise the **temperature** of 1 kilogram of the substance by 1 degree Celsius.
- Different substances have different specific heat capacities. The greater the specific heat capacity, the more energy required for each degree temperature change of a given **mass**.
- The greater the mass of substance being heated, the more energy required for each degree temperature change.
- The equation for specific heat capacity is:

$$E = m \times c \times \theta$$

where E is energy transferred, J
m is mass, kg
c is specific heat capacity, J/kg°C
θ is temperature change, °C.

▶ **1** *How much energy is needed to raise the temperature of*
a *1 kg of oil by* **i** *1°C?* **ii** *5°C?*
b *1 kg of aluminium by 5°C?*
The specific heat capacity of oil is 2100 J/kg°C and of aluminium is 900 J/kg°C.

Practical

Measuring the specific heat capacity of aluminium

A 12V heater and a **thermometer** are placed in slots in an insulated aluminium block. The heater is connected to a **joulemeter** to measure the energy transfer to the block when the heater is switched on for 5 minutes.

The readings of the thermometer and the joulemeter are measured and recorded before switching the heater on and after switching the heater off.

The readings are used to calculate the energy transfer to the block and its temperature change, then to calculate the specific heat capacity of aluminium.

∞ links

Revise more on energy and temperature in 14.6 'Energy transfer by design'.

▶ **2** *How could you test if the insulation stops energy transfer by heating from the block?*

▶ **3** *How much energy is needed to raise the temperature of 2 kg of water by 5°C? The specific heat capacity of water is 4200 J/kg°C.*

Maths skills

Worked example

Here are some measurements using an aluminium block of mass 1.0 kg.
Starting temperature = 14°C
Final temperature = 22°C
Energy supplied = 7200 J
Use these measurements to calculate the specific heat capacity of aluminium.

Solution

E = energy supplied = 7200 J
θ = temperature change = 22°C − 14°C = 8°C

Rearranging the equation $E = m \times c \times \theta$ gives $c = \dfrac{E}{m \times \theta}$

Substituting the values of E, m and θ into the rearranged equation gives:

$$c = \frac{7200\,\text{J}}{1.0\,\text{kg} \times 8°C} = 900\,\text{J/kg°C}$$

Study tip

Note that in the equation θ is the temperature change.

Key words: specific heat capacity, temperature

P13.3 Change of state

Key points

- For a pure substance:
  - its melting point is the temperature at which it melts or solidifies
  - its boiling point is the temperature at which it boils or condenses.
- Energy is needed to melt a solid or to boil a liquid.
- Boiling occurs throughout a liquid at its boiling point. Evaporation occurs from the surface of a liquid when its temperature is below the boiling point.

Study tip

Evaporation takes place at any temperature; boiling occurs only at the boiling point.

∞ links

Revise more on evaporation in 14.3 'Evaporation and condensation'.

▶ **2 What is the difference between evaporation and boiling?**

▶ **3 What feature of the graph gives the melting point of the substance?**

Key words: change of state, melting point, freezing point, boiling point, fusion, evaporation

- For any **pure** substance undergoing a **change of state**, its temperature stays the same. As shown in Table 1, depending on the change of state, we refer to this temperature as the **melting point** (or **freezing point**) or the **boiling point** of the substance.
- The melting point of a solid and the boiling point of a liquid are affected by impurities. For example, the melting point of water is lowered if salt is added to the water.
- Most pure substances when heated produce a **temperature–time** graph with flat sections which is where a change of state occurs.

▶ **1 a Ice melts at 0 °C. What is the freezing point of pure water?**
b What can you say about the freezing point of salt water?

Table 1

Change of state	Initial and final state	Temperature
Melting	Solid to liquid	Melting point
Freezing (also called solidification)	Liquid to solid	Melting point
Boiling	Liquid to vapour	Boiling point
Condensation	Vapour to liquid	Boiling point

- The energy supplied to a substance when it changes its state is called **latent heat**.
- **Fusion** is a word often used to describe melting because different solids can be joined or 'fused' together when they melt.
- **Evaporation** from a liquid occurs at its surface when the liquid is below its boiling point. At its boiling point, a liquid boils because bubbles of vapour form inside the liquid and rise to the surface to release the gas.

Practical

Measuring the melting point of a substance

Place a test tube containing the substance in its solid state in a beaker of water, as shown in Figure 1a. Heat the water and measure the temperature of the substance every minute until it has all melted.

Plot the measurements on a graph, as shown in Figure 1b. Use the graph to find the melting point of the substance.

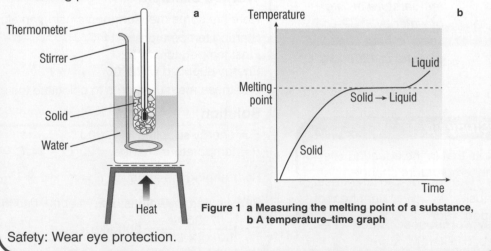

Figure 1 a Measuring the melting point of a substance, b A temperature–time graph

Safety: Wear eye protection.

P13.4 # Specific latent heat

Key points

- Latent heat is the energy needed or released when a substance changes its state without changing its temperature.
- Specific latent heat of fusion (or of vaporisation) is the energy needed to melt (or to boil) 1 kg of a substance with no change in temperature.

- When a solid substance is heated, its particles vibrate more and more vigorously as its temperature increases. At its melting point, the particles break free from each other and the substance changes from a solid to a liquid.
- When the liquid is heated, its temperature increases as particles move about faster and faster. At its boiling point, the particles break away from each other and the liquid changes to a gas.
- The **specific latent heat of fusion, L_f,** of a substance is the energy needed to melt 1 kg of the substance at its melting point. The specific latent heat of fusion of water is sometimes just referred to as the specific latent heat of ice.
- The **specific latent heat of vaporisation, L_v,** of a substance is the energy needed to change 1 kg of the substance at its boiling point from liquid to vapour. The specific latent heat of vaporisation of water is sometimes just referred to as the specific latent heat of steam.
- The unit of specific latent heat is the joule per kilogram (J/kg). The equation for specific latent heat is:

$$L = \frac{E}{m}$$

where E is energy transferred, J

m is mass, kg

L is specific latent heat of fusion or vaporisation, J/kg

Note that rearranging this equation gives $E = mL$

▶ **1** *How much energy is needed to boil away 0.10 kg of water at its boiling point? The specific latent heat of vaporisation of water is 2.3 MJ/kg.*

Practical

Measuring the specific latent heat of ice

A 12 V heater is surrounded by crushed ice in a funnel. The melted ice is collected using a beaker under the funnel. A **joulemeter** is used to measure the energy supplied to the heater.

With the heater off, water from the funnel is collected in the beaker for a measured time (for example, 10 minutes). The mass of the beaker and water, m_1, is then measured. The beaker is then emptied for the next stage.

With the heater on, the procedure is repeated for exactly the same time. The joulemeter readings before and after the heater is switched on are recorded. After the heater is switched off, the mass of the beaker and the water, m_2, is measured once more.

Study tip

In the practical, energy transfer from the surroundings is taken account of by making measurements without and with the heater on.

The mass of ice melted due to the heater, $m (= m_2 - m_1)$ and the energy supplied (= the difference between the joulemeter readings) are calculated, and then the specific latent heat of fusion of ice can be calculated.

▶ **2** *How is energy transfer from the surroundings to the ice taken account of?*

Key words: specific latent heat of fusion, specific latent heat of vaporisation

▶ **3** *1700 J of energy is needed to melt 0.005 kg of ice at 0 °C. What is the specific latent heat of fusion of water?*

Use the following data where appropriate in the questions below:
- The specific heat capacity of water is 4200 J/kg °C.
- The specific heat capacity of aluminium is 900 J/kg °C.
- The specific latent heat of vaporisation of water is 2300 kJ/kg.
- The specific latent heat of ice is 340 kJ/kg.

1 State two differences between the motion of the particles in a liquid and in a gas.

2 State two properties of a liquid that are not properties of a gas.

3 What happens to the particles of a substance when energy is transferred:
a to it at its boiling point?
b from it at its melting point?

4 What two changes of state occur when you breathe on a cold window and mist forms?

5 What is evaporation?

6 How much energy must be transferred to 12 kg of water to raise the water temperature from 15 °C to 45 °C?

7 Aluminium has a greater specific heat capacity than steel. An aluminium panel and a steel panel have the same mass and are at the same initial temperature. If the same amount of energy is transferred to each panel, which of the two panels becomes warmer?

8 What do we mean by the specific latent heat of fusion of a substance?

9 How much energy is needed to boil away 0.40 kg of water? (The latent heat of vaporisation of water is 2.3 MJ/kg.)

10 An insulated aluminium can of mass 0.070 kg contains 0.016 kg of water at 20 °C.
a Calculate the energy needed to heat the can from 20 °C to 60 °C.
b Calculate the energy needed to heat the water from 20 °C to 60 °C.
c A heater supplies 100 J of energy each second to the can and the water. Calculate the time taken for the temperature of the can and the water to increase from 20 °C to 60 °C.

11 What mass of ice could be melted by the energy transferred from 1 kg of water cooled from 4 °C to 0 °C?

12 Which would freeze faster when placed in a refrigerator, 0.10 kg of water at 20 °C in a plastic beaker (X) or an identical beaker containing 0.15 kg of water at 10 °C (Y)?

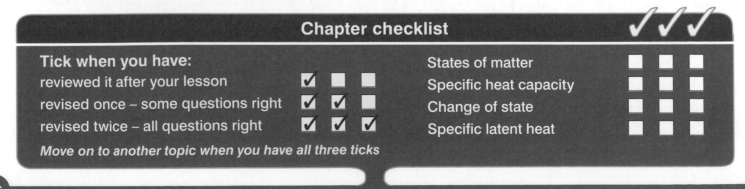

Chapter checklist				✔ ✔ ✔
Tick when you have:				
reviewed it after your lesson	✔ ☐ ☐	States of matter	☐ ☐ ☐	
revised once – some questions right	✔ ✔ ☐	Specific heat capacity	☐ ☐ ☐	
revised twice – all questions right	✔ ✔ ✔	Change of state	☐ ☐ ☐	
Move on to another topic when you have all three ticks		Specific latent heat	☐ ☐ ☐	

P14.1

Conduction

Key points

- Metals are the best conductors.
- Materials such as wool and fibre glass are the best insulators.
- Conduction in a metal is mainly due to free electrons transferring energy inside the metal.
- Non-metals are poor conductors because they do not contain free electrons.

- **Conduction** occurs mainly in solids. Most liquids and all gases are poor **conductors**. Metals are good conductors.
- Materials that are poor conductors are called **insulators**. Materials such as wool and fibreglass are the best insulators because they contain trapped air.
- If one end of a solid is heated, the particles at that end gain kinetic energy and vibrate more. This energy is passed to neighbouring particles and in this way the energy is transferred through the solid. This process occurs in metals and non-metals.
- In addition, when metals are heated, their **free electrons** gain kinetic energy and move through the metal transferring energy by colliding with other particles. Hence all metals are good conductors.

⟫ 1 a *Why are saucepans often made of metal with wooden handles?*
  b *Why are insulators not good conductors like metals?*

⟫ 2 a *Why are materials that trap air good insulators?*
  b *What makes a duvet a poor conductor of heat?*

Study tip

Make sure that you:
- know some examples of insulators and how they are used
- can explain the difference between conduction in metals and conduction in non-metals.

links

Revise more on conduction in 14.6 'Energy transfer by design' and 15.4 'Heating and insulating buildings'.

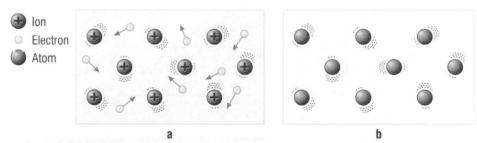

Figure 1 Energy transfer in **a** a metal and **b** a non-metal

Practical

Testing sheets of materials as insulators

- Use different materials to insulate identical cans (or beakers) of hot water. The volume of water and its temperature at the start should be the same. Use a thermometer to measure the water temperature after a fixed time. The results should tell you which insulator was best.
- Safety: Take care if using very hot water.

⟫ 3 *Why must the volume of water be the same in each test?*

Key words: conduction, conductor, insulator, free electron

P14.2 | ## Convection

Key points

- Convection is the circulation of a fluid caused by heating it.
- Convection takes place only in liquids and gases (fluids).
- Heating a liquid or a gas makes it less dense so it rises and causes circulation.

- **Convection** occurs in **fluids**. Fluids are liquids and gases.
- When a fluid is heated it expands because the particles move further apart.
- The fluid becomes less dense and rises. The warm fluid is replaced by cooler, denser fluid.
- The resulting **convection current** transfers energy throughout the fluid.

> **1** **a** *Why does convection not occur in solids?*
> **b** *Why does a fluid become less dense when it is heated?*

- Convection currents can be on a very small scale, such as heating water in a beaker, or on a very large scale, such as heating the air above land and sea.
- Convection currents in the air are responsible for onshore and offshore breezes.
- Convection currents in the oceans are responsible for transferring energy from tropical regions to other parts of the world.

> **2** *A chimney is designed to take away unwanted gases from a gas fire or solid fuel fire. Why does air from the outside not flow down the chimney?*

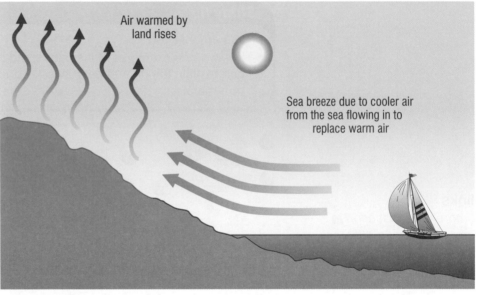

Air warmed by land rises

Sea breeze due to cooler air from the sea flowing in to replace warm air

Figure 1 Sea breezes

links

Revise more on convection in 14.6 'Energy transfer by design' and 15.4 'Heating and insulating buildings'.

Study tip

Remember that convection cannot occur in solids. Also, make sure that you can explain how convection currents are set up in terms of the changes in density when a fluid is heated.

Key words: convection, fluid, convection current

Evaporation and condensation

Key points

- Evaporation is when a liquid turns into a gas at the surface of the liquid.

- Condensation is when a gas turns into a liquid.

- The cooling of a liquid by evaporation is caused by faster-moving particles escaping from the liquid.

- **Evaporation** is when a liquid turns into a gas at the surface of the liquid. Evaporation takes place because the more energetic liquid molecules escape from the liquid's surface and enter the air. Therefore the average kinetic energy of the remaining molecules is less so the **temperature** of the liquid decreases. This means that evaporation causes cooling.

The rate of evaporation is increased by:
- increasing the surface area of the liquid
- increasing the temperature of the liquid
- creating a draught of air across the liquid's surface.

> **1** *What effect would increasing the surface area of a liquid have on its rate of evaporation?*

> **2** *What effect would blowing across the surface of a liquid have on the liquid?*

- **Condensation** is when a gas turns into a liquid. This often takes place on cold surfaces such as windows and mirrors.
- The rate of condensation is increased by:
- increasing the surface area
- reducing the surface temperature.

> **3 a** *When someone first sits in a car on a cold morning, why does the windscreen mist up?*
> **b** *Why does a flow of warm air across a misted windscreen clear the mist?*

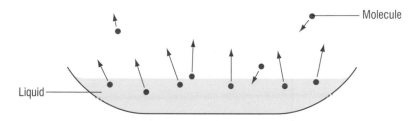

Liquid

Molecule

Figure 1 Water molecules escaping from a liquid

links

Revise more on evaporation in 14.6 'Energy transfer by design'.

Practical

Testing cooling by evaporation of water

Smear a drop of lukewarm water onto the palm of your hand. Blow gently across the water and you should find your palm becomes cooler.

Study tip

Make sure you know the factors that affect the rate of evaporation and condensation.

> **4** *How is the cooling effect affected if air is blown faster across the water? Give a reason for your answer.*

Key words: evaporation, condensation

P14.4 Infrared radiation

Key points

- Infrared radiation is energy transfer by electromagnetic waves.
- All objects emit infrared radiation.
- The hotter an object is, the more infrared radiation it emits in a given time.

- **Infrared** waves are part of the electromagnetic spectrum. They are the part of the spectrum just beyond visible red light. We can detect infrared radiation with our skin as it makes us feel warm.
- All objects give out (**emit**) infrared **radiation**.
- The hotter an object is, the more infrared radiation it emits in a given time.

▶ **1** *How does the temperature of an object affect the rate at which it emits infrared radiation?*

- Infrared radiation can travel through a vacuum, as in travelling through space. This is how we get energy from the Sun.
- Short wavelength infrared radiation from the Sun passes through the Earth's atmosphere and heats the Earth. Long wavelength infrared radiation from the Earth is unable to pass through the Earth's atmosphere into space as it is absorbed by some gases, such as carbon dioxide. This makes the Earth warmer than it would be if it had no atmosphere.

▶ **2** *Why does the temperature of the Moon's surface decrease much more than that of the Earth's surface when darkness falls?*

Practical

Detecting infrared radiation

Split a narrow beam of white light into the colours of the spectrum using a glass prism, as shown in Figure 1. Use a thermometer with a blackened bulb to detect infrared radiation just beyond the red part of the spectrum.

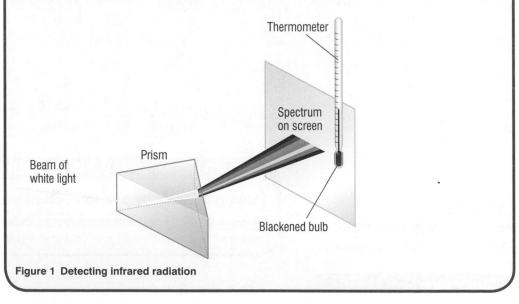

Figure 1 Detecting infrared radiation

Study tip

Remember that the transfer of energy by infrared radiation does **not** involve particles.

▶ **3** *Why is it difficult to detect the infrared radiation in the spectrum if the spectrum is spread out too much?*

⬤⬤ links

Revise more on radiation in 8.2 'Light, infrared, microwaves and radio waves'.

Key words: infrared, emit, radiation

Surfaces and radiation

Key points

- All objects absorb infrared radiation.
- Dark, matt surfaces emit infrared radiation more quickly than light, shiny surfaces.
- Dark, matt surfaces absorb infrared radiation more quickly than light, shiny surfaces.
- Light, shiny surfaces reflect more infrared radiation than dark, matt surfaces.

- Dark, matt surfaces are good **absorbers** of infrared radiation. An object painted dull black and left in the Sun will become hotter than the same object painted shiny white.

> **1 a** *Why are houses in hot countries often painted white?*
> **b** *Why are car radiators often painted black?*

- Dark, matt surfaces are also good **emitters** of infrared radiation. So an object that is painted dull black will transfer energy and cool down more quickly than the same object painted shiny white.

> **2** *Why are the pipes on the back of a fridge usually painted black?*

- Light, shiny surfaces are good **reflectors** of infrared radiation.

> **3** *Why is a shiny surface more suitable than a black surface for a flat roof?*

Practical

Comparing radiation from two different surfaces

Two identical beakers (and lids) containing the same mass of hot water are used; one beaker with a shiny silvered surface and the other with a matt black surface. With a **thermometer** in each beaker and a **stopwatch**, the temperature of the water in each beaker is measured every minute. The measurements are recorded then plotted on a temperature against time graph to give a line for each beaker. The results should show that the temperature of the matt black beaker decreases faster than the other one.

> **4** *Why must the mass of water be the same in the beakers?*

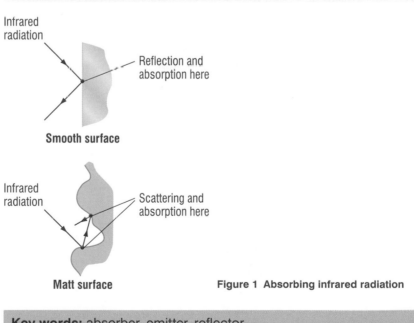

Figure 1 Absorbing infrared radiation

links

Revise more on radiation in 14.6 'Energy transfer by design' and 15.4 'Heating and insulating buildings'.

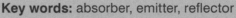

Key words: absorber, emitter, reflector

Student's book
pages 146–147

P14.6 Energy transfer by design

Key points

- The rate of energy transfer to or from an object depends on:
  – the shape, size and type of material of the object
  – the materials the object is in contact with
  – the temperature difference between the object and its surroundings.

Figure 1 Motorcycle engine fins

- The greater the **temperature difference** between an object and its surroundings, the greater the rate at which energy is transferred.
- The rate at which energy is transferred also depends on:
  – the materials the object is in contact with
  – the object's shape
  – the object's surface area.
- To **maximise** the rate of energy transfer to keep things cool, use materials that:
  – are good conductors
  – are painted dull black
  – have the air flow around them maximised.

> **1** *Why does a motorcycle engine have fins?*

- To **minimise** the rate of energy transfer to keep things warm, the transfer of energy by conduction, convection and radiation needs to be minimised by using things that:
  – are good insulators
  – are white and shiny
  – prevent convection currents by trapping air in small pockets.

> **2** *Why does painting an object dull black maximise the rate of energy transfer?*

> **3** *Why does trapping air in small pockets minimise the rate of energy transfer?*

- **The vacuum flask** is designed to minimise energy transfer by conduction, convection and radiation.
- The inside surfaces of the flask are silvered to reduce energy transfer by radiation.

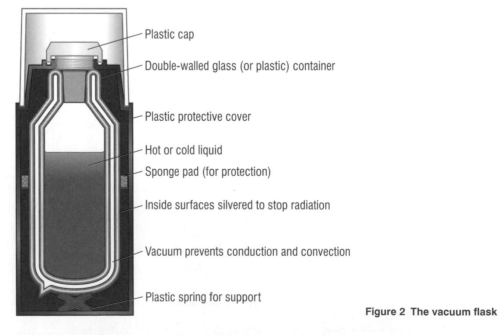

Plastic cap

Double-walled glass (or plastic) container

Plastic protective cover

Hot or cold liquid

Sponge pad (for protection)

Inside surfaces silvered to stop radiation

Vacuum prevents conduction and convection

Plastic spring for support

Figure 2 The vacuum flask

- The vacuum reduces energy transfer by conduction and radiation.

> **4** *In Figure 2, list the parts of the vacuum flask made from materials chosen to reduce conduction.*

Student's book
pages 148–149 **P14.7**

Expansion by heating

Key points

- Gases expand on heating much more than solids and liquids.
- Applications of expansion by heating include liquid-in-glass thermometers and thermostats containing liquids.
- Expansion by heating must be allowed for in buildings and bridges by using expansion gaps.

- Different substances expand by different amounts. In general: gases expand much more than liquids, liquids expand slightly more than solids.
- The greater the increase in temperature of a solid, liquid or gas, the greater the expansion is.

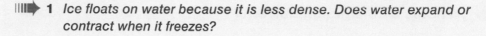

> 1 *Ice floats on water because it is less dense. Does water expand or contract when it freezes?*

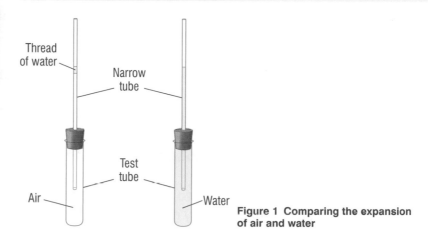

Figure 1 Comparing the expansion of air and water

- The longer the length of a solid, the greater its expansion. Applications of expansion by heating include: 1) expansion gaps in buildings and bridges, otherwise long beams and sections would buckle against each other; 2) heating of steel tyres so they expand and can be fitted on the wheels; 3) bimetallic strips in thermostats in which two joined strips of different metals bend as they expand.

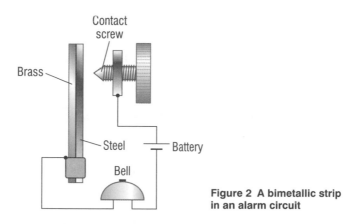

Figure 2 A bimetallic strip in an alarm circuit

> 2 *In a bimetallic strip metal X expands more than metal Y. When it becomes hotter, does the strip bend with X on the inside or the outside of the bend?*

- The greater the volume of a liquid or a gas, the greater the expansion.
- In a liquid-in-glass thermometer, the liquid expands when heated into a narrow tube in a glass stem.
- In a radiator thermostat, the liquid expands when heated against the force of a spring to close a valve and so turn off the flow of hot water.
- A gas expands when heated unless it is in a sealed container.

Study tip

Make sure you can describe and explain the applications above.

> 3 *Why is the spring necessary in a thermostat valve?*

1 How does a non-metal conduct?

2 Why is dry wool a good insulator?

3 What is a convection current?

4 A cup of tea in a beaker cools more slowly if a lid is placed on the beaker. What methods of energy transfer does the lid prevent?

5 Why do wet clothes on a washing line dry faster if there is a wind?

6 How does the vacuum in a vacuum flask reduce energy losses?

7 Why does a black car in a car park heat up in sunshine faster than a silvered car?

8 A marathon runner is given a silvered foil blanket to wear at the end of a race. How does this stop the runner from losing energy?

9 A heat sink is a device used to stop electrical components over-heating.

   a Why is a heat sink made of metal?

   b Why does a heat sink have fins?

10 Why does closing the curtains at night in winter reduce energy loss from a house?

11 In a bimetallic strip designed to switch a heater off, metal X bends more than metal Y.

   a Which metal X or Y is in contact with the contact screw when the heater is on?

   b What adjustment needs to be made so that the heater switches off at a lower temperature?

12 How does the air in a hot air balloon become cooler when it is not being heated?

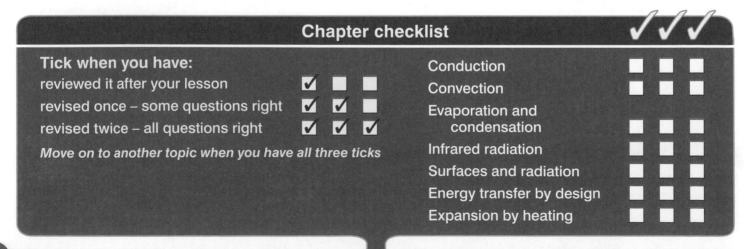

Chapter checklist	✓	✓	✓
Tick when you have:			
reviewed it after your lesson	✓	☐	☐
revised once – some questions right	✓	✓	☐
revised twice – all questions right	✓	✓	✓
Move on to another topic when you have all three ticks			
Conduction	☐	☐	☐
Convection	☐	☐	☐
Evaporation and condensation	☐	☐	☐
Infrared radiation	☐	☐	☐
Surfaces and radiation	☐	☐	☐
Energy transfer by design	☐	☐	☐
Expansion by heating	☐	☐	☐

Student's book
pages 152–153

P15.1 Conservation of energy

Key points

- Energy cannot be created or destroyed.
- Conservation of energy applies to all energy changes.
- Energy can be stored in various ways.

Study tip

Never use the terms 'movement energy' or 'motion energy' in an exam; you will only gain marks by using 'kinetic energy'.

⃝⃝ links

Revise more on kinetic energy in 5.4 'Kinetic energy'.

Key word: conservation of energy, electrical energy

- Energy exists in different forms such as: light, sound, kinetic, electrical, gravitational potential, elastic potential, chemical and nuclear.
- The principle of **conservation of energy** states that **energy cannot be created or destroyed**. It is only possible to change it from one form to another, or transfer (move) it from one place to another.
- This means that the total amount of energy is always the same.

⟫ 1 *What energy transfers take place when **a** you turn on a torch? **b** you burn a fuel?*

Conservation of energy applies to all energy changes. For example:

- The energy of a swinging pendulum changes from gravitational potential energy to kinetic energy and back again as it swings.
- Stretching an elastic band changes chemical energy to elastic potential energy.
- In a solar cell, light energy is changed to **electrical energy**.

⟫ 2 *A swinging pendulum gradually comes to rest. What energy changes take place each time it swings from its highest position on one side to the highest position on the other side?*

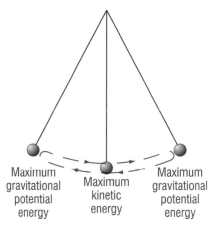

Maximum gravitational potential energy

Maximum kinetic energy

Maximum gravitational potential energy

Figure 1 A pendulum in motion

Student's book
pages 154–155

P15.2 Useful energy

Key points

- Useful energy is energy in the place we want it and the form we need it.
- Wasted energy is energy that is not useful energy.
- Wasted energy is eventually transferred to the surroundings, which become warmer.
- As energy spreads out (dissipates), it gets less and less useful.

⃝⃝ links

Revise more on energy and friction in 5.1 'Energy and work'.

Key words: machine, useful energy, wasted energy

- **Machines** transfer energy from one place to another or from one form to another. The energy we get out of a machine consists of:
  useful energy, which is transferred to the place we want and in the form we want it.
  wasted energy, which is not usefully transferred.

⟫ 1 *What happens to the electrical energy transferred to a light bulb?*

- Both the useful energy and the wasted energy will eventually be transferred to the surroundings, and make them warm up. As the energy spreads out, it becomes more difficult to use for further energy transfers.
- Energy is often wasted because of friction between the moving parts of a machine. This energy warms the machine and the surroundings.
- Sometimes friction may be useful, for example in the brakes of a bicycle or a car. Some of the kinetic energy of the vehicle is transferred to energy heating the brakes.

⟫ 2 *What happens to the gravitational potential energy of a lift when it descends at constant speed?*

Study tip

Sometimes wasted energy is transferred as sound, but the amount of energy is usually very small. Remember that this energy will also eventually be transferred to the surroundings making them warmer.

P15.3 # Energy and efficiency

Key points

- The efficiency of a device =

$$\frac{\text{useful energy transferred by the device}}{\text{total energy supplied to the device}} \times 100\%$$

- No machine can be more than 100% efficient.
- Sankey diagrams are used to show energy flow in a system.

⫸ **2** *A low-energy light bulb is supplied with 60 J of electrical energy every second and emits 12 J of light energy every second.* **a** *What is the total power supplied to the light bulb?* **b** *What is the percentage efficiency of the light bulb?*

Study tip

In an efficiency calculation, an answer greater than 1 or 100% means you have made an error and should check your working.

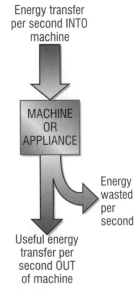

Energy transfer per second INTO machine

MACHINE OR APPLIANCE

Energy wasted per second

Useful energy transfer per second OUT of machine

Figure 1 A Sankey diagram

- The energy supplied to a machine is often called the **input energy**. From the conservation of energy we know that:

  input energy = useful energy delivered + wasted energy

- The less energy that is wasted by a machine, the more efficient the machine is.

- For any device that transfers energy, its **efficiency** $= \dfrac{\text{useful power out}}{\text{total power in}} \times 100\%$

- The efficiency can be given as a fraction or multiplied by 100 to give a percentage.

- Power $= \dfrac{\text{energy transferred}}{\text{time taken}}$. The unit of power is the watt (W). See topic P5.1.

⫸ **1** *In a light bulb, for every 25 joules of energy that are supplied to the bulb, 5 joules are usefully transferred into light energy.* **a** *What is the efficiency of the bulb?* **b** *What percentage of the energy supplied to it is wasted?*

- No device can be more than 100% efficient. Table 1 shows why machines waste energy and how to reduce wastage of energy.

Maths skills

Worked example

An electric motor transfers 60 J of gravitational potential energy to raise an object when the motor is supplied with 200 J of electrical energy. Calculate the percentage efficiency of the motor.

Solution

Total energy supplied to the device = 200 J

Useful energy transferred by the device = 60 J

$$\text{Percentage efficiency} = \frac{\text{useful energy transferred by the device}}{\text{total energy supplied to the device}} \times 100\% = \frac{60\,\text{J}}{200\,\text{J}} \times 100\%$$
$$= 30\%$$

Table 1

	Why machines waste energy	How to reduce the problem
1	Friction between the moving parts causes heating.	Lubricate the moving parts to reduce friction.
2	The resistance of a wire causes the wire to get hot when a current passes through it.	In circuits, use wires with as little electrical resistance as possible.
3	Air resistance causes energy transfer to the surroundings.	Streamline the shapes of moving objects to reduce air resistance.
4	Sound created by machinery causes energy transfer to the surroundings.	Cut out noise (for example, tighten loose parts to reduce vibration).

∞ **links**

Revise more on energy and power in 5.2 'Power'.

Key words: efficiency, Sankey diagram

- The energy transfer through a device can be represented with a **Sankey diagram**.

Heating and insulating buildings

Key points

- The rate of energy transfer to or from our homes can be reduced by fitting loft insulation, cavity wall insulation, double glazing, draught proofing and aluminium foil behind radiators.

- U-values tell us how much energy per second passes through different materials. The lower the U-value, the better the material is as an insulator.

- Solar heating panels do not use fuel to heat water but their payback time is high because they are expensive to buy and install.

⚮ links

Revise more on energy transfer by heating in 14.1 'Conduction', 14.2 'Convection' and 14.5 'Surfaces and radiation'.

Energy transfer out of homes can be reduced by fitting:

- loft insulation, such as fibreglass, to reduce energy transfer by conduction
- cavity wall insulation that traps air in small pockets to reduce energy transfer by convection
- double glazing to reduce energy transfer by conduction through windows
- draught proofing to reduce energy transfer by convection
- aluminium foil behind radiators to reflect infrared radiation back into the room.

> **1 a** *Why is fibreglass a good insulator?*
> **b** *Why is aluminium foil suitable for reflecting infrared radiation?*

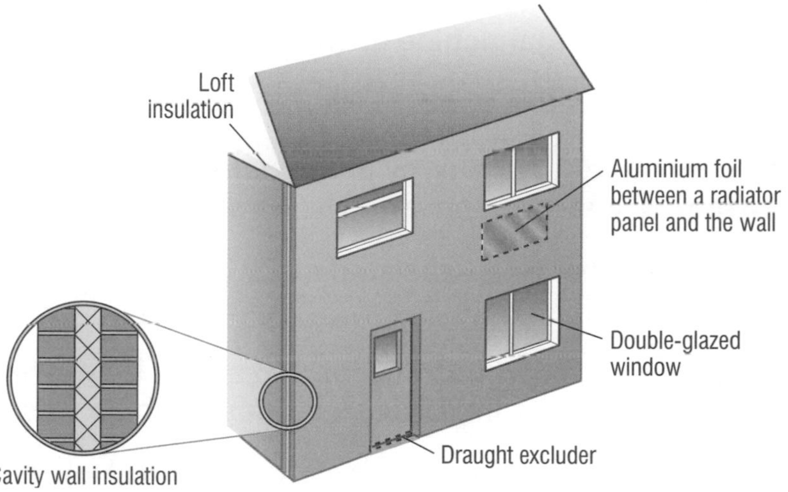

Loft insulation

Aluminium foil between a radiator panel and the wall

Double-glazed window

Draught excluder

Cavity wall insulation

Figure 1 Saving money

- The **U-value** of a material tells us how much energy per second passes through it. Knowing the U-values of different materials allows us to compare them. The lower the U-value, the better the material is as an insulator.

- **Solar heating panels** contain water that is heated by radiation from the Sun. This water may then be used to heat buildings or provide domestic hot water. Solar heating panels are cheap to run because they do not use fuel. However, they are expensive to buy and install and the water is not heated at night.

- The payback time of an 'energy saving' device is the time taken to recover the cost of buying and installing the device from the savings on the subsequent energy bills.

> **2** *A solar heating panel costs £2000 to install. What would be the payback time if the device reduces energy bills by £100 per year?*

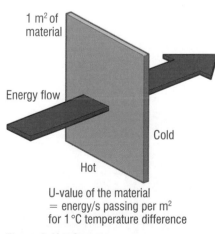

1 m² of material

Energy flow

Cold

Hot

U-value of the material
= energy/s passing per m²
for 1 °C temperature difference

Figure 2 U-values

Study tip

Be prepared to look at tables of U-values and decide which would be the best material to use in a particular situation. You may also have to take into account other things such as cost-effectiveness and pay-back time.

Key words: U-value, solar heating panel

1 **a** What form of energy does a moving car have?
b What form of energy does a stretched spring have?

2 What are the useful energy transfers that take place in:
a a hairdryer?
b a television?

3 What energy transfers take place when a bungee jumper descends?

4 **a** What is meant by useful energy?
b What is meant by wasted energy?

5 When an electric sewing machine is used, in what forms is the useful energy it transfers?

6 When a microwave oven is used, in what form or forms is the wasted energy it transfers?

7 In an electric motor 250 J of energy are transferred to the surroundings by heating for every 1000 J of electrical energy supplied. What is the efficiency of the motor as a fraction?

8 Why is the efficiency of a fan-assisted electric heater less when the fan is on than when it is off?

9 60 J of energy are supplied each second to a light bulb. The bulb transfers 18 J of energy to light each second. How much energy does the bulb waste each second?

10 An 800 W microwave oven has an efficiency of 80%. How much energy does it waste each minute?

11 When a kettle full of cold water is brought to boiling point, 720 000 J of energy are transferred to the water.
a If the kettle has an efficiency of 96%, how much energy is supplied to the kettle to boil the water?
b If the power supplied to the kettle is 3000 W, how long does the kettle take to heat the water from cold to boiling point?

12 An 800 W microwave oven takes 40 s to heat 0.150 kg of water in a plastic beaker from 15 °C to 55 °C. The specific heat capacity of water is 4200 J/kg °C.
a How much electrical energy is supplied to the oven?
b How much energy is transferred by heating to the water?
c Calculate the efficiency of the oven.
d How is the energy wasted?

Chapter checklist ✓ ✓ ✓

Tick when you have:				Conservation of energy	☐	☐	☐
reviewed it after your lesson	✓	☐	☐	Useful energy	☐	☐	☐
revised once – some questions right	✓	✓	☐	Energy and efficiency	☐	☐	☐
revised twice – all questions right	✓	✓	✓	Heating and insulating buildings	☐	☐	☐

Move on to another topic when you have all three ticks

1 A 3000 W electric kettle is capable of heating 1.5 kg of water from 20 °C to 100 °C in 280 seconds.

  a Calculate the electrical energy supplied to the kettle in this time. *(1 mark)*

  b **i** The specific heat capacity of water is 4200 J/kg °C. Calculate the energy needed to heat 2.0 kg of water from 20 °C to 100 °C. *(2 marks)*

    ii The empty kettle has a mass of 1.5 kg and is made of steel which has a specific heat capacity of 490 J/kg °C. Calculate the energy needed to heat the kettle from 20 °C to 100 °C. *(2 marks)*

    iii Give reasons why more energy is supplied to the kettle than is used to heat the kettle and the water in it. *(3 marks)*

  c The kettle circuit is fitted with a bimetallic strip that switches the kettle off a few seconds after the water temperature reaches 100 °C. Explain what a bimetallic strip is and describe how it works in the kettle. *(3 marks)*

2 **a** **i** State two differences between evaporation and boiling. *(2 marks)*

    ii A volatile liquid evaporates easily. Explain why such a liquid in a shallow container becomes cooler when a steady wind blows across its surface. *(3 marks)*

  b In an air conditioning system in a building, a volatile substance is pumped round a closed circuit of pipes which includes an air conditioning unit in the building and a heat exchanger outside the building. Figure 1 shows an outline of the system.

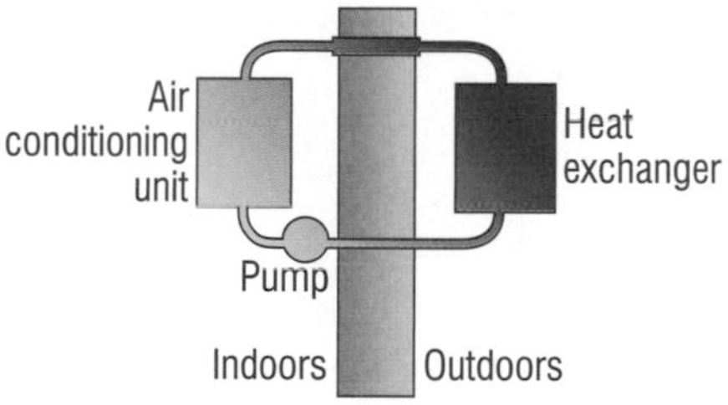

    i In the air conditioning unit, energy is transferred from hot air blown through the unit to the substance in the pipes in the unit. What change of state occurs in the volatile substance when it passes through the air conditioning unit? *(1 mark)*

Figure 1

    ii Energy is transferred to the surroundings of the heat exchanger when the substance passes through the pipes inside the heat exchanger. What change of state occurs in the volatile substance when it passes through these pipes? *(1 mark)*

    iii How is energy transferred between the inside and the outside of the pipes in the air conditioning unit? *(1 mark)*

    iv Why is it necessary to insulate the indoor pipe that takes the substance from the inside to the outside of the building? *(1 mark)*

    v Explain why energy transfer from pipes is more effective if the heat exchanger pipes are painted black. *(2 marks)*

3 The U-value of a double-glazed window is half that of a single-glazed window of the same size.

  a What does the statement above tell you about energy transfer through the double-glazed window compared with the single-glazed window under the same conditions? *(1 mark)*

  b The double-glazed window consists of two glass panes spaced 5 mm apart with a vacuum between the panes which are sealed at the edges, as shown in Figure 2.

  Describe the different ways energy transfer occurs through the window and explain why energy transfer through the double-glazed window is less than through a single-glazed window of the same area.

  In this question, you will be assessed on using good English, organising information clearly and using specialist terms where appropriate *(6 marks)*

Single-glazed window   Double-glazed window

Figure 2

P16.1 Electrical charges

Key points

- Certain insulating materials become charged when rubbed together.
- Electrons are transferred when objects become charged:
  - Insulating materials that become positively charged when rubbed lose electrons.
  - Insulating materials that become negatively charged when rubbed gain electrons.
- Like charges repel; unlike charges attract.

- When certain electrically **insulating** materials are rubbed with a dry cloth, electrons transfer between the insulating material and the cloth. Some materials lose electrons (which the cloth gains) and some materials gain electrons (which the cloth loses).
- Electrons have a **negative** charge so an insulating material that gains electrons becomes negatively charged. A material that loses electrons is left with a **positive** charge. This process is called charging by friction.

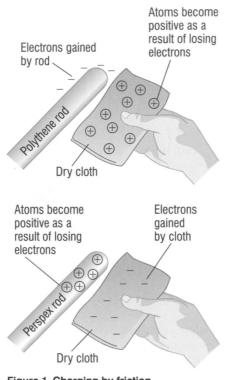

Figure 1 Charging by friction

> 1 *A polythene rod becomes negatively charged when it is rubbed with a dry cloth. Where do the electrons it gains come from?*

- Two objects that have opposite electric charges (unlike charges) **attract** each other. Two objects that have the same electric charges (like charges) **repel** each other.
- The bigger the distance between the objects, the weaker the force between them.

> 2 *What will happen when two charged objects are brought close together if:*
> *a they are both negatively charged? b one is negatively charged and the other is positively charged?*

links

Revise more on electrical insulators in '17.2 Cables and plugs'.

Study tip

Remember it is only ever electrons that move to produce the positive and negative charges on objects.

Key words: insulating, negative, positive, attract, repel

P16.2

Electric circuits

Key points

- Every electrical component has its own agreed symbol. A circuit diagram shows how components are connected together.
- A battery consists of two or more cells connected together.
- The size of an electric current is the rate of flow of charge.
- Electric current = $\dfrac{\text{charge flow}}{\text{time taken}}$

- An **electric current** is a flow of charge due to electrons being forced to move.
- Electric current is measured in **amperes** (A).
- **Electric charge** is measured in **coulombs** (C).

To calculate the electric current in a circuit when charge flows, we use the equation:

$$I = \frac{Q}{t}$$

where I is the current in amperes, A
Q is the charge in coulombs, C
t is the time in seconds, s.

> **1** *A current of 2A passes through a wire for 30 seconds. Calculate the total charge that passes through a point on the wire.*

Every component in a circuit has an agreed **circuit symbol**. These are put together in a circuit diagram to show how the components are connected together in a circuit.

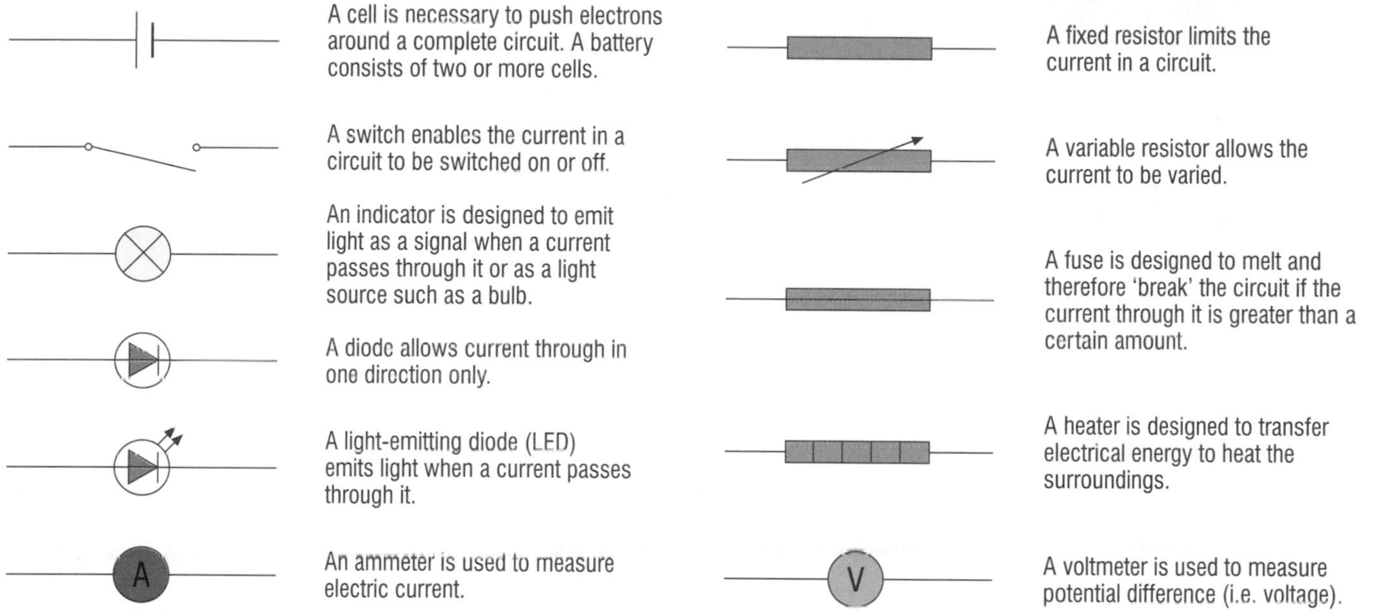

A cell is necessary to push electrons around a complete circuit. A battery consists of two or more cells.

A switch enables the current in a circuit to be switched on or off.

An indicator is designed to emit light as a signal when a current passes through it or as a light source such as a bulb.

A diode allows current through in one direction only.

A light-emitting diode (LED) emits light when a current passes through it.

An ammeter is used to measure electric current.

A fixed resistor limits the current in a circuit.

A variable resistor allows the current to be varied.

A fuse is designed to melt and therefore 'break' the circuit if the current through it is greater than a certain amount.

A heater is designed to transfer electrical energy to heat the surroundings.

A voltmeter is used to measure potential difference (i.e. voltage).

Figure 1 Components and symbols

> **2** *What is the circuit symbol for **a** a variable resistor? **b** a battery of three cells?*

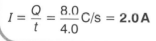

Maths skills

Worked example

A charge of 8.0 C passes through a bulb in 4.0 seconds. Calculate the current through the bulb.

Solution

$$I = \frac{Q}{t} = \frac{8.0}{4.0}\,\text{C/s} = \textbf{2.0\,A}$$

Study tip

We mark the current direction in a circuit from + to −. This convention was agreed long before electrons were discovered.

⃝⃝ links

Revise more on circuits in 16.5 'Series circuits' and 16.6 'Parallel circuits'.

Key words: electric current, ampere, electric charge, coulomb, circuit symbol

Potential difference and resistance

Key points

- Potential difference (volts)

$= \dfrac{\text{energy transferred (joules)}}{\text{charge (coulombs)}}$

- Resistance (ohms)

$= \dfrac{\text{potential difference (volts)}}{\text{current (amperes)}}$

- Ohm's law states that the current through a resistor at constant temperature is directly proportional to the potential difference across the resistor.

- Reversing the current through a component reverses the potential difference across it.

Maths skills

Worked example

The energy transferred to a bulb is 24 J when 8.0 C of charge passes through it. Calculate the potential difference across the bulb.

Solution

$V = \dfrac{E}{Q} = \dfrac{24\,\text{J}}{8.0\,\text{C}} = 3.0\,\text{V}$

Study tip

'Directly proportional' means the graph is a straight line **that passes through the origin.**

⬤⬤ links

Revise more on potential difference in 17.4 'Electrical power and potential difference'.

Key words: ammeter, series, potential difference, voltmeter, parallel, voltage, resistance, ohmic conductor

---

- The current through a component is measured with an **ammeter**. Ammeters are always placed in **series** with the component. The unit of current is the ampere (or amp), A.

- The **potential difference** across a component is measured with a **voltmeter**. Voltmeters are always placed in **parallel** with the component. The unit of potential difference is the volt, V.

> **1** *When an ammeter is used to measure the current through a component, why must it be connected in series with the component?*

The potential difference (pd or **voltage**) across a component is the energy transferred to it (or work done on it) by each coulomb of charge that passes through it.

We can use the following equation to calculate potential difference:

$$V = \frac{E}{Q}$$

where V is the potential difference in volts, V

E is the energy transferred in joules, J

Q is the charge in coulombs, C.

> **2** *How much energy is transferred to a 12 V lamp when 4 C of charge passes through it?*

- **Resistance** is the opposition to current flow. The unit of resistance is the ohm, Ω.

The resistance of a component is calculated using the equation:

$$R = \frac{V}{I}$$

where R is resistance in ohms, Ω

V is the potential difference in volts, V

I is current in amps, A.

> **3 a** *What is the resistance of a resistor when the current through it is 4.0 A and the pd across it is 6.0 V?*
>
> **b** *What is the potential difference across the resistor in part **a** when the current through it is 0.5 A?*

- Current–potential difference graphs are used to show how the current through a component varies with the potential difference across it.

Ohm's law

- The current through a resistor at constant temperature is directly proportional to the potential difference across the resistor.

- The above statement is known as Ohm's law. Any component that obeys Ohm's law is called an **ohmic conductor**.

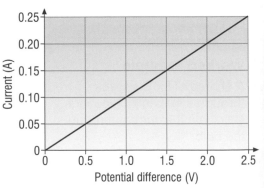

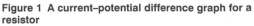

Figure 1 A current–potential difference graph for a resistor

More current–potential difference graphs

Key points

- *Filament bulb*: resistance increases with increase of the filament temperature.
- *Diode*: 'forward' resistance low; 'reverse' resistance high.
- *Thermistor*: resistance decreases if its temperature increases.
- *LDR*: resistance decreases if the light intensity on it increases.

- The line on a current–potential difference graph for a **filament bulb** is a curve. So the current is not directly proportional to the potential difference.
- The resistance of the filament increases as the current increases. So the line curves away from the current axis. This is because the resistance increases as the temperature increases. This happens because the metal ions in the filament of the lamp vibrate more as the filament temperature increases. So they resist the passage of the electrons through the filament more.
- Reversing the potential difference makes no difference to the shape of the curve.

▶ **1** *The current through a lamp is 2.0 A when the potential difference across the lamp is 12.0 V. State whether the current is less than, equal to, or more than 1.0 A when the potential difference across the lamp is 6.0 V.*

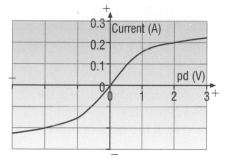

Figure 1 A current–potential difference graph for a filament bulb

Practical

Investigate the resistance of a filament bulb

Connect a low voltage filament bulb in series with a switch, a battery, a variable resistor and an ammeter. Connect a voltmeter in parallel with the bulb.

Use the variable resistor to change the current. Measure the potential difference across the bulb, as well as the current through it for different currents. Record the measurements in a table.

Plot a graph of current on the vertical (*y*) axis against potential difference on the horizontal (*x*) axis. The graph should be a curve with a decreasing gradient, showing the resistance increases as the current increases.

Study tip

Current–potential difference may be plotted with the current on the *x*-axis or the *y*-axis. Make sure you know the shape either way round and check which way round they are given in exam questions.

▶ **2** *What would you do if one of the graph points was anomalous?*

The current through a **diode** flows in one direction only. In the reverse direction the diode has a very high resistance so the current is virtually zero.

- A **light-emitting diode** (LED) emits light when a current passes through it.

▶ **3** *Why is an LED used in circuits as a current indicator?*

∞ links

Revise more on diodes in 17.1 'Alternating current'.

- As the light falling on it gets brighter, the resistance of a **light-dependent resistor** (LDR) decreases.
- As the temperature goes up, the resistance of a **thermistor** goes down.

▶ **4 a** *What happens to the resistance of an LDR if its surroundings become darker?*
b *What effect does reversing the pd across a thermistor have on the current through it?*

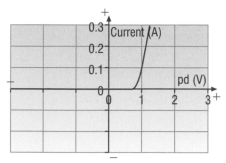

Figure 2 A current–potential difference graph for a diode.

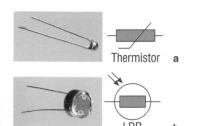

Figure 3 a A thermistor and its symbol, **b** An LDR and its symbol

Key words: filament bulb, diode, light-emitting diode, light-dependent resistor, thermistor

P16.5 # Series circuits

Key points

- For components in series:
  - the current is the same in each component
  - adding the potential differences gives the total potential difference.
- Adding the resistances gives the total resistance of resistors in series.
- For cells in series, acting in the same direction, the total potential difference is the sum of their individual potential differences.

- In a series circuit the components are connected one after another. Therefore if there is a break anywhere in the circuit, charge stops flowing.
- There is no choice of route for the charge when it flows around the circuit so the current through each component is the same.

⟫ **1** *What happens in a series circuit if one component stops working?*

- The current *I* in a series circuit is given by the equation:

$$I = \frac{V}{R}$$

where *V* is the potential difference of the **supply** and *R* is the total resistance of the circuit.

- The potential difference of the supply is shared between all the components in the circuit. So the potential differences across individual components add up to give the potential difference of the supply.
- The resistances of the individual components in series add up to give the total resistance of the circuit.
- The bigger the resistance of a component, the bigger its share of the supply potential difference.

⟫ **2 a** *Draw a circuit diagram to show a battery consisting of three 2.0 V cells in series with a 4 Ω resistor and an 8 Ω resistor.*
   b *Calculate* **i** *the total resistance of the circuit,* **ii** *the current in the circuit.*

Study tip

Remember that in a series circuit the current is the same at any position in the circuit.

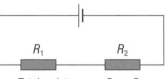

Total resistance = $R_1 + R_2$

Figure 1 Resistors in series

links

Revise more on series circuits in 17.3 'Fuses'.

Key word: supply

Parallel circuits

- For components in parallel:
  - the total current is the sum of the currents through the separate components,
  - the potential difference is the same across each component.
- The bigger the resistance of a component the smaller the current is.
- To calculate the current through a resistor in a parallel circuit:
- $current = \dfrac{potential\ difference}{resistance}$

Study tip

In everyday life parallel circuits are much more useful than series circuits. That is because a break in one part of the circuit does not stop charge flowing in the rest of the circuit. Make sure that you understand the difference between series and parallel circuits.

- In a parallel circuit each component is connected across the supply, so if there is a break in one part of the circuit, charge can still flow in the other parts.
- Each component is connected across the supply pd, so the pd across each component is the same.

Maths skills

Worked example

The circuit diagram in Figure 1 shows three resistors $R_1 = 1\,\Omega$, $R_2 = 2\,\Omega$ and $R_3 = 6\,\Omega$ connected in parallel to a 6V battery.
Calculate:

a the current through each resistor

b the current through the battery.

Solution

a $I_1 = \dfrac{V_1}{R_1} = \dfrac{6}{1} = \mathbf{6\,A}$

$I_2 = \dfrac{V_2}{R_2} = \dfrac{6}{2} = \mathbf{3\,A}$

$I_3 = \dfrac{V_3}{R_3} = \dfrac{6}{6} = \mathbf{1\,A}$

b The total current from the battery $= I_1 + I_2 + I_3 = 6\,A + 3\,A + 1\,A = \mathbf{10\,A}$

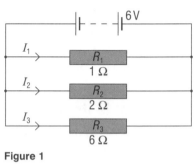

Figure 1

⟫ **1** *What happens in a parallel circuit if one component stops working?*

- There are junctions in the circuit so different amounts of charge can flow through different components.
- The current I through a component of resistance R in a parallel circuit can be calculated using the equation $I = \dfrac{V}{R}$ where V is the pd across the component.
- The total current through the whole circuit is equal to the sum of the currents through the separate components.

⟫ **2** *In a parallel circuit what is the relationship between:*
   a *the supply pd and the pd across each parallel component?*
   b *the supply current and the current through each component?*

⟫ **3** *Two $4\,\Omega$ resistors are connected in parallel across a 12V battery.*
   a *Draw the circuit diagram.*
   b *Calculate **i** the current through each resistance, **ii** the total current through the battery.*

1 When a glass rod is rubbed with a dry cloth, electrons transfer from the rod to the cloth.
 a What type of charge does an electron have?
 b Does the rod become negatively or positively charged?

2 A polythene rod P becomes negatively charged when it is rubbed with a dry cloth. A rod X of a different material is also charged. When X is held near P, the two objects repel each other. What type of charge does X have?

3 Calculate the charge flow when a current of 6.0 A passes through a component for 500 s.

4 Two cells, a lamp, a diode and a switch are connected in series so the lamp is on when the switch is closed.
 a Draw the circuit diagram for this circuit.
 b A student connects the components in series but finds that the lamp remains off when the switch is closed. Give two possible reasons why the lamp stays off.

5 If the current through a resistor is 0.2 A when the potential difference across it is 12 V, what is its resistance?

6 The energy transferred to a bulb is 36 J when 8.0 C of charge passes through it. Calculate the potential difference across the bulb.

7 A thermistor is connected in series with a battery and an ammeter. State and explain what change occurs to the ammeter reading if the temperature of the thermistor is reduced.

8 What can you say about the resistance of a diode in its forward direction compared with its resistance in its reverse direction?

9 A series circuit consists of a battery, a resistor R and a variable resistor V. If the resistance of V is increased, what happens to:
 a the current in the circuit?
 b the pd across R?

10 A 5 Ω resistor and a 7 Ω resistor are connected in series with a 6.0 V battery. Calculate the current in the circuit.

11 An ammeter and a voltmeter are used to measure the current through and the pd across a resistor when it is connected in series with a cell and a switch. Draw the circuit diagram for this circuit.

12 A 4 Ω resistor and a 12 Ω resistor are connected in parallel with a 12 V battery.
 a Draw the circuit diagram for this circuit.
 b **i** Calculate the current through each resistor.
 ii Calculate the current through the battery.

Chapter checklist ✔ ✔ ✔

Tick when you have:

reviewed it after your lesson	✔	☐	☐
revised once – some questions right	✔	✔	☐
revised twice – all questions right	✔	✔	✔

Move on to another topic when you have all three ticks

Electrical charges	☐	☐	☐
Electric circuits	☐	☐	☐
Potential difference and resistance	☐	☐	☐
More current–potential difference graphs	☐	☐	☐
Series circuits	☐	☐	☐
Parallel circuits	☐	☐	☐

Alternating current

Key points

- Direct current (dc) is in one direction only. Alternating current (ac) repeatedly reverses its direction.

- A mains circuit has a live wire that is alternately positive and negative every cycle and a neutral wire at zero volts.

- A diode can be used for half-wave rectification of ac.

- The peak potential difference of an ac supply is the maximum voltage measured from zero volts.

- To measure the frequency of the ac supply, we measure the time period of the waves then use the formula frequency
$$= \frac{1}{\text{time taken for 1 cycle}}$$

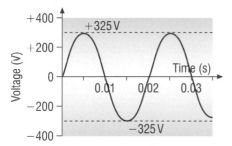

Figure 1 Mains voltage against time

Study tip

Make sure that you can make readings from diagrams of oscilloscope traces.

∞ links

Revise more on frequency in 7.2 'Measuring waves'.

Cells and batteries supply **direct current**. This is current that passes round the circuit in one direction only.

The current from the mains supply is **alternating current**. This is current that alternates, meaning it repeatedly passes in one direction, then reverses and passes in the other direction.

- The **frequency** of the UK mains supply is 50 hertz (Hz), which means it alternates direction 50 times each second. The 'voltage' of the mains is 230 V.
- The potential difference between the live wire and 'earth' is usually referred to as the 'potential' or 'voltage' of the live wire.
- The **live wire** of the mains supply alternates between a positive and a negative potential, as shown in Figure 1.
- The voltage of the **live wire** alternates between +325 volts and –325 volts. In terms of electrical power, this is equivalent to a direct potential difference of 230 volts. The **neutral wire** stays at zero volts.

> **1 a** *What is the potential of the neutral wire?*
> **b** *What is the change of potential of the live wire from a positive peak to a negative peak?*

- The frequency of an ac supply can be determined by connecting the supply to an oscilloscope. The time taken for one cycle, *T*, can be found from the oscilloscope trace by measuring the time taken for as many complete cycles as possible.
- The frequency *f* (in hertz, Hz) is calculated using the equation:

$$f = \frac{1}{T}$$

where *T* is the time for one cycle in seconds, s.

Half-wave rectification

A diode in series with a resistor may be used to convert alternating current to direct current as shown in Figure 2. An oscilloscope may be used to show how the potential difference across the resistor varies with time.

The diode conducts in the half of each cycle when it is forward biased. The current is said to be **half-wave rectified.**

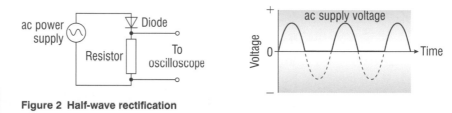

Figure 2 Half-wave rectification

> **2** *How would the waveform in Figure 2 differ if the diode were reversed in the circuit?*

Key words: direct current, alternating current, frequency, live wire, neutral wire

P17.2 # Cables and plugs

Key points

- Sockets and plugs are made of stiff plastic materials, which enclose the electrical connections.
- Mains cable consists of two or three insulated copper wires surrounded by an outer layer of flexible plastic material.
- In a three-pin plug or a three-core cable: the live wire is brown; the neutral wire is blue; the earth wire is green and yellow.
- The earth wire is used to earth the metal case of a mains appliance.

- Most electrical appliances are connected to the **sockets** of the mains supply using **cable** and a **three-pin plug**.
- The outer cover of a three-pin plug is made of a stiff electric insulator such as plastic or rubber.
- The pins of the **plug** are made of brass. Brass is a good electrical conductor. It is also hard and will not rust or oxidise.
- The **earth wire** is connected to the longest pin.
- The cable grip must be fastened tightly over the cable. There should be no bare wires showing inside the plug and the correct wire must be connected firmly to the terminal of the correct pin.

▐▐▐▶ **1** *Why are the pins made of brass instead of iron or copper?*

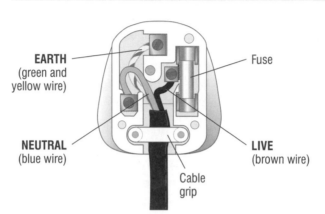

EARTH
(green and
yellow wire)

Fuse

NEUTRAL
(blue wire)

LIVE
(brown wire)

Cable
grip

Figure 1 Inside a three-pin plug

- Appliances with metal cases must be earthed (to prevent the case becoming live if the live wire touches it). The case is attached to the earth wire in the cable.
- The green-yellow wire (of a three-core cable) is connected to the earth pin. Note that a two-core cable does not have an earth wire.
- Appliances with plastic cases do not need to be earthed. They are said to be double insulated and are connected to the supply with two-core cable containing just a live and a neutral wire.

▐▐▐▶ **2** *What type of cable, two-core or three-core, is needed for **a** a plastic hair dryer? **b** a fridge freezer?*

Cables of different thicknesses are used for different purposes. The more current to be carried, the thicker the cable needs to be, otherwise the cable would overheat.

> ### Study tip
>
> Make sure that you can identify faults in the wiring of a three-pin plug.

links
Revise more on electrical faults in 17.7 'Electrical issues'.

Key words: socket, cable, three-pin plug, plug, earth wire

P17.3 | Fuses

Key points

- A fuse contains a thin wire that heats up and melts if too much current passes through it. This cuts the current off.

- A circuit breaker is an electromagnetic switch that opens ('trips') and cuts the current off if too much current passes through it.

- A **fuse** is always fitted in series with the live wire. This cuts off the appliance from the live wire if the fuse blows.

- Appliances with metal cases need to be earthed. Otherwise if a fault develops, and the live wire touches the metal case, the case becomes live and could give an electric shock to anyone who touches it.

- If a fault develops in an earthed appliance, a large current flows to earth and melts the fuse. This disconnects the supply.

- A mains appliance with a plastic case does not need to be earthed because plastic is an insulator and cannot become live.

- The rating of the fuse should be slightly higher than the normal working current of the appliance. If it is much higher, it will not melt soon enough. If it is not higher than the normal current, it will melt as soon as the appliance is switched on.

> **1** *The current supplied to an appliance is 2.8 A when it works normally. Which fuse rating (1 A, 3 A or 5 A) would be suitable for this appliance?*

- A **circuit breaker** can be used in place of a fuse. This is an electromagnetic switch that opens and cuts off the supply if the current is bigger than a certain value. It can be reset once the fault that caused the current to be cut off is fixed.

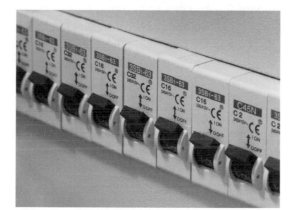

Figure 1 A circuit breaker

Study tip

Make sure you can explain how the earth wire and the fuse protect an appliance.

- A **residual current circuit breaker (RCCB)** cuts off the current in the live wire if it is different to the current in the neutral wire. It works faster than a fuse or an ordinary circuit breaker and is more sensitive than an ordinary circuit breaker.

> **2** **a** *State one advantage of a circuit breaker compared with a fuse.*
> **b** *State one advantage of a residual current circuit breaker compared with an ordinary circuit breaker.*

⚬⚬ links

Revise more on fuses in 17.4 'Electrical power and potential difference'.

Key words: fuse, circuit breaker, residual current circuit breaker (RCCB)

Student's book
pages 182–183 **P17.4**

Electrical power and potential difference

Key points

- The power supplied to a device is the energy transferred to it each second.
- Electric power supplied (watts) = current (amperes) × potential difference (volts).
- Correct rating (in amperes) for a fuse
  $$= \frac{\text{electrical power (watts)}}{\text{potential difference (volts)}}$$

An electrical appliance transfers electrical energy into other forms of energy. The rate at which it does this is called the **power**.

Power can be calculated using the equation:

$$P = \frac{E}{t}$$

where P is the power in watts, W
E is the energy transferred in joules, J
t is the time in seconds, s.

> **1 a** *What is the power, in kW, of an appliance that transfers 90 000 J of energy in 30 seconds?*
> **b** *How much energy is supplied to a 3 kW electric kettle in 3 minutes?*

We can also use current and pd to calculate the power of the appliance using the equation:

$$P = I \times V$$

where P is the power in watts, W
I is the current in amperes, A
V is the potential difference in volts, V.

- Electrical appliances have their power rating shown on them. The pd of the mains supply is 230 V.
- This equation can be used to calculate the normal current through an appliance and so work out the size of fuse to use. The fuse is chosen so that its value is slightly higher than the calculated current.

> **2 a** *What is the current in a 230 V steam wallpaper stripper that has a power of 2 kW?*
> **b** *Which fuse rating 3 A, 5 A or 13 A would be suitable for this appliance?*

> **3** *What is the power of a mains appliance that takes a current of 10 A?*

Maths skills

Worked example

A light bulb transfers 30 000 J of electrical energy when it is on for 300 s. Calculate its power.

Solution

$$\text{Power} = \frac{\text{energy transferred}}{\text{time}}$$

$$= \frac{30\,000\,\text{J}}{300\,\text{s}}$$

$$= \textbf{100 W}$$

Study tip

Practise calculating the current in appliances of different powers so you can choose the correct fuse.

Practical

Measure the power of a low voltage electric heater

Set up a 12 V low voltage heater in series with a switch, a battery, a variable resistor and an **ammeter**. Connect a **voltmeter** in parallel with the heater and adjust the variable resistor to increase the heater pd to exactly 12 V.

Record the heater current and pd. Use these values to calculate the power of the heater at 12.0 V.

links

Revise more on potential difference and power in 16.3 'Potential difference and resistance' and 5.2 'Power'.

> **4** *How would you use your result to check the accuracy of a joulemeter used to measure the energy supplied to the heater?*

Key word: power

P17.5

Electrical energy and charge

Key points

- An electric current is the rate of flow of charge.
- Charge (coulombs) = current (amperes) × time (seconds).
- When an electrical charge flows through a resistor, energy transferred to the resistor makes it hot.
- Energy transferred (joules) = potential difference (volts) × charge flow (coulombs).
- When charge flows round a circuit for a certain time, the electrical energy supplied by the battery is equal to the electrical energy transferred to all the components in the circuit.

The equation relating charge, current and time is:

$$Q = I \times t$$

where Q is the charge in **coulombs**, C
I is the current in amperes, A
t is the time in seconds, s.

> **1** *How much charge flows past a particular point in a circuit when a current of 2A flows for 2 minutes?*

- When charge flows through an appliance, electrical energy is transferred to other forms. In a resistor, electrical energy is transferred to the resistor so the resistor becomes hotter.
- The amount of energy transferred can be calculated using the equation:

$$E = V \times Q$$

where E is the energy in joules, J
V is the potential difference in volts, V
Q is the charge in coulombs, C.
Note that combining the two equations gives $E = V \times I \times t$

Maths skills

Worked example

Calculate the charge flow when the current is 8 A for 80 s.

Solution

Charge flow = current × time
= 8 A × 80 s
= 640 C

> **2** *How much energy is transferred when:*
> **a** *a charge of 200 C flows through a resistor that has a potential difference across it of 230 V?*
> **b** *a current of 5 A passes through a 12 V lamp for 20 minutes?*

Maths skills

Worked example

Calculate the energy transferred in a component when the charge passing through it is 30 C and the potential difference is 20 V.

Solution

Energy transferred = 20 V × 30 C
= **600 J**

⚲ links

Revise more on potential difference and energy in 16.3 'Potential difference and resistance'.

Study tip

When charge flows in a circuit, the components will heat up because of their resistance. This means that most electrical appliances have vents to keep them cool.

Key word: coulomb

Using electrical energy

Key points

- The kilowatt-hour (kWh) is the energy supplied to a 1 kW appliance in 1 hour.
- Energy transferred = power × time
- Total cost of energy used = number of kWh used × cost per kWh.

- For any appliance, the energy supplied to it depends on:
  - how long it is switched on for,
  - the power supplied to it.
- We use the **kilowatt-hour** (kWh) as the unit of energy supplied by mains electricity.

The energy E transferred to a mains appliance is given by the equation:

$$E = P \times t$$

where E is the energy transferred in kWh
P is the power in **kilowatts** (kW)
t is the time in hours.

Maths skills

Worked example

To calculate the power of an appliance, just rearrange the equation $E = P \times t$ as below:

Divide both sides by t: $\dfrac{E}{t} = \dfrac{Pt}{t}$

This is the same as: $P = \dfrac{E}{t}$

links

Revise more on power and energy in 5.2 'Power'.

1 *How much energy in kWh is supplied to **a** a 3.0 kW electric heater in 4 hours? **b** a 60 W electric lamp for 12 hours?*

- An electricity meter in your home records the total electrical energy supplied to your home in kilowatt-hours.
- The difference between two meter readings gives the number of kilowatt-hours in the time between the two readings.
- The cost of the electrical energy supplied is calculated using the equation:

  Total cost = number of kWh used × cost per kWh

2 *An electricity meter reads 2508 kWh a month after it read 1502 kWh.*
  a How much electrical energy in kWh was supplied in the month?
  *b The electrical energy cost 14p per kWh. What was the cost of the energy supplied in **a**?*

Study tip

Remember, kilowatt-hours = number of kilowatts × number of hours

Key words: kilowatt-hour, kilowatt

P17.7

Electrical issues

Key points

- Electrical faults are dangerous because they can cause electric shocks and fires.
- Never touch a mains appliance (or plug or socket) with wet hands. Never touch a bare wire or a terminal at a potential of more than 30 V.
- Check cables, plugs and sockets for damage regularly.
- When choosing an electrical appliance, the power and efficiency rating of the appliance need to be considered.
- Filament bulbs and halogen lamps are much less efficient than low energy lamps.

- Electrical faults may occur as a result of damage to sockets, plugs, cables or appliances.
- Electrical equipment should be checked regularly for wear. Worn or damaged items should be replaced or repaired by a qualified electrician.
- Avoid overloading sockets as this may cause overheating and a risk of fire.
- Electrical appliances should be handled safely and never used in a bathroom or with wet hands.
- The cable should always be appropriate for the intended use.

> **1** *Why should you never touch a mains appliance with wet hands?*

- When choosing an electrical appliance, the power and efficiency rating need to be considered, as well as the cost.
- Filament bulbs and halogen lamps are much less efficient than low energy compact fluorescent lamps and do not last as long.

> **2** *Why is a filament bulb very inefficient?*

Study tip

You may have to identify the best appliance to use in a particular situation from information given in a question.

P17.8 ## The National Grid

Key points

- The National Grid transmits electricity from power stations to our homes.
- Step-up and step-down transformers are used in the National Grid.
- A high grid voltage reduces the current needed, therefore reducing energy wastage and making the system more efficient.

- The **National Grid** is a network of pylons and cables that connects power stations to homes, schools, factories and other buildings. Since the whole country is connected to the system, power stations can be switched in or out according to demand.
- The cables cover long distances across the countryside supported by overhead pylons. In towns and close to homes the cables are buried underground.

> 1 *Give two advantages of overhead cables compared with underground cables.*

- The National Grid's voltage is 132 000 V or more. Power stations produce electricity at a voltage of 25 000 V.
- In power stations, electricity is generated at a particular voltage. The voltage is increased by **step-up transformers** before the electricity is transmitted across the National Grid. This is because transmission at high voltage reduces the current in the cables and therefore reduces the energy wasted in the cables, making the system more efficient.
- It would be dangerous to supply electricity to consumers at these very high voltages. So, at local sub-stations, **step-down transformers** are used to reduce the voltage to 230 volts for use in homes and offices.

> 2 *What sort of transformers are used* **a** *at local sub-stations?* **b** *power stations?*

Study tip

Remember that:
- the grid voltage is much higher than the voltage of the power stations and much much higher than in homes
- the mains voltage in homes is 230 V
- step-up transformers increase the voltage and step-down transformers decrease the voltage.

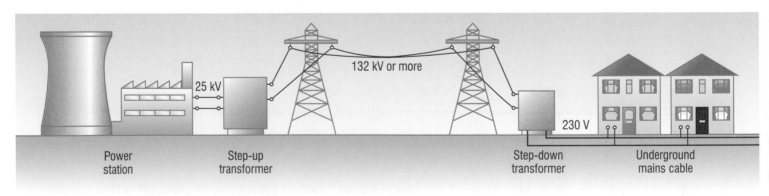

Figure 1 The National Grid

⚭ links

Revise more on transformers in 18.6 'Transformers' and 18.7 'Transformers in action'.

Key words: National Grid, step-up transformer, step-down transformer

1 **a** What is the frequency of the mains supply?
  b What is the peak voltage of the mains supply?

2 What do we mean when we say the mains voltage is 230 V?

3 **a** What colour is the neutral wire?
  b What is the potential of the neutral wire?

4 **a** Which wire in a 3-pin plug is yellow and green in colour?
  b Why is it important to earth the case of any mains appliance that has a metal case?

5 State four possible faults in either the cable or the plug of a mains appliance.

6 A box contains four mains fuses rated at 1 A, 3 A, 5 A and 13 A.
  a Which fuse would be most suitable for a 230 V 1000 W microwave oven?
  b Why would it be dangerous if one of the other fuses were used instead?

7 A 12 V 36 W lamp is connected to a 12 V battery. Calculate:
  a the lamp current
  b the charge flow through the lamp in 5 minutes.

8 **a** State one advantage and one disadvantage of a circuit breaker compared with a fuse.
  b What does a residual current circuit breaker do that an ordinary circuit breaker does not do?

9 A 3 kW appliance is used for 600 seconds. Calculate the energy transferred in joules.

10 The potential difference across a 200 Ω resistor in a circuit is 12 V. Calculate:
  a the current through the resistor
  b the energy transferred to the resistor each second.

11 A student uses a 2300 W mains heater for 2 hours, a 60 W lamp for 4 hours and an 800 W microwave oven for 15 minutes.
  a Calculate the energy transferred to each appliance in kilowatt-hours.
  b If each kilowatt-hour of electrical energy costs 12p, calculate the cost of the total energy transferred in **a**.

12 Why is power transmitted through the National Grid at very high voltage?

Chapter checklist	✓	✓	✓
Tick when you have:			
reviewed it after your lesson	✓	☐	☐
revised once – some questions right	✓	✓	☐
revised twice – all questions right	✓	✓	✓
Move on to another topic when you have all three ticks			

Alternating current	☐	☐	☐
Cables and plugs	☐	☐	☐
Fuses	☐	☐	☐
Electrical power and potential difference	☐	☐	☐
Electrical energy and charge	☐	☐	☐
Using electrical energy	☐	☐	☐
Electrical issues	☐	☐	☐
The National Grid	☐	☐	☐

P18.1 # Magnetic fields

Key points

- Like poles repel and unlike poles attract.
- The magnetic field lines of a bar magnet curve round from the north pole of the bar magnet to the south pole.
- In a uniform magnetic field, the lines of the magnetic field are parallel.

- Any iron or steel object can be magnetised or demagnetised.
- The space around a **magnet** is called a **magnetic field**. The Earth has a magnetic field which is most concentrated at the magnetic **north pole** and **south pole**.
- The north-seeking pole of a bar magnet is the end that points north when the magnet is freely suspended. The other end is the south-seeking pole.
- A plotting compass is a tiny magnet that lines up with the Earth's magnetic field and its tip points to the Earth's magnetic north pole.
- The **lines of force** of a magnetic field are the lines along which a plotting compass would point.

When two magnets are held near each other like poles repel; unlike poles attract.

> **1** *A bar magnet attracts the tip of a plotting compass when one end is held near the compass. What is the magnetic polarity of the end of the magnet nearest the plotting compass?*

The magnetic field lines around two bar magnets when they are lined up with each other, with unlike poles facing each other is shown in Figure 1. The lines across the gap are:
– from the N-pole of one magnet to the S-pole of the other
– parallel to each other in the central part of the gap.

- With like poles facing each other across the gap between them, the lines across the gap are absent in the central part of the gap. The effect of one of the magnets on a plotting compass placed here is cancelled out by the other magnet.

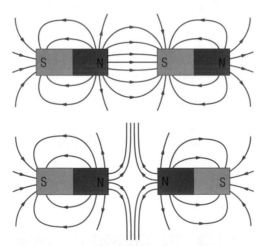

Figure 1 Magnets in line

> **2** *A plotting compass is placed midway between two identical bar magnets A and B which are in line with each other. The plotting compass points towards A.*
> **a** *What is the magnetic polarity of the end of each bar magnet nearest the plotting compass?*
> **b** *What can you say about the magnetic field where the plotting compass is?*

links

Revise more on magnetic fields in 18.2 'Electromagnets'.

Key words: magnet, magnetic field, north pole, south pole, line of force

Electromagnets

Key points

- The magnetic field lines around a current-carrying wire are circles centred on the wire, in a plane perpendicular to the wire.
- Increasing the current makes the magnetic field stronger
- Reversing the direction of the current reverses the magnetic field lines
- An electromagnet consists of a coil of insulated wire wrapped round an iron core.
- Electromagnets are used in scrapyard cranes, circuit breakers, electric bells and relays.

- When a current flows through a wire, a magnetic field is produced around the wire. The magnetic field lines are circles around the wire – see Figure 1.
- The circles are centred on the wire and are in a plane perpendicular to the wire.
- Increasing the current makes the magnetic field stronger.
- The corkscrew rule gives the direction of the field lines.
- Reversing the direction of the current reverses the direction of the magnetic field.

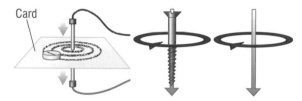

Figure 1 The magnetic field near a long straight wire

1 *A vertical wire carries a current downwards. When the wire is seen from above, in what direction, clockwise or anticlockwise, are the magnetic field lines?*

Electromagnets

- An **electromagnet** is made by wrapping insulated wire around a piece of iron, called the core. When a current flows through the wire the iron becomes strongly magnetised. When the current is switched off the iron loses its magnetism. This temporary magnetism makes electromagnets very useful.
- Electromagnets are used in devices such as scrapyard cranes, circuit breakers, electric bells and **relays**. A relay is an electrically operated switch.

2 a *What is the purpose of the make and break switch in an electric bell?*
   b *What is a relay and what is it used for?*

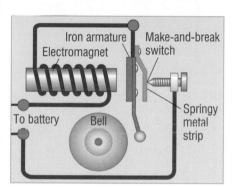

Iron armature
Electromagnet
Make-and-break switch
To battery
Bell
Springy metal strip

Figure 2 An electric bell

⊂⊃ **links**

Revise more on electromagnets in 17.3 'Fuses'.

Study tip

In the exam you may be given a diagram of an appliance that contains an electromagnet and asked to explain how it works.

Practical

Investigate the magnetic field near a long straight wire

A vertical wire through a horizontal card is set up as shown in Figure 1. The wire is connected in series with an **ammeter**, a switch, a variable resistor and a cell. A **plotting compass** is placed near the wire so it points at the wire when the current is off. The current is switched on and a **protractor** is used to measure the angle of deflection *A* of the plotting compass needle for different measured currents. The results are recorded and used to plot a graph of *A* on the vertical axis and current *I* on the horizontal axis.

3 *Sketch the graph you would expect and explain its shape.*

Key words: electromagnet, relay

P18.3 # The motor effect

Key points

- In the motor effect, the force:
  - is increased if the current or the strength of the magnetic field is increased
  - is at right angles to both the direction of the magnetic field and to the wire
  - is reversed if the direction of either the current or the magnetic field is reversed.
- An electric motor has a coil which turns when a current is passed through it.

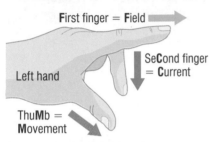

First finger = Field

Left hand

SeCond finger = Current

ThuMb = Movement

Figure 1 Fleming's left-hand rule

- When we place a wire carrying an electric current in a magnetic field, it may experience a force. This is called the **motor effect**.
- The force is at its maximum if the wire is at an angle of 90° to the magnetic field, and zero if the wire is parallel to the magnetic field.
- Fleming's left-hand rule is used to determine the direction of the force. The thumb and first two fingers of the left hand are held at right angles to each other:
  - the first finger represents the magnetic field (pointing north to south)
  - the second finger represents the current (pointing positive to negative)
  - the thumb represents the direction of the force.
- The size of the force can be increased by: 1) increasing the strength of the magnetic field; 2) increasing the size of the current.
- The direction of the force on the wire is reversed if either the direction of the current or the direction of the magnetic field is reversed.
- The motor effect is used in different devices.

> **1 a** If the wire is in front of you and the current is vertically upwards and the magnetic field is horizontal and away from you, what is the direction of the force on the wire?
>
> **b** What happens to the direction of the force on the wire carrying a current in **a** if the direction of the current and the magnetic field are both reversed?

The electric motor

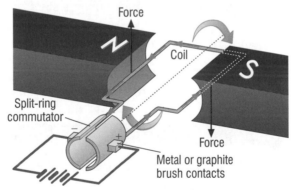

Force

Coil

N

S

Split-ring commutator

Force

Metal or graphite brush contacts

Figure 2 The electric motor

- Figure 2 shows a simple electric motor with a direct current passing through it. The speed of the motor is increased by increasing the size of the current. The direction of the motor can be reversed by reversing the direction of the current.
- When a current passes through the coil, the coil spins because:
  - A force acts on each side of the coil due to the motor effect.
  - The force on one side of the coil is in the opposite direction to the force on the other side.
- The **'split-ring' commutator** reverses the direction of the current around the coil every half turn. Because the sides swap over each half-turn, the coil is always pushed in the same direction.

Study tip

Make sure you practise using Fleming's left-hand rule.

Key words: motor effect, 'split-ring' commutator

> **2** When the plane of the coil in a motor is parallel to the magnetic field, what can you say about the force on each side of the coil?

P18.4

The generator effect

Revise more on the generator effect in 18.5 'The alternating current generator'.

Key points

- The generator effect is the effect of inducing a potential difference using a magnetic field.
- When a wire cuts the lines of a magnetic field, a potential difference is induced across the ends of the wire.
- The faster a wire cuts across the lines of a magnetic field, the greater the induced pd is.
- When an electromagnet is used, it needs to be switched on or off to induce a pd.

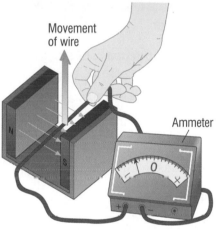

Figure 1 The generator effect

Study tip

Remember a potential difference is induced only when the wire or coil and the magnetic field move relative to each other.

∞ links

Revise more on the generator effect in 18.5 'The alternating current generator'.

Key words: electromagnetic induction

- When an electrical conductor such as a wire or a coil 'cuts' through magnetic field lines, a potential difference (pd) is induced across the ends of the conductor. This process is called **electromagnetic induction**.
- If the direction of movement of the conductor is reversed, the direction of the induced pd is also reversed. A pd is only induced while there is movement of the conductor relative to the magnetic field and the conductor cuts across the lines of force of the magnetic field.
- If the conductor is part of a complete circuit, a current passes through it.
- The size of the induced pd is increased by increasing:
  - the speed of movement
  - the strength of the magnetic field
  - the number of turns on the coil.

1 *When a wire is moved so it cuts across the magnetic field lines, what is the effect on the induced current of reversing the direction of movement of the wire?*

Figure 2 shows a coil of insulated wire connected to a centre-reading ammeter. When one end of a bar magnet is pushed into one end of the coil, the ammeter pointer deflects.

- This is because the movement of the bar magnet causes an induced pd in the coil and the induced pd causes a current in the circuit.
- The current in the coil produces a magnetic field in the coil. The field of the coil acts against the field of the magnet. The work done to keep the magnet moving generates electrical energy.
- Table 1 shows the results of testing each direction of motion of the magnet, with the magnet each way round.

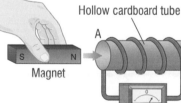

Meter pointer deflects when the magnet is pushed into the coil

Figure 2 Testing the generator effect

Table 1

Magnetic pole entering or leaving the coil	pushed in or pulled out	induced polarity of end A of the coil	magnet and coil
north pole	in	north pole	repel
north pole	out	south pole	attract
south pole	in	south pole	repel
south pole	out	north pole	attract

2 a *In Figure 2, what do you think happens if the magnet is left at rest in the coil?*
   b *Give two ways in which the induced current could be increased.*

The alternating current generator

Key points

- A simple ac generator is made up of a coil that spins in a uniform magnetic field.
- The waveform, seen using an oscilloscope, of the ac generator's induced potential difference is at
  - its peak value when the sides of the coil cut directly across the magnetic field lines
  - its zero value when the sides of the coil move parallel to the field lines.
- The simple dc generator has a split-ring commutator instead of two slip rings.

- A simple **alternating current generator** consists of a rectangular coil which is forced to spin in a magnetic field, as shown in Figure 1. The coil is connected continuously to a centre-reading meter via metal 'brushes' that press on two metal slip rings.
- When the coil turns steadily in one direction, an alternating potential difference is induced in the coil.
- In one complete rotation of the coil (or 'one full cycle'), the induced potential difference (pd) increases from zero to a peak then decreases to zero, reverses and increases to a negative peak and then becomes zero again.
- **The magnitude of the induced potential difference is greatest** when the plane of the coil is parallel to the direction of the magnetic field, as shown in Figure 1. The sides of the coil parallel to the axis of rotation cut directly across the magnetic field lines. So the induced emf is at its peak value.
- **The magnitude of the induced potential difference is zero** when the plane of the coil is perpendicular to the magnetic field lines. The sides of the coil do not cut the field lines. So the induced emf is zero.
- The alternating pd may be displayed on an oscilloscope screen. If the generator is rotated faster, the screen display will show more waves on the screen (because the frequency of the induced pd will be greater), and the waves will be taller (because the peak value of the induced pd will be greater.

> **1** *How would the oscilloscope display change if **a** the coil rotated more slowly? **b** the direction of rotation of the coil was reversed?*

A **direct current generator** is the same as an ac generator except it has a split-ring commutator, as shown in Figure 3. This reconnects the coil the opposite way round in the circuit every half-turn. This happens each time the coil is perpendicular to the magnetic field lines. As a result, the induced pd does not reverse its direction as in the ac generator. The induced pd varies from zero to a maximum twice each cycle, never changing polarity.

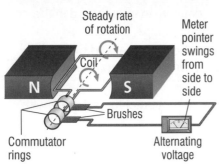

Figure 1 The construction of a simple ac generator

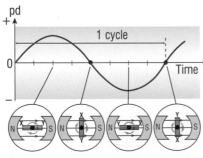

Figure 2 Alternating voltage

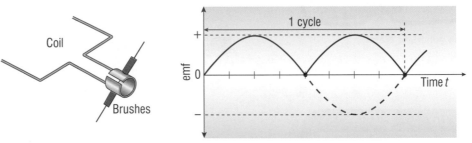

Figure 3 The dc generator

> **2** *What difference would it make to the waveform in Figure 3 if the coil rotated continuously in the opposite direction?*

In a **cycle dynamo**, a magnet spins near the end of a fixed coil so an alternating pd is induced in the coil. This happens because the magnetic field lines cut across the wires of the coil. When the dynamo is connected to a lamp, a current passes round the circuit when the lamp is on.

> **3** *What difference would it make to the brightness of the lamp if the magnet rotated **a** faster? **b** in the opposite direction?*

⚭ links

Revise more on alternating current in 17.1 'Alternating current'.

Study tip

Make sure you can explain how an ac generator works.

Key words: alternating current generator, direct current generator, cycle dynamo

Transformers

- A transformer only works on alternating current because a changing magnetic field is necessary to induce alternating current in the secondary coil.

- A transformer has an iron core unless it is a switch mode transformer which has a ferrite core.

- A switch mode transformer is lighter and smaller than an ordinary transformer. It operates at high frequency.

- A **transformer** consists of two coils of insulated wire, called the **primary coil** and the **secondary coil**. These coils are wound on to the same iron core. When an alternating current passes through the primary coil, it produces an alternating magnetic field in the core. This field continually expands and collapses.

- The alternating magnetic field lines pass through the secondary coil and induce an alternating potential difference across its ends. If the secondary coil is part of a complete circuit an alternating current is produced.

- The coils of wire are insulated so that current does not short across either the iron core or adjacent turns of wire, but flows around the whole coil.

- The core is made of iron so it is easily magnetised and demagnetised.

1 *Why would a transformer not work if a steady direct current is used instead of alternating current?*

- Transformers are used in the National Grid:
  - a step-up transformer makes the pd across the secondary coil greater than the pd across the primary coil. Its secondary coil has more turns than its primary coil.
  - a step-down transformer makes the pd across the secondary coil less than the pd across the primary coil. Its secondary coil has fewer turns than its primary coil.

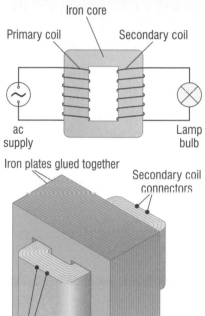

Figure 1 Transformer action

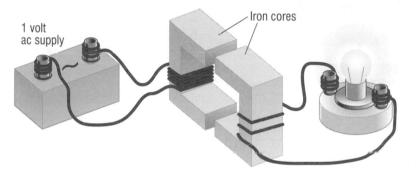

Figure 2 A model transformer

2 *Why is a transformer core made of iron better than one made of steel?*

- A **switch mode transformer** has a ferrite core. Compared with a traditional transformer, a switch mode transformer:
  - operates at a much higher frequency
  - is lighter and smaller
  - uses very little power when there is no device connected across its output terminals.

3 *A step-down transformer has a coil with 100 turns and a coil with 800 turns. Which coil is used as the primary coil?*

Study tip

- Remember there is no current in the iron core, just a changing magnetic field.
- Transformers do not work with dc, but only ac. If a dc passes through the primary coil a magnetic field is produced in the core, but it would not be continually expanding and collapsing, so no pd would be induced in the secondary coil.

∞ **links**
Revise more on transformers in 17.8 'The National Grid'.

Key words: transformer, switch mode transformer

P18.7 **Transformers in action**

Student's book pages 206–207

Key points

- Transformers are used to step alternating potential differences up or down.
- $\dfrac{\text{primary pd } V_p}{\text{secondary pd } V_s} = \dfrac{n_p}{n_s}$

  where n_p is the number of primary turns and n_s is the number of secondary turns.
- For a step-down transformer, n_s is less than n_p
- For a step-up transformer n_s is greater than n_p
- For a 100% efficient transformer:

  $$V_p \times I_p = V_s \times I_s$$

  where I_p is the primary current and I_s is the secondary current.

🖩 Maths skills

Worked example

A transformer is used to step a potential difference of 230 V down to 10 V. The secondary coil has 60 turns. Calculate the number of turns of the primary coil.

Solution

$V_p = 230\,\text{V}$, $V_s = 10\,\text{V}$, $n_s = 60$ turns

Using $\dfrac{V_p}{V_s} = \dfrac{n_p}{n_s}$ gives $\dfrac{230}{10} = \dfrac{n_p}{60}$

Therefore $n_p = 230 \times \dfrac{60}{10}$

$\qquad\quad = \textbf{1380 turns}$

- Transformers are used in the National Grid to step-up the pd from power stations to the grid cables and to step-down the pd from the grid cables so that it is safe to be used by consumers.
- For a given amount of power transferred through the Grid, the higher the pd at which electrical energy is transmitted across the Grid, the smaller the current through the cables. So the smaller the energy wasted in the cables.
- The pd across, and the number of turns on, the primary and secondary coils are related by the equation:

  $$\frac{V_p}{V_s} = \frac{n_p}{n_s}$$

  where V_p is the pd across the primary coil in volts, V
  V_s is the pd across the secondary coil in volts, V
  n_p is the number of turns on the primary coil
  n_s is the number of turns on the secondary coil.
- A step-down transformer has fewer turns on the secondary coil than on the primary coil.
- A step-up transformer has more turns on the secondary coil than on the primary coil.

> **1 a** *Why is a transformer used to step-up the pd from a power station?*
> **b** *A step-down transformer is used to change a pd of 230 V to a pd of 11.5 V. If there are 5000 turns on the primary coil, how many turns are there on the secondary coil?*

Transformers are almost 100% efficient.
- The power supplied to the primary coil = $V_p \times I_p$
- The power supplied to the secondary coil = $V_s \times I_s$

For 100% efficiency:

$$V_p \times I_p = V_s \times I_s$$

where I_p is the current in the primary coil in amperes, A
$\quad\;\; I_s$ is the current in the secondary coil in amperes, A.

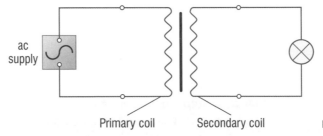

Primary coil　　　Secondary coil　　**Figure 1 Transformer efficiency**

> **2** *A transformer has 100 turns on the primary coil and 400 turns on the secondary coil. The pd across the primary coil is 2 V.*
> **a** *What is the pd across the secondary coil?*
> **b** *Assuming the transformer is 100% efficient, what is the current in the secondary coil if the primary current is 1 A?*

🔗 links

Revise more on electrical power in 17.4 'Electrical power and potential difference'.

Study tip

Make sure you can describe how transformers are used in the National Grid.

1   **a**   Why is an electromagnet made from iron not steel?
      b   Why is an electromagnet, not a permanent magnet, used in a scrapyard?

2   Describe the magnetic field lines near a straight current-carrying wire.

3   **a**   A direct current passes down a vertical wire that is perpendicular to the lines of a uniform horizontal magnetic field which is directed due east. What direction is the force on the wire?
      b   How would the force differ if the current was reversed?

4   What is the purpose of a split-ring commutator in a dc electric motor?

5   One end of a bar magnet is pushed into a coil of wire connected to an ammeter. What is observed if:
      a   the magnet is pushed quickly into the coil?
      b   the magnet is held stationary then pulled out of the coil slowly?

6   How does the induced pd of an ac generator change if:
      a   the coil is turned more slowly?
      b   a stronger magnet had been fitted?

7   How does the waveform of a dc generator differ from an ac generator in terms of the waveform of the induced pd?

8   **a**   How does the frequency of operation of a switch mode transformer compare with a traditional transformer?
      b   State two advantages of a switch mode transformer compared with an iron core transformer.

9   A transformer is used to step down a 240V supply to a 12V applianoc. There are 1000 turns on the primary coil.
      a   How many turns are there on the secondary coil?
      b   What would be the output pd if the coils were connected the wrong way round?

10   A transformer that is 100% efficient is used to step down a 240V supply to a 6V 2A lamp.
      a   What is the current in the primary coil?
      b   How much power is supplied to the primary coil?

11   Why is the transmission of electric power through the National Grid made more efficient by using step-up and step-down transformers?

Chapter checklist	✓ ✓ ✓

Tick when you have:				Magnetic fields	☐ ☐ ☐
reviewed it after your lesson	☑	☐	☐	Electromagnets	☐ ☐ ☐
revised once – some questions right	☑	☑	☐	The motor effect	☐ ☐ ☐
revised twice – all questions right	☑	☑	☑	The generator effect	☐ ☐ ☐
Move on to another topic when you have all three ticks				The alternating current generator	☐ ☐ ☐
				Transformers	☐ ☐ ☐
				Transformers in action	☐ ☐ ☐

1 A student set up the circuit shown in Figure 1 to measure the potential difference across a filament lamp for different currents up to 0.060 A through it.

   a Describe the procedure the student should follow to make and record these measurements.

   In this question, you will be assessed on using good English, organising information clearly and using specialist terms where appropriate. *(6 marks)*

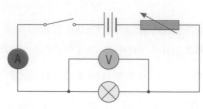
Figure 1

   b The table below shows a set of results obtained by the student.

Current/A	0	0.010	0.021	0.032	0.042	0.052	0.057
Potential difference/V	0	0. 60	1.40	2.35	3.50	4.90	5.90

   i Plot a graph of these measurements. *(3 marks)*

   ii Calculate the resistance of the lamp at 3.0 V and at 6.0 V. *(2 marks)*

   iii Explain in terms of electrons why the resistance of the lamp is greater at 6.0 V than at 3.0 V. *(3 marks)*

   c The battery in the circuit is a rechargeable battery that can supply a current of 0.06 A for a maximum of 10 hours.

   i Calculate the charge that would flow through the battery when the current is 0.06 A for 10 hours. *(2 marks)*

   ii How much energy would be supplied to a lamp operating at 6.0 V when this amount of charge passes through it? *(2 marks)*

2 In a low voltage lighting circuit, two lamps A and B are connected in parallel to a 12 V battery, as shown in Figure 2. Each lamp is switched on or off using a switch in series with it.

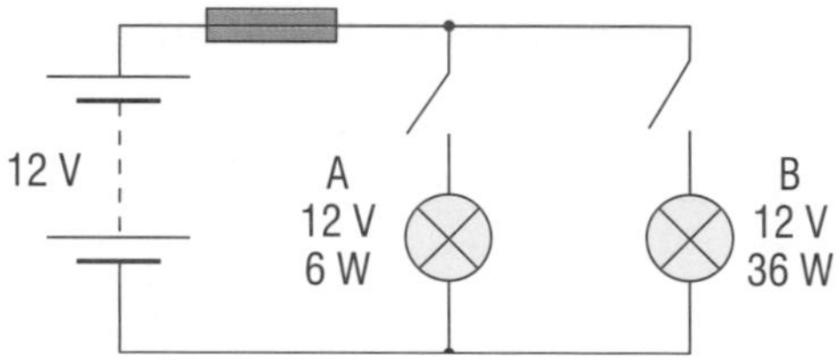

   a Lamp A is a 12 V 6 W lamp. Lamp B is a 12 V 36 W lamp.

   i What is the current through each lamp when it is switched on? *(2 marks)*

   ii What is the current through the battery when both lamps are switched on? *(1 mark)*

   iii What is the purpose of the fuse in the circuit? *(1 mark)*

   iv Why would a 5 A fuse be more suitable in this circuit rather than a 3 A fuse or a 13 A fuse? *(3 marks)*

   b A student suggests the two lamps could be connected in series with the battery, a switch and a fuse.

   i Give one reason why this series circuit would be less useful than a parallel circuit. *(1 mark)*

   ii What difference would be made to the brightness of each lamp if they are connected in series to the battery as suggested above instead of in parallel? *(3 marks)*

Figure 2

P19.1

Atoms and radiation

Key points

- A radioactive substance contains unstable nuclei that become stable by emitting radiation.

- There are three main types of radiation from radioactive substances – alpha, beta and gamma radiation.

- Radioactive decay is a random event – we cannot predict or influence when it happens.

- Background radiation is from radioactive substances in the environment or from space or from devices such as X-ray machines.

- The basic structure of an atom is a small positively charged central **nucleus**, made up of **protons** and **neutrons**, surrounded by **electrons** which are negatively charged.

- The nuclei of radioactive substances are unstable. They become stable (or less unstable) by **radioactive decay**. When an unstable nucleus undergoes radioactive decay, it emits radiation. There are three types of radiation emitted: **alpha radiation** (symbol α) **beta radiation** (symbol β) **gamma radiation** (symbol γ).

- An unstable nucleus that emits alpha radiation or beta radiation forms a nucleus of a different element.

- Radioactive decay is a **random** process and is not affected by external conditions.

⟶ **1 a** *Which part of an atom might emit alpha radiation?*
    b *What can you say about a nucleus that does not emit radiation?*

- **Background radiation** is around us all the time. This is radiation from radioactive substances that are in the environment (e.g. radon gas in the air, food and drink, and the ground) or are used in hospitals, from devices such as X-ray tubes, from nuclear reactors and from space.

⟶ **2** *What is a random process?*

Study tip

Remember that it is not possible to predict when any particular nucleus will decay and it is not possible to make any particular nucleus decay.

Practical

Investigating radioactivity

Observe a **Geiger counter** being used to detect radioactivity. Look at Figure 2. The counter clicks each time a particle of radiation from a radioactive substance enters the Geiger tube. **Safety:** Avoid touching and inhaling radioactive material.

⟶ **3** *Why are the clicks unpredictable?*

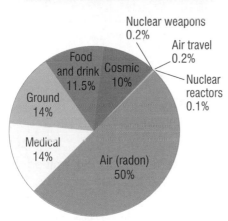

Figure 1 The origins of background radiation

Figure 2 Using a Geiger counter

Geiger tube

∞ links

Revise more on background radiation in 19.3 'More about alpha, beta and gamma radiation'.

Key words: nucleus, proton, neutron, electron, radioactive decay, alpha radiation, beta radiation, gamma radiation, random, background radiation

Nuclear reactions

Key points

- Isotopes of an element are atoms with the same number of protons but different numbers of neutrons. Therefore they have the same atomic numbers but different mass numbers.

	Change in the nucleus	Particle emitted
alpha (α) decay	The nucleus loses 2 protons and 2 neutrons.	2 protons and 2 neutrons emitted as an α particle
beta (β) decay	A neutron in the nucleus changes into a proton.	An electron is created in the nucleus and instantly emitted.

Table 1

	Relative mass	Relative charge
proton	1	+1
neutron	1	0
electron	0.0005	−1

Study tip

Make sure you can use nuclear equations to show how the atomic number and mass number change when alpha or beta particles are emitted.

⃝⃝ links

Revise more on gamma radiation in 8.4 'Ultraviolet rays, X-rays and gamma rays'.

Table 1 below gives the relative masses and charges of the subatomic particles.

- In an atom the number of protons and electrons are equal so the atom has no overall charge. If an atom loses or gains electrons it becomes charged and is called an **ion**.
- All atoms of a particular element have the same number of protons in their nuclei. Atoms of the same element with different numbers of neutrons are called **isotopes**.
- The number of protons in an atom is its **atomic number** or **proton number** (symbol Z).
- The total number of protons and neutrons in an atom is its **mass number** (symbol A).
- The symbol for an isotope of element X can be shown as: ^A_ZX

> **1** *How many protons and how many neutrons are in the nucleus of the uranium isotope $^{238}_{92}$U?*

- **Alpha radiation** consists of particles which each consist of two protons and two neutrons.
- Its relative mass is 4 and relative charge is +2. We represent it as $^4_2\alpha$
- When a nucleus ^A_ZX emits an alpha particle, the nucleus loses 2 protons and 2 neutrons so the atomic number goes down by two and the mass number goes down by four.
- The equation for this change is:

$$^A_Z\text{X} \rightarrow {}^{A-4}_{Z-2}\text{Y} + {}^4_2\alpha$$

where $^{A-4}_{Z-2}$Y represents the nucleus formed.

> **2** *The uranium isotope $^{238}_{92}$U emits α radiation. When a nucleus of this isotope emits an α particle, what is **a** the atomic number, **b** the mass number of the nucleus formed?*

- **Beta radiation consists of particles which are high speed electrons** emitted from the nucleus when a neutron in the nucleus changes to a proton and an electron. The proton stays in the nucleus.
- The relative mass of a beta particle is 0 and its relative charge is −1. We represent it as $^0_{-1}\beta$
- When a nucleus emits a beta particle, the atomic number goes up by one and the mass number is unchanged.
- The equation for this change is:

$$^A_Z\text{X} \rightarrow {}^{A}_{Z+1}\text{Y} + {}^0_{-1}\beta$$

where $_{Z+1}^A$Y represents the nucleus formed.

> **3** *The carbon isotope $^{14}_6$C emits β radiation. When a nucleus of this isotope emits a β particle, what is **a** the atomic number, **b** the mass number of the nucleus formed?*

- **When a nucleus emits gamma radiation** there is no change in the atomic number or the mass number. A gamma ray is an electromagnetic wave which has no charge and no mass. Its symbol is γ.

Key words: ion, isotope, atomic number, proton number, mass number

Student's book
pages 214–215 **P19.3**

More about alpha, beta and gamma radiation

DOUBLE AWARD

Key points

- α radiation is stopped by paper or a few centimetres of air. It is more ionising than β radiation or γ radiation.

- β radiation is stopped by thin metal or about a metre of air. It is more ionising than γ radiation.

- γ radiation is stopped by thick lead and has an unlimited range in air.

- A magnetic or an electric field can be used to separate a beam of alpha, beta and gamma radiation.

- Alpha, beta and gamma radiation ionise substances they pass through. Ionisation in a living cell can damage or kill the cell.

- When nuclear radiation travels through a material it will collide with atoms of the material, knocking electrons off the atoms, creating charged atoms or ions. This process is called **ionisation**.

- Ionisation in a living cell can damage or kill the cell.

- Alpha particles are more strongly ionising than beta particles because they have twice as much charge and they move more slowly than beta particles. So they collide with atoms more often than beta particles do.

- Beta particles are more strongly ionising than gamma rays because they are charged whereas gamma rays are uncharged. They are also slower than gamma rays which travel at the speed of light.

- The absorption of nuclear radiation by materials depends on the ionising effect of the radiation on the material and on the thickness of the material. Table 1 gives examples of a material that stops each type of radiation.

- The greater the absorbing effect of a material is, the less penetrating the radiation is.

Table 2

Type of radiation	Ionising effect	Absorber	Range in air	Deflection by the electric field between a positive and a negative plate
alpha (α)	strong	thin paper, human skin	about 5 cm	towards the negative plate
beta (β)	less strong	5 mm of aluminium	about 1 m	towards the positive plate
gamma (γ)	weak	several cm of lead or several metres of concrete.	unlimited	No deflection

> **1 a** Which type of radiation can penetrate a thin sheet of aluminium?
> **b** Which types of radiation are not stopped by human skin?

- Alpha and beta particles have opposite types of charge so they are deflected by electric and magnetic fields in opposite directions.

- Gamma rays are uncharged because they are electromagnetic waves. So they are not deflected by electric and magnetic fields.

Figure 1 shows the effect of a magnetic field on different types of radiation.

> **2 a** Which type of nuclear radiation is the least penetrating?
> **b** Why is gamma radiation not deflected by a magnetic field?

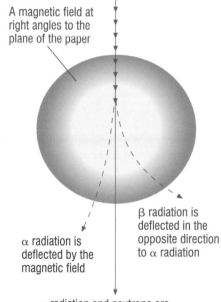

Beam of radiation enters a magnetic field

A magnetic field at right angles to the plane of the paper

α radiation is deflected by the magnetic field

β radiation is deflected in the opposite direction to α radiation

γ radiation and neutrons are undeflected by the magnetic field

Figure 1 Deflection of particles by a magnetic field

Study tip

Make sure you can explain the different paths taken by alpha, beta and gamma radiation in magnetic and electric fields.

⚬⚬ **links**

Revise more on radioactive risks in 20.3 'Nuclear issues'.

Key word: ionisation

Half-life

Key points

- The half-life of a radioactive isotope is the average time it takes for the number of nuclei of the isotope in a sample to halve.
- The activity of a radioactive source is the number of nuclei that decay per second.
- The count rate of a Geiger counter due to a radioactive source decreases as the activity of the source decreases.
- The number of atoms of a radioactive isotope and the activity both decrease by half every half-life.

- We can measure the radioactivity of a sample of a radioactive material by measuring the **count rate** from it with a Geiger counter.
- The activity of a sample decreases over time. How quickly the count rate falls to nearly zero depends on the isotope.

The **half-life** of a radioactive isotope is the time taken for the count rate from the original isotope to fall to half its initial value.

- Half-life can also be defined as the time it takes for the number of unstable nuclei in a sample of the isotope to halve.
- The half-life of an isotope is the same for any sample of a particular isotope.

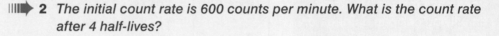

1 *What has happened to the original count rate of a radioactive sample after two half-lives have passed?*

Figure 1 shows how the count rate varies with time for a radioactive isotope with a half-life of 45 minutes. The count rate
- after 1 half-life is ½ × the initial count rate
- after 2 half-lives is ¼ × the initial count rate
- after 3 half-lives is ⅛ × the initial count rate.

2 *The initial count rate is 600 counts per minute. What is the count rate after 4 half-lives?*

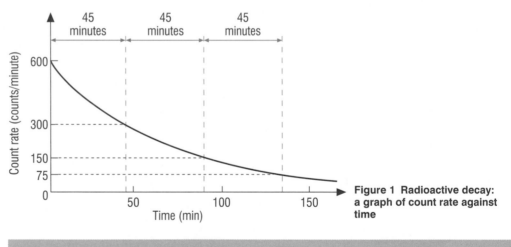

Figure 1 Radioactive decay: a graph of count rate against time

Key words: count rate, half-life

P19.5

Radioactivity at work

Key points

- The use we can make of a radioactive isotope depends on its half-life, and the type of radiation it gives out.

- For monitoring, the isotope should have a long half-life.

- Radioactive tracers should be β or γ emitters that last long enough to monitor, but not too long.

- For radioactive dating of a sample, we need a radioactive isotope that is present in the sample which has a half-life about the same as the age of the sample.

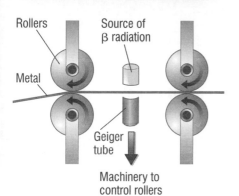

Figure 1 Thickness monitoring using a radioactive source

∞ links

Revise more on radioactivity in 20.3 'Nuclear issues'.

Alpha sources are used in smoke alarms. The alpha particles ionise the air molecules in a circuit gap so an ionisation current passes across the gap. Smoke absorbs the ions and reduces the current to zero which switches the alarm on.

- Alpha particles are not dangerous here because they are easily absorbed and have a small range.
- The source needs a half-life of several years.

▷ **1** *Why is a beta or a gamma source unsuitable for use in a smoke alarm?*

Beta sources are used for **thickness monitoring** in the manufacture of things like paper or metal foil. In the production process, rollers squeeze the material so a thin continuous sheet of material emerges. A radiation detector monitors the radiation passing through the material from the source on the other side of the sheet.

- Alpha particles would be stopped by a thin sheet of paper and the gamma rays would all pass through it.
- The source needs a half-life of many years so that decreases in count rate are due to changes in the thickness of the paper.

▷ **2** *If the detector reading is less than it should be, is the sheet too thin or too thick?*

Gamma and beta sources are used as **tracers** in medicine. The source is injected or swallowed by the patient. Its progress around the body is monitored by a detector outside the patient.

- The source needs a half-life of a few hours so that the patient is not exposed to unnecessary radioactivity.

▷ **3** *Why isn't an alpha source used as a tracer in medicine?*

Radioactive dating is used to find the age of ancient material.

- Carbon dating is used to find the age of wood and other organic material.
- Uranium dating is used to find the age of igneous rocks.

▷ **4** *Why is uranium dating unsuitable for finding the age of wood?*

Study tip

For each type of radiation you should know an application, why a particular source is used and the approximate half-life.

Key words: thickness monitoring, tracer, radioactive dating

1 **a** What does an α particle consist of?
  b What does a β particle consist of?
  c What is γ radiation?

2 **a** How many protons and how many neutrons are in a nucleus of the cobalt isotope $^{60}_{27}$Co?
  b In terms of protons and neutrons, what change takes place in an unstable nucleus when it emits:
    i a β particle?
    ii γ radiation?

3 When a nucleus emits an α particle, what happens to:
  a the mass number of the nucleus?
  b the atomic number of the nucleus?

4 Copy and complete the following equation:
$$^{60}_{27}\text{Co} \rightarrow {^{0}_{...}}\beta + {^{...}_{...}}\text{Ni}$$

5 **a** What is background radiation?
  b State two sources of background radiation in the environment.

6 Which type of nuclear radiation:
  a is more ionising than the other types?
  b has an unlimited range?
  c can pass through paper but not through several centimetres of aluminium?

7 **a** Why is γ radiation not deflected by an electric field?
  b Why is an α particle deflected in a magnetic field in the opposite direction to a β particle?

8 A radioactive isotope has a half-life of 7 hours. A sample of the isotope has a mass of 32 milligrams. How long would it take for the mass of the isotope to decrease from 32 milligrams to 1 milligram?

9 A sample of a radioactive isotope contains 100 million atoms of the isotope which has a half-life of 1000 years.
  a How many atoms of the isotope will remain after 2000 years?
  b Estimate to the nearest 1000 years how long it would take for the number of atoms of the isotope to decrease to 1 million.

10 **a** Why is alpha radiation unsuitable for monitoring the thickness of metal foil?
  b Why is a γ-emitting isotope with a short half-life suitable for use as a tracer in medicine?

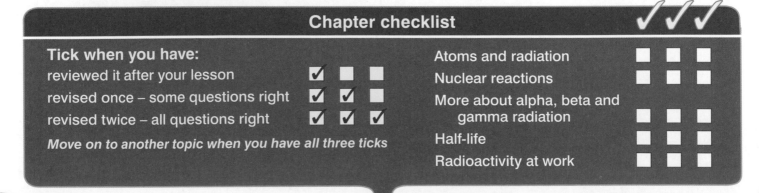

Chapter checklist

Tick when you have:				Atoms and radiation	☐ ☐ ☐
reviewed it after your lesson	☑	☐	☐	Nuclear reactions	☐ ☐ ☐
revised once – some questions right	☑	☑	☐	More about alpha, beta and gamma radiation	☐ ☐ ☐
revised twice – all questions right	☑	☑	☑	Half-life	☐ ☐ ☐
Move on to another topic when you have all three ticks				Radioactivity at work	☐ ☐ ☐

Student's book
pages 222–223 **P20.1** # Nuclear fission

Key points

- Nuclear fission is the splitting of a nucleus into two approximately equal fragments and the release of two or three neutrons.

- Nuclear fission occurs when a neutron hits a uranium-235 nucleus or a plutonium-239 nucleus and the nucleus splits.

- A chain reaction occurs when neutrons from the fission go on to cause further fission.

- In a nuclear reactor, control rods absorb fission neutrons to ensure that, on average, only one neutron per fission goes on to produce further fission.

Nuclear fission is the splitting of an atomic nucleus.

- Most nuclear reactors use uranium-235 as the fissionable isotope. Some reactors use plutonium-239 instead.

- Naturally occurring uranium is mostly uranium-238, which is non-fissionable. Uranium reactors use 'enriched' uranium that contains 2–3% uranium-235.

- For fission to occur, the uranium-235 or plutonium-239 nucleus must absorb a neutron. The nucleus then splits into two smaller nuclei. In this process:
  - two or three neutrons are emitted which can go on to cause further fission, and
  - energy is released in much greater quantities than the energy released in a chemical process such as burning.

➡ **1 a** *What is enriched uranium?*
   b *What needs to happen for fission to occur?*

A **chain reaction** occurs when each fission event causes further fission events. In a **nuclear fission reactor** the process is controlled by control rods which absorb neutrons. The rods ensure that, on average, only one neutron per fission goes on to produce further fission. In this way, energy is released at a steady rate.

➡ **2** *What would happen if more than one fission neutron per fission in a nuclear reactor goes on to produce further fission?*

Study tip

Make sure that you can draw a simple diagram to show a chain reaction.

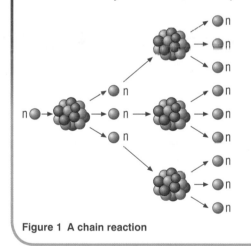

Figure 1 A chain reaction

⬯ links

Revise more on nuclear fission in 20.3 'Nuclear issues'.

Key words: nuclear fission, chain reaction, nuclear fission reactor

Nuclear fusion

DOUBLE AWARD

Key points

- Nuclear fusion is the process of forcing two nuclei close enough together so they form a single larger nucleus.

- Nuclear fusion can be brought about by making two light nuclei collide at very high speed.

- Energy is released when two light nuclei are fused together. Nuclear fusion in the Sun's core releases energy.

- A fusion reactor needs to be at a very high temperature before nuclear fusion can take place.

- The nuclei to be fused are difficult to contain.

- **Nuclear fusion** is the process of forcing two nuclei close enough together so they form a single larger nucleus.
- The force of repulsion between the two nuclei due to their electric charge must be overcome so they can get close enough to fuse.
- Nuclear fusion can be brought about by making two light nuclei collide at very high speed.
- **Fusion is the process by which energy is released in stars.** In stars such as the Sun, hydrogen nuclei (i.e. protons) are fused together in the core to form helium nuclei.
- The core of a star is so hot that it consists of a plasma of 'bare' nuclei with no electrons.
- The nuclei in the core move fast enough to fuse.

> **1** *Why does fusion not take place outside the core of a star?*

Fusion reactors at present can maintain fusion for no more than a few minutes.
- The plasma of nuclei in the reactor is heated to very high temperatures by passing an electric current through it. If this gives the nuclei enough kinetic energy to overcome their repulsion, they fuse when they collide.
- The plasma is contained by a magnetic field inside the reactor. This prevents the plasma touching the reactor walls and losing energy which would cause fusion to stop.

> **2** *Why is an electric current passed through the plasma of a fusion reactor?*

Study tip

Make sure that you can explain the difference between nuclear fission and nuclear fusion.

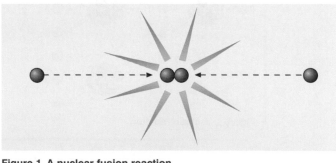

Figure 1 A nuclear fusion reaction

Key word: nuclear fusion

 links

Revise more on nuclear fusion in 20.6 'How the chemical elements formed'.

Student's book
pages 226–227 **P20.3** # Nuclear issues

Key points

- Radon gas is an α-emitting isotope that seeps into houses in certain areas through the ground.

- There are thousands of fission reactors safely in use throughout the world. None of them are of the same type as the Chernobyl reactor that exploded.

- Nuclear waste must be stored in safe and secure conditions for many years, after the unused uranium and plutonium (to be used in the future) is removed from it.

- **Ionising radiation damages or kills living cells**. The effect on living cells depends on the type and the **radiation dose** received. The larger the dose of radiation someone receives, the greater the risk of cancer.

- The dose depends on the amount of radiation, how long the cells are exposed and whether the source is inside or outside the body.

Table 1

Source	Inside the body	Outside the body
Alpha radiation	Very dangerous due to short range and strong ionisation	Some danger – absorbed by outer layers of the skin; damages retinal cells
Beta radiation Gamma radiation	Dangerous – reaches cells throughout the body	

- **Sources of background radiation** are shown in Topic 19.1 Figure 1. The major source is radon gas which seeps up from radioactive substances in rocks deep underground. Radon gas emits alpha particles so is a health hazard if breathed in.

||||➡ **1** *Why is radon gas a health hazard?*

- **Radioactive waste** must be stored in secure conditions for many years. Uranium and plutonium are chemically removed from used fuel rods from nuclear reactors, as these substances can be used again. The remaining radioactive waste must be stored in secure conditions for many years.

To reduce exposure to nuclear radiations, workers should:

- keep as far as possible from sources of radiation
- spend as little time exposed as possible
- shield themselves with materials such as concrete and lead.

||||➡ **2** *Why must radioactive waste be stored securely?*

Study tip

Make sure that you can explain some measures that can be taken to reduce exposure to nuclear radiations.

⊂⊃ **links**

Revise more on half-life in 19.4 'Half-life'.

Key word: radiation dose

The early universe

- A galaxy is a collection of billions of stars held together by their own gravity.
- Before galaxies and stars formed, the universe was a dark patchy cloud of hydrogen and helium.
- The force of gravity pulled matter into galaxies and stars.

- Most scientists believe that the universe was created by the Big Bang about 13 thousand million (13 billion) years ago.
- At first the universe was a hot glowing ball of radiation. In the first few minutes the nuclei of the lightest elements formed. As the universe expanded, over millions of years, its temperature fell. Uncharged atoms were formed.

▯▯▯➡ **1** *What happened to the temperature of the universe as it expanded?*

- Before galaxies and stars formed, the universe was a dark patchy cloud of hydrogen and helium. Eventually dust and gas were pulled together by **gravitational attraction** to form **stars**. The resulting intense heat in each star started nuclear fusion reactions so they began to emit visible light and other radiation.
- Very large groups of stars are called galaxies. Our Sun is one of the many billions of stars in the Milky Way galaxy. The universe contains billions of galaxies.
- A galaxy is a collection of billions of stars held together by their own gravity. There are billions of galaxies in the universe, with vast empty spaces between them.

▯▯▯➡ **2** *What is a galaxy?*

> **Study tip**
>
> You should understand that the universe is mostly empty space. The distance between neighbouring stars is usually millions of times greater than the distance between planets in our Solar System. The distance between neighbouring galaxies is usually millions of times greater than the distance between stars within a galaxy. So the universe is mostly empty space.

Key words: gravitational attraction, star

⬭⬭ **links**

Revise more on the universe and the Big Bang in 12.1 'The expanding universe' and 12.2 'The Big Bang'.

P20.5

The life history of a star

Key points

- A protostar is a gas and dust cloud in space that can go on to form a star.
- The Sun is a main sequence star that will eventually become a black dwarf.
- A supernova is the explosion of a supergiant after it collapses.

Protostar
⇩
main sequence star

low mass	high mass
⇩	⇩
red giant	red supergiant
⇩	⇩
white dwarf	supernova
⇩	⇩
black dwarf	neutron star
	black hole
	(if sufficient mass)

Figure 1 The life cycle of a star

∞ **links**

Revise more on stars in 20.6 'How the chemical elements formed'.

- Gravitational forces pull clouds of dust and gas together to form a **protostar**. The protostar becomes denser and the nuclei of hydrogen atoms and other light elements start to fuse together. Energy is released in the process so the core gets hotter and brighter.
- Stars radiate energy because of hydrogen fusion in the core. This stage can continue for billions of years until the star runs out of hydrogen nuclei. The star is stable because the inward force of gravity is balanced by the outward force of radiation from the core and is called a **main sequence star**.
- Eventually a star that runs out of hydrogen nuclei swells, cools down and turns red. Helium and other light elements fuse in its core to form heavier elements.

▸ **1** *Why are stars in the main sequence stable?*

- What happens next in the life cycle of the star depends on its mass, as shown in Figure 1.
- A low mass star (e.g. the Sun) will become a **red giant**. After fusion stops, the star will contract to form a **white dwarf**. Eventually no more light is emitted and the star becomes a **black dwarf**.
- A high mass star will swell to become a **red supergiant**. After fusion stops, it collapses and eventually explodes in a **supernova**. The outer layers are thrown out into space. The core is left as a **neutron star**. If the core is massive enough it becomes a **black hole**. The gravitational field of a black hole is so strong not even light can escape from it.

▸ **2** *What is **a** a neutron star? **b** a black hole?*

Key words: protostar, main sequence star, red giant, white dwarf, black dwarf, red supergiant, supernova, neutron star, black hole

Study tip

Make sure you can put the stages of the life cycle of a star in the correct order.

P20.6

How the chemical elements formed

Key points

- Elements as heavy as iron are formed inside stars as a result of nuclear fusion.
- Elements heavier than iron are formed in supernovas, along with lighter elements.
- The Sun and the rest of the Solar System were formed from the debris of a supernova.

∞ **links**

Revise more on nuclear fusion in 20.2 'Nuclear fusion'.

- The nuclei of chemical elements are formed by fusion processes in stars. Small nuclei fuse to form nuclei as large as iron nuclei. The process releases large amounts of energy.
- Nuclei larger than iron nuclei are only formed in the collapse of a high mass star. This is because the fusion process requires the input of energy. All the elements get distributed through space by the supernova explosion.
- The presence of the heavier elements in the Sun and inner planets is evidence that they were formed from debris scattered by a supernova.

▸ **1** *What is the heaviest element formed by fusion in a main sequence star?*

▸ **2** *How was the uranium now used in nuclear reactors created?*

Study tip

In the process of fusion, light nuclei fuse to form heavier nuclei and energy is released. For elements heavier than iron to be formed there must be an input of energy.

1 Which two fissionable isotopes are used in nuclear reactors?

2 When a uranium-235 nucleus undergoes fission:
   a what happens to the nucleus?
   b what is released?

3 **a** What is a chain reaction in a nuclear reactor?
   b When fission events occur at a steady rate in a nuclear reactor, how many fission neutrons on average must go on to produce further fission?

4 **a** What do the control rods in a nuclear reactor do?
   b What happens to the used fuel rods from a nuclear reactor?

5 **a** What is nuclear fusion?
   b What type of particles are fused in the core of the Sun and what do they form?

6 **a** Why is nuclear fusion in a fusion reactor difficult to achieve?
   b How is the plasma heated in a fusion reactor?

7 **a** Why is a source of alpha radiation less dangerous outside the body than inside?
   b Why is exposure to beta and gamma radiation from a source outside the body dangerous?

8 What did the stars form from?

9 **a** What is the main stage in the life of a star called?
   b What will happen to a low mass star after **a**?

10 A high mass star eventually becomes a neutron star.
   a What stages does a high mass star go through after 9a?
   b What is a black hole?

11 **a** What is a supernova?
   b What evidence is there that the Sun formed from the debris of a supernova?

12 **a** How were chemical elements lighter than iron formed?
   b How were chemical elements heavier than iron formed?

Chapter checklist	✓	✓	✓
Tick when you have:			
reviewed it after your lesson ✔ ☐ ☐			
revised once – some questions right ✔ ✔ ☐			
revised twice – all questions right ✔ ✔ ✔			
Move on to another topic when you have all three ticks			
Nuclear fission	☐	☐	☐
Nuclear fusion	☐	☐	☐
Nuclear issues	☐	☐	☐
The early universe	☐	☐	☐
The life history of a star	☐	☐	☐
How the chemical elements are formed	☐	☐	☐

1 The phosphorus isotope $^{33}_{15}$P emits β radiation.

  a **i**   What is an isotope? *(1 mark)*

     ii How many protons and how many neutrons are in the nucleus of a phosphorus-33 atom? *(2 marks)*

  b **i**   β radiation consists of β particles. What is a β particle and what change in a nucleus takes place when one is emitted? *(2 marks)*

     ii A phosphorus-33 nucleus becomes a nucleus of sulfur (S) after it emits a β particle. Copy and complete the equation below to represent this change.

       $^{33}_{15}$P → $^{...}_{...}$S + $^{...}_{...}$β *(2 marks)*

  c **i**   What is meant by the half-life of a radioactive isotope? *(2 marks)*

     ii Figure 1 shows how the percentage of phosphorus-33 nuclei in a sample of the isotope decreases with time.

       Determine the half-life of the isotope $^{33}_{15}$P. *(2 marks)*

     iii Estimate the time taken for the percentage to decrease to 10%. *(2 marks)*

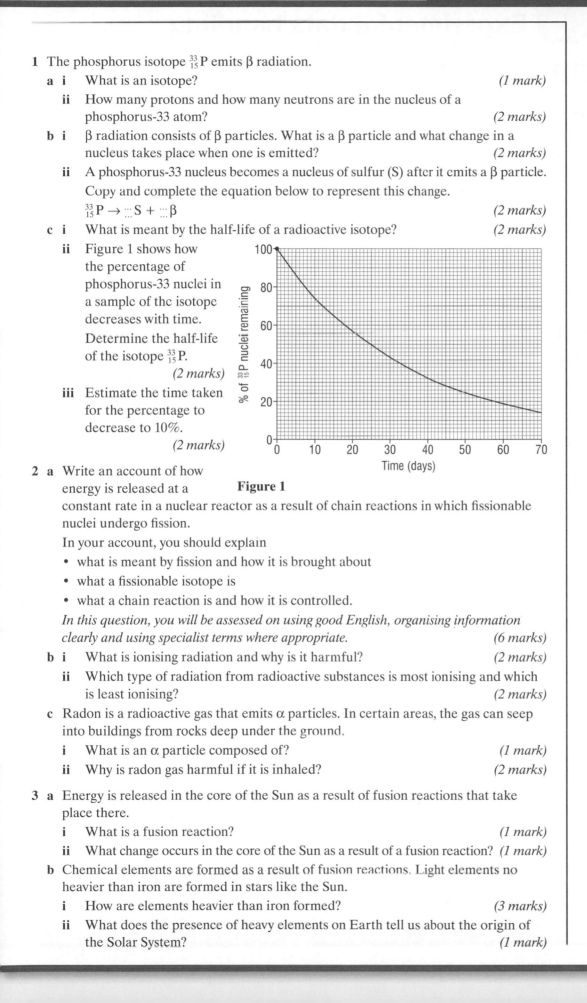

Figure 1

2 **a** Write an account of how energy is released at a constant rate in a nuclear reactor as a result of chain reactions in which fissionable nuclei undergo fission.

    In your account, you should explain

    • what is meant by fission and how it is brought about

    • what a fissionable isotope is

    • what a chain reaction is and how it is controlled.

    In this question, you will be assessed on using good English, organising information clearly and using specialist terms where appropriate. *(6 marks)*

  b **i**   What is ionising radiation and why is it harmful? *(2 marks)*

     ii Which type of radiation from radioactive substances is most ionising and which is least ionising? *(2 marks)*

  c Radon is a radioactive gas that emits α particles. In certain areas, the gas can seep into buildings from rocks deep under the ground.

    i   What is an α particle composed of? *(1 mark)*

    ii Why is radon gas harmful if it is inhaled? *(2 marks)*

3 **a** Energy is released in the core of the Sun as a result of fusion reactions that take place there.

    i   What is a fusion reaction? *(1 mark)*

    ii What change occurs in the core of the Sun as a result of a fusion reaction? *(1 mark)*

  b Chemical elements are formed as a result of fusion reactions. Light elements no heavier than iron are formed in stars like the Sun.

    i   How are elements heavier than iron formed? *(3 marks)*

    ii What does the presence of heavy elements on Earth tell us about the origin of the Solar System? *(1 mark)*

Student's book
pages 236–241

Experimental data handling

Key points

- Plan investigations to produce repeatable, reproducible and valid results. Take care to ensure fair testing.

- Careful use of the correct equipment can improve accuracy. The mean of a repeat set of readings is the sum of the values divided by how many values there are.

- Human error can produce random and systematic errors. Examine anomalous results and discard them if necessary.

- The reproducibility of data can be checked by looking at similar work done by others, by using a different method or by others checking your method.

Study tip

Trial runs will tell you a lot about how your investigation might work out. They should get you to ask yourself:
- Do you have the correct conditions?
- Have you chosen a sensible range?
- Have you got readings that are close together?
- Will you need to repeat your readings?

Study tip

When you draw a results table, put the independent variable in the first column, and the dependent variable in the other column(s). When you draw a graph, plot the independent variable along the horizontal axis and the dependent variable up the vertical axis.

Investigations

- The **independent variable** is the one you choose to vary in your investigation.
- The **dependent variable** is used to judge the effect of varying the independent variable.
- A fair test is one in which only the independent variable affects the dependent variable. All other variables are controlled and kept constant if at all possible. (In fieldwork, the best you can do is to make sure that each of the many control variables change in much the same way.)
- If you are investigating two variables in a large population then you will need to do a survey. Again, it is impossible to control all of the variables. So here, the larger the sample size tested, the more valid the results will be.
- Variables can be one of two different types:
  – A **categoric variable** is one that is best described by a label (usually a word). A type of metal (for example, magnesium or zinc) is a categoric variable.
  – A **continuous variable** is one that we measure, so its value could be any number.
- When you are designing an investigation you must make sure that others can repeat any results you get – this makes it **reproducible**. You should also plan to make each result **repeatable**. You can do this by getting consistent sets of repeat measurements.
- You must also make sure you are measuring the actual thing you want to measure. You need to make sure that you have controlled as many other variables as you can, so that no-one can say that your investigation is not **valid**.
- A precise set of results is grouped closely together.
- An accurate set of results will have a mean (average) close to the true value.

Setting up investigations

- Even when an instrument is used correctly, the results can still show differences. Results may differ because of a random error. This could be due to poor measurements being made. It could be due to not carrying out the method consistently. The error may be a systematic error. This means that the method was carried out consistently but an error was being repeated.
- Anomalous results are clearly out of line with the rest of the data collected. If they are simply due to a random error then they should be ignored. If anomalies can be identified while you are doing an investigation, then it is best to repeat that part of the investigation. If you find anomalies after you have finished collecting the data for an investigation (perhaps when drawing your graph), then they must be discarded.

Using data

- If you have a categoric independent variable and a continuous dependent variable then you should use a bar chart.
- If you have a continuous independent and a continuous dependent variable then use a line graph.
- If you are still uncertain about a conclusion, you could check reproducibility by:
  – looking for other similar work on the Internet or from others in your class,
  – getting somebody else to redo your investigation,
  – trying an alternative method to see if you get the same results.
- You will find Paper 2-style questions designed to test your understanding of practical skills included in the pages of Examination-style questions in this Revision Guide.

Key words: reproducible, repeatable, valid

1 A student carried out an experiment to measure the refractive index of glass. He directed a narrow beam of light into a semi-circular glass block as shown in Figure 1.

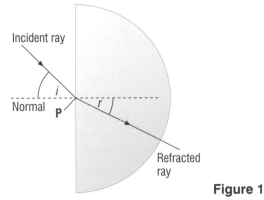

Figure 1

1 (a) He measured the angle of incidence *i* and the angle of refraction *r* using a protractor. He repeated the measurements two more times for the same angle of incidence. Table 1 shows the measurements he made.

Table 1

Angle of incidence *i*/degree	Angle of refraction *r*/degree
30.0	19.5
30.0	19.5
30.0	18.5

1 (a) (i) Calculate the mean value of *r*.

19.2°

(1)

1 (a) (ii) The refractive Index, *n*, of a transparent substance is given by the equation $n = \sin i/\sin r$
Use this equation to calculate the refractive index of the glass block.

$n = \sin 30.0/\sin 19.2 = 1.52$

(3)

1 (a) (iii) Why was it important to make sure the incident ray enters the block exactly at the midpoint of the flat side of the block?

The ray would refract again where it leaves the block if the point of entry into the block was not exactly at the centre.

(2)

1 (b) To obtain a more accurate value of *n* for the glass block, outline what further measurements you would make and explain how you would use them.

Repeat the experiment in (a) and Figure 1 for six different angles of incidence.
For each angle of incidence *i*, measure the angle of refraction *r*.
Calculate the mean value of the angle of incidence *i* and the angle of refraction *r* and use the mean values in the equation $n = \sin i/\sin r$ to calculate *n*.

(3)

The answer is correct and gains the mark.

The answer gains 3 marks (1 for use of mean value of *r*; 1 for correct use of: $n = \sin i/\sin r$; 1 for correct answer).

The answer gains 1 mark. The candidate needed to state that further refraction would invalidate the calculation in **(a)(ii)**.

The answer gains 2 marks. Repeating for five or more different values of *i* gains a mark and measuring angle *r* for each angle *i* gains a mark. The third mark is not given because the equation $n = \sin i/\sin r$ should have been used for each of the six values of *i* and then the mean value of *n* worked out.

Glossary

Absorb: To take in and 'soak up'.

Acceleration: Change of velocity per second (in metres per second per second, m/s^2).

Acceleration due to gravity, g: The acceleration of a falling object when no other forces other than the force of gravity acts on it.

Air bag: Car safety feature to reduce the force on a driver's/passenger's head in a collision.

Alpha radiation: Alpha particles, each composed of two protons and two neutrons, emitted by unstable nuclei.

Alternating current: An electric current that repeatedly reverses its direction.

Alternating current generator: A generator that produces alternating current.

Ammeter: Meter that measures current.

Ampere: The unit of electric current (unit symbol A).

Amplitude: The height of a wave crest or a wave trough of a transverse wave from the rest position. For oscillating motion, it is the maximum distance moved by an oscillating object from its equilibrium position.

Angle of incidence: The angle between the incident ray and the normal.

Angle of reflection: The angle between the reflected ray and the normal.

Anomalous results: Results that do not match the pattern seen in the other data collected or are well outside the range of other repeat readings. They should be retested and if necessary discarded.

Atomic number: The number of protons in a nucleus, symbol Z (also called the proton number).

Attract: Move towards.

Average speed: Total distance travelled ÷ by total time taken.

Background radiation: Ionising radiation from substances around us.

Band: Division of the microwave or radio spectrum.

Beta radiation: Beta particles emitted by a radioactive isotope; a beta particle is an electron created and emitted when a nucleus undergoes radioactive decay.

Big Bang theory: The theory that the universe was created in a massive explosion (the Big Bang) and that the universe has been expanding ever since.

Black dwarf: A star that has faded and gone cold.

Black hole: An object in space that has so much mass that nothing, not even light, can escape from its gravitational field.

Blue-shift: Decrease in the wavelength of electromagnetic waves emitted by a star or galaxy due to its motion towards us. The faster the speed of the star or galaxy, the greater the blue-shift is.

Boiling point: Temperature at which a pure substance boils or condenses.

Boundary: Dividing line between two different materials.

Braking distance: The distance travelled by a vehicle during the time its brakes act.

Cable: Two or three insulated wires surrounded by an outer layer of rubber or flexible plastic.

Cancellation: When a wave crest and a wave trough pass through each other, they cancel each other out where they meet.

Centre of mass: The point where an object's mass may be thought to be concentrated.

Centripetal acceleration: The acceleration due to the centripetal force on an object moving at constant speed round a circle.

Centripetal force: The resultant force towards the centre of a circle acting on an object moving in a circular path.

Chain reaction: Reactions in which one reaction causes further reactions, which in turn cause further reactions, etc. A nuclear chain reaction occurs when fission neutrons cause further fission, so more fission neutrons are released. These go on to produce further fission.

Change of state: For example, boiling, freezing, condensing.

Charge-coupled device: A device that processes a signal to convert it to a digital image.

Ciliary muscle: Controls shape of lens in the eye.

Circuit breaker: An electromagnetic switch that opens and cuts the current off if too much current passes through it.

Circuit symbol: A diagram that represents an electrical component.

Compression: Squeezing together.

Condensation: Turning from vapour into liquid.

Conduction: Heat transfer by movement of free electrons or vibrations.

Conductor: Material that conducts heat or electricity.

Conservation of energy: Energy cannot be created or destroyed.

Conservation of momentum: In a closed system, the total momentum before an event is equal to the total momentum after the event. Momentum is conserved in any collision or explosion provided no external forces act on the objects that collide or explode.

Contrast medium: An X-ray absorbing substance used to fill a body organ so the organ can be seen on a radiograph.

Convection: Circulation of a liquid or gas by increasing its thermal energy.

Convection current: Flow of a liquid or gas due to heating.

Converging (convex) lens: A lens that makes light rays parallel to the principal axis converge to (meet at) a point; also referred to as a convex lens.

Cornea: Carries out initial focusing of light entering the eye.

Cosmic microwave background radiation (CMBR): Electromagnetic radiation that has been travelling through space ever since it was created shortly after the Big Bang.

Coulomb (C): The unit of electrical charge, equal to the charge passing a point in a (direct current) circuit in 1 second when the current is 1 A.

Count rate: The number of counts per second detected by a Geiger counter.

Critical angle: The angle of incidence of a light ray in a transparent medium that produces refraction along the boundary.

Crumple zone: Parts of a vehicle that fold in a collision.

CT scanner: A medical scanner that uses X-rays to produce a digital image of any cross-section through the body or a three-dimensional image of an organ.

Cycle dynamo: Small-scale generator that runs a cycle lamp.

Deceleration: Change of velocity per second when an object slows down.

Density: Mass per unit volume of a substance.

Dependent variable: See Variable – dependent.

Diffraction: The spreading of waves when they pass through a gap or around the edges of an obstacle which has a similar size to the wavelength of the waves.

Diffusion: Spreading out of particles away from each other.

Diode: A non-ohmic conductor that has a much higher resistance in one direction (the reverse direction) than in the other direction (its forward direction).

Dioptre: The unit of lens power, D.

Direct current: Electric current in a circuit that is in one direction only.

Direct current generator: A generator that produces direct current.

Directly proportional: A graph will show this if the line of best fit is a straight line through the origin.

Dispersion: The splitting of white light into the colours of the spectrum.

Displacement: Distance in a given direction.

Diverging (concave) lens: A lens that makes light rays parallel to the axis diverge (i.e. spread out) as if from a single point; also referred to as a concave lens.

Doppler effect: The change of wavelength (and frequency) of the waves from a moving source due to the motion of the source.

Drag force: See Resistive force.

Driving force: Force of a vehicle that makes it move; sometimes referred to as motive force.

Earth wire: A wire used to connect the metal case of an appliance to earth so that the case cannot become live.

Echo: Reflection of sound that can be heard.

Efficiency: Useful energy transferred by a device ÷ total energy supplied to the device.

Effort: The force applied to a device used to raise a weight or shift an object.

Elastic: A material is elastic if it is able to regain its shape after it has been squashed or stretched.

Elastic potential energy: Energy stored in an elastic object when work is done to change its shape.

Electric charge: Amount of electricity, measured in coulombs.

Electric current: The rate of flow of electric charge (in amperes, A).

Electrical energy: Energy transferred by the movement of charge.

Electromagnet: An insulated wire wrapped round an iron bar that becomes magnetic when there is a current in the wire.

Electromagnetic induction: The process of inducing a potential difference in a wire by moving the wire so it cuts across the lines of force of a magnetic field.

Electromagnetic spectrum: The continuous spectrum of electromagnetic waves.

Electromagnetic waves: Electric and magnetic disturbances that transfer energy from one place to another. The spectrum of electromagnetic waves, in order of increasing wavelength, is as follows: gamma rays, X-rays, ultraviolet radiation, visible light, infrared radiation, microwaves, radio waves.

Electrons: Tiny negatively-charged particles that move around the nucleus of an atom.

Emit: Give out.

Endoscope: A medical instrument that uses optical fibres to see inside the body.

Equal: The same in value.

Equilibrium (of forces): The state of an object when it is at rest.

Evaporate: Turn from liquid into vapour.

Expansion of the universe: The motion of galaxies away from each other, discovered from the observations that the red-shift (and therefore the speed) of distant galaxies increases with their distance.

Explosion: A sudden rapid expansion.

Extension: The increase in length of a spring (or a strip of material) from its original length.

Eye lens: Fine focuses light in the eye.

Fair test: A test in which only the independent variable has been allowed to affect the dependent variable.

Far point: The furthest point from an eye at which an object can be seen in focus by the eye. The far point of the normal eye is at infinity.

Field lines: See Line of force.

Filament bulb: Bulb containing a wire that glows when electric current passes through.

Fleming's left-hand rule: A rule that gives the direction of the force on a current-carrying wire in a magnetic field according to the directions of the current and the field.

Fluid: A liquid or a gas.

Focal length: The distance from the centre of a lens to the point where light rays parallel to the principal axis are focused (or, in the case of a convex mirror or a diverging lens, appear to diverge from).

Force: A force can change the motion of an object (in newtons, N).

Force diagram: A diagram showing the forces on an object.

Force multiplier: A lever used so that a weight or force can be moved by a smaller force.

Free electron: Electron that moves about freely inside a metal and is not held inside an atom.

Freezing point: Temperature at which a liquid changes to a solid.

Frequency: The number of wave crests passing a point each second. The unit of frequency is the hertz (Hz).

Friction: The force opposing the relative motion of two solid surfaces in contact.

Fuse: A fuse contains a thin wire that melts and cuts the current off if too much current passes through it.

Fusion (change of state): Melting.

Fusion (nuclear): See Nuclear fusion.

Gamma radiation: Electromagnetic radiation emitted from unstable nuclei in radioactive substances.

Gas: State of matter in which particles are spread out and move at random.

Generator effect: The production of a potential difference using a magnetic field.

Gradient: Change of the quantity plotted on the y-axis divided by the change of the quantity plotted on the x-axis.

Gravitational attraction: Attraction of two objects due to the force of gravity on each other.

Gravitational field strength: The force of gravity on an object of mass 1 kg (in newtons per kilogram, N/kg).

Gravitational potential energy: Energy of an object due to its position in a gravitational field. Near the Earth's surface, change of GPE (in joules, J) = weight (in newtons, N) × vertical distance moved (in metres, m).

Half-life: Average time taken for the number of nuclei of the isotope (or mass of the isotope) in a sample to halve.

Half-wave rectification: The use of a diode in a circuit with an alternating supply pd to allow current only in one direction every other half-cycle of the supply pd.

Hooke's law: Hooke's law states that the extension of a spring is directly proportional to the force applied to it, as long as its limit of proportionality is not exceeded.

Hydraulic pressure: The pressure in the liquid in a hydraulic arm.

Impact time: Time during which a force acts, for example in a collision.

Induced potential difference: The potential difference generated in a wire or coil when the wire or coil cuts across the lines of a magnetic field.

Infrared radiation: Electromagnetic waves between visible light and microwaves in the electromagnetic spectrum.

Input energy: Energy supplied to a device.

Insulator: Material that does not conduct (heat or electricity).

Interference: Reinforcement or cancellation of waves when two sets of identical waves overlap.

Ion: A charged atom.

Ionisation: Any process in which atoms become charged.

Ionising radiation: Radiation that ionises substances it passes through. Alpha, beta, gamma and X-radiation are all ionising.

Iris: Coloured part of the eye that controls amount of light entering.

Isotopes: Atoms of an element that contain different numbers of neutrons in their nuclei.

Joule (J): The unit of energy.

Kilowatt: 1000 watts.

Kilowatt-hour (kWh): Electrical energy supplied to a 1 kW electrical device in 1 hour.

Kinetic energy: Energy of a moving object due to its motion; kinetic energy (in joules, J) = ½ mass (in kilograms, kg) × (speed)^2 (in m^2/s^2).

Latent heat of fusion: Energy supplied to a substance to melt it; also, energy removed from a substance to solidify or freeze it.

Latent heat of vaporisation: Energy supplied to a liquid substance to vaporise it; also, energy removed from a vapour to liquefy it.

Law of conservation of momentum: The total momentum before the interaction is equal to the total momentum afterwards, provided no external forces act on the objects.

Law of force between charged objects: Like charges repel; unlike charges attract.

Lens formula: Formula that relates object distance u, image distance v and focal length f:

$$\frac{1}{u} + \frac{1}{v} = \frac{1}{f}$$

Light-dependent resistor (LDR): A resistor whose resistance depends on the intensity of the light incident on it.

Light-emitting diode (LED): A diode that emits light when it conducts.

Limit of proportionality: The limit for Hooke's law applied to the extension of a stretched spring.

Line of action: The line along which a force acts.

Line of force: Line in a magnetic field along which a magnetic compass points; also called a magnetic field line.

Liquid: State of matter in which particles are close together but not held in a rigid structure.

Live wire: The mains wire that has a voltage that alternates repeatedly from positive to negative and back (between +325 V and –325 V in Europe).

Load: The weight of an object raised by a device used to lift the object, or the force applied by a device when it is used to shift an object.

Long sight: An eye that cannot focus on nearby objects but can focus on distant objects.

Longitudinal wave: Waves in which the vibrations are parallel to the direction of energy transfer.

Loudness: Property of sound related to amplitude.

Machine: Device that transfers or transforms energy.

Magnet: An object that creates a magnetic field.

Magnetic field: The space around a magnet or a current-carrying wire.

Magnetic field line: See Line of force.

Magnetic poles: The ends of a magnet or a magnetic compass.

Magnification: The image height ÷ the object height.

Magnifying glass: A converging lens used to magnify a small object which must be placed between the lens and its focal point.

Magnitude: The size or amount of a physical quantity.

Main sequence: The main stage in the life of a star during which it radiates energy because of fusion of hydrogen nuclei in its core.

Mass: The quantity of matter in an object; a measure of the difficulty of changing the motion of an object (in kilograms, kg).

Mass number: The number of protons and neutrons in the nucleus of an atom (symbol A).

Mechanical wave: Vibration that travels through a substance.

Medium: A substance.

Melting point: Temperature at which a pure substance melts or freezes (solidifies).

Microwaves: Electromagnetic waves between infrared radiation and radio waves in the electromagnetic spectrum.

Moment: The turning effect of a force defined by the equation: Moment of a force (in newton metres) = force (in newtons) × perpendicular distance from the pivot to the line of action of the force (in metres).

Momentum: Mass (in kilograms, kg) × velocity (in m/s). The unit of momentum is the kilogram metre per second (kg m/s).

Monitor: To make observations over a period of time.

Motive force: See Driving force.

Motor effect: When a current is passed along a wire in a magnetic field and the wire is not parallel to the lines of the magnetic field, a force is exerted on the wire by the magnetic field.

National Grid: The network of cables and transformers used to transfer electricity from power stations to consumers (homes, shops, offices, factories, etc.).

Near point: The nearest point to an eye at which an object can be seen in focus by the eye. The near point of the normal eye is 25 cm from the eye.

Negative: Type of charge carried by an electron.

Neutral wire: The wire of a mains circuit that is earthed at the local sub-station so its potential is close to zero.

Neutrons: Uncharged particles of the same mass as protons. The nucleus of an atom consists of protons and neutrons.

Neutron star: The highly compressed core of a massive star that remains after a supernova explosion.

Newton (N): The unit of force.

Normal: Straight line through a surface or boundary that is perpendicular to the surface or boundary.

North pole: North-pointing end of a freely-suspended bar magnet or a magnetic compass.

Nuclear energy: Energy released from an unstable atom as a result of a change in its nucleus.

Nuclear fission: The process in which certain nuclei (uranium-235 and plutonium-239) split into two fragments when struck by a neutron, releasing energy and two or three neutrons as a result.

Nuclear fission reactors: Reactors that release energy steadily due to the fission of a suitable isotope such as uranium-235.

Nuclear fusion: The process in which small nuclei are forced together so they fuse with each other to form a larger nucleus, releasing energy in the process.

Nucleus: The positively charged object composed of protons and neutrons at the centre of every atom.

Ohm: The unit of electrical resistance (unit symbol Ω).

Ohm's law: The current through a resistor at constant temperature is directly proportional to the potential difference across the resistor.

Ohmic conductor: A conductor that has a constant resistance and therefore obeys Ohm's law.

Opposite: The other type or direction (where there are just two types or the two directions along a line).

Optical fibres: Thin transparent fibres used to transmit light.

Oscillating motion: Motion of any object that moves to and fro along the same line.

Oscillation: Move to and fro about a certain position along a line.

Oscilloscope: A device used to display the shape of an electrical wave.

Parallel: Components connected in a circuit so that the potential difference is the same across each one.

Parallelogram of forces: A geometrical method used to find the resultant force of two forces that do not act along the same line.

Pascal (Pa): The unit of pressure, equal to 1 newton per square metre.

Pay-back time: The time taken to pay back the cost of an energy-saving device from the savings on fuel bills.

Peak potential difference: The maximum voltage of an ac supply measured from zero volts.

Period: See Time period.

Perpendicular: At right angles.

Pitch: The pitch of a sound increases if the frequency of the sound waves increases.

Pivot: The point about which an object turns when acted on by a force that makes it turn.

Plane mirror: A flat mirror.

Planet: A large object that moves in an orbit round a star. A planet reflects light from the star and does not produce its own light.

Plasma: A very hot gas consisting of bare nuclei (atoms stripped of their electrons).

Plug: A plug has an insulating case and is used to connect the cable from an appliance to a socket.

Positive: Type of charge carried by a proton.

Potential difference: A measure of the work done or energy transferred to a lamp by each coulomb of charge that passes through it. The unit of potential difference is the volt (V).

Power: The energy transformed or transferred per second. The unit of power is the watt (W).

Power of a lens: The unit of lens power is the dioptre (D) – the reciprocal of the focal length of a lens in metres.

Prediction: A forecast or statement about the way something will happen in the future. In science it is not just a simple guess because it is based on some prior knowledge or on a hypothesis.

Pressure: Force per unit cross-sectional area for a force acting on a surface at right angles to the surface. The unit of pressure is the pascal (Pa) or newton per square metre (N/m^2).

Principal axis: A line through the centre of the lens and at right angles to it.

Principal focus: The point where light rays parallel to the principal axis of a lens are focused (or, in the case of a diverging lens, appear to diverge from).

Principle of moments: For an object in equilibrium, the sum of all the clockwise moments about any point = the sum of all the anticlockwise moments about that point.

Proton: Positively charged particle with an equal and opposite charge to that of the electron. The nucleus of an atom consists of protons and neutrons. Protons and neutrons have the same approximate mass which is about 2000 times that of the electron.

Proton number: See Atomic number.

Protostar: The concentration of dust clouds and gas in space that forms a star.

Pupil: Part of the eye through which light enters.

Radiation: Energy transfer by means of waves.

Radiation dose: Amount of ionising radiation a person receives.

Radio waves: Electromagnetic waves of wavelengths greater than 0.10 m.

Radioactive dating: Dating of material using radioactive decay (for example, of carbon or uranium).

Radioactive decay: Unstable nuclei are said to undergo radioactive decay when they emit alpha or beta or gamma radiation.

Radioactive substances: Substances with unstable nuclei that emit alpha, beta or gamma radiation becoming more stable as a result.

Radiograph: An X-ray picture.

Random: Cannot be predicted.

Range of measurements: The maximum and minimum values of the independent variable; important in ensuring that any pattern is detected.

Range of vision: Distance between near point and far point of the eye.

Rarefaction: Stretched apart.

Residual Current Circuit Breaker (RCCB): Cuts off the current in the live wire when it is different from the current in the neutral wire.

Reactor core: The thick steel vessel used to contain the fuel rods, the control rods and the moderator of a nuclear reactor.

Real image: An image formed by a lens that can be projected on a screen.

Red giant: A star after the main sequence stage that has expanded and cooled, resulting in it becoming red and much larger and cooler than it was before it expanded.

Red supergiant: A star much more massive than the Sun that has swollen out after the main sequence stage to become a red supergiant before it collapses.

Red-shift: Increase in the wavelength of electromagnetic waves emitted by a star or galaxy due to its motion away from us. The faster the speed of the star or galaxy, the greater the red-shift is.

Reflection: The change of direction of a light ray or a wave at a boundary when the ray or wave stays in the incident medium.

Refraction: The change of direction of a light ray or a wave due to change of speed when it passes across a boundary (for example, a light ray passing between two transparent substances (including air).

Refractive index, _n_: A measure of how much a substance can refract a light ray:

$$n = \frac{\text{speed of light in vacuum (air)}}{\text{speed of light in the substance}}$$

Reinforcement: The meeting of two or more crests or two or more troughs of a wave.

Relay: A switch opened by an electromagnet (in a separate circuit) when a current passes through the electromagnet.

Repeatable: A measurement is repeatable if the original experimenter repeats the investigation using the same method and equipment and obtains the same results.

Repel: Push apart.

Reproducible: A measurement is reproducible if the investigation is repeated by another person or by using different equipment or techniques and the same results are obtained.

Resistance: Resistance (in ohms, Ω)

$$= \frac{\text{potential difference (in volts, V)}}{\text{current (in amperes, A)}}$$

Resistive force: Force such as friction or air resistance that opposes the motion of an object.

Resistors in parallel: Resistors in a circuit with the same potential difference across each one. The bigger the resistance of a resistor, the smaller the current that passes through it.

Resistors in series: Resistors in a circuit with the same current passing through them. Their combined resistance = sum of the individual resistances.

Resolution: This is the smallest change in the quantity being measured (input) of a measuring instrument that gives a perceptible change in the reading.

Resonance: When sound vibrations build up in a musical instrument and cause the sound from the instrument to become much louder.

Resultant force: The combined effect of the forces acting on an object.

Resultant moment: The difference between the sum of the clockwise moments and the sum of the anticlockwise moments about the same point.

Retina: Light sensitive region in the eye.

Sankey diagram: An energy transfer diagram.

Scalar: A scalar is a physical quantity such as mass or energy that has magnitude only, unlike a vector that has magnitude and direction.

Seat belt: Belts to reduce the force of an impact, worn by travellers in vehicles.

Sensitivity: The smallest change that an instrument can detect, e.g. 0.1 mm.

Series: Components connected in a circuit so that the same current passes through them are in series with each other.

Series circuit rules: 1. The current through components in series is the same. 2. The total potential difference across components in series is shared between the components.

Short-circuit: A circuit fault in which two wires at different potentials touch and a large current passes between them at the point of contact.

Short sight: A condition where an eye cannot focus on distant objects but can focus on nearby objects.

Sign convention: Real images have positive values. Virtual images have negative values.

Simple pendulum: A pendulum consisting of a small spherical bob suspended by a thin string from a fixed point.

Socket: A mains socket is used to connect the mains plug of a mains appliance to the mains circuit.

Solar cell: Electrical cell that produces a voltage when in sunlight; solar cells are usually connected together in solar cell panels.

Solar heating panel: Sealed panel designed to use sunlight to heat water running through it.

Solid: State of matter in which particles are close together, and have fixed positions.

Sound: Wave produced by vibrations.

South pole: South-pointing end of a freely-suspended bar magnet or a magnetic compass.

Specific heat capacity: Energy needed by 1 kg of a substance to raise its temperature by 1°C.

Specific latent heat of fusion: Energy needed to melt 1 kg of a substance at its melting point.

Specific latent heat of vaporisation: Energy needed to boil away 1 kg of a substance with no change of temperature.

Speed: Distance moved ÷ time taken (metres/second, m/s).

Split-ring commutator: Metal contacts on the coil of a direct-current motor that connects the rotating coil continuously to its electrical power supply.

Spring constant: The force per unit extension needed to stretch a spring.

Star: A ball of gas held together by gravity.

States of matter: The states that matter can exist in: solid, liquid and gas.

Static electricity: Charge 'held' by an insulator or an insulated conductor.

Step-down transformer: Electrical device that is used to step down the size of an alternating voltage.

Step-up transformer: Electrical device that is used to step up the size of an alternating voltage.

Stopping distance: Thinking distance + braking distance.

Supernova: The explosion of a massive star after fusion in its core ceases and the matter surrounding its core collapses on to the core and rebounds.

Supply: In electric circuits, the battery or mains.

Suspensory ligament: Attaches the eye lens to the ciliary muscles.

Switch mode transformer: A transformer that works at much higher frequencies than a traditional transformer. It has a ferrite core instead of an iron core.

Tangent: A straight line drawn to touch a point on a curve so it has the same gradient as the curve at that point.

Temperature: Measure of hotness.

Terminal velocity: The velocity reached by an object when the drag force on it is equal and opposite to the force making it move.

Thermal expansion: Increase of length of a solid or increase of volume of a liquid or gas due to an increase in temperature.

Thermistor: A resistor whose resistance depends on the temperature of the thermistor.

Thickness monitoring: Method to control thickness of materials by detection of radiation from a beta source.

Thinking distance: The distance travelled by the vehicle in the time it takes the driver to react.

Three-pin plug: A three-pin plug has a live pin, a neutral pin and an earth pin. The earth pin is used to earth the metal case of an appliance so the case cannot become live.

Time base control: An oscilloscope control used to space the waveform out horizontally.

Time period: The time taken for one complete cycle of the motion of an oscillating object (e.g. a simple pendulum) or of an object moving round a circle (e.g. a satellite in orbit).

Total internal reflection: The total reflection of a light ray in a transparent substance when it reaches a boundary with air or another transparent substance. Total reflection only happens if the angle of incidence is greater than the critical angle.

Tracer: Radioactive source used in medical diagnosis.

Transformer: Electrical device used to change an alternating voltage. See also Step-up transformer and Step-down transformer.

Transverse wave: Wave in which the vibration is perpendicular to the direction of energy transfer.

Turbine: A machine that uses steam or hot gas to turn a shaft.

Ultrasound wave: Sound waves at a frequency above the upper frequency limit of the human ear (above 20 000 Hz).

Useful energy: Energy transferred to where it is wanted in the form it is wanted.

U-value: A measure of the energy per second (per square metre) that passes through a material when the temperature difference across it is 1°C. A good insulator has a lower U-value than a poor insulator.

Valid: Suitability of the investigative procedure to answer the question being asked.

Vector: A vector is a physical quantity such as displacement or velocity that has a magnitude and direction unlike a scalar which has magnitude only.

Velocity: Speed in a given direction (in metres/second, m/s).

Vibrate: Oscillate rapidly (or move to and fro rapidly about a certain position).

Virtual image: An image, seen in a lens or a mirror, from which light rays appear to come after being refracted by the lens or reflected by the mirror.

Visible light: Electromagnetic waves that can be detected by the normal human eye. Visible light has a wavelength range from about 350 nm for violet light to about 650 nm for red light. (1 nm = 1 nanometre = 1 millionth of 1 millimetre).

Volt (V): The unit of potential difference, equal to energy transfer per unit charge in joules per coulomb.

Voltage: The pd across a component.

Voltmeter: Meter that measures voltage.

Wasted energy: Energy that is not usefully transferred or transformed.

Watt (W): The unit of power.

Wave speed: The distance travelled per second by a wave crest or wave trough.

Waveform: The shape of a wave.

Wavelength: The distance from one wave crest to the next wave crest (along the waves).

Weight: The force of gravity on an object (in newtons, N).

White dwarf: A star that has collapsed from the red giant stage to become much hotter and denser than it was.

Work: Energy transferred by a force, given by: Work done (in joules, J) = force (in newtons, N) × distance moved in the direction of the force (in metres, m).

X-ray: Electromagnetic wave shorter in wavelength than ultraviolet radiation, produced by X-ray tubes.

Y-gain control: An oscilloscope control used to adjust the height of the waveform.

Answers

1 Motion

⟫ 1.1
1 a The speed of X is greater than that of Y.
   b The speed of Y is constant. The speed of Z is zero from 500 s to 1000 s and is less than that of Y in the first 500 s and in the last 500 s.
2 a 24 m/s
   b 13.3 m/s

⟫ 1.2
1 Speed is distance travelled per unit of time. Velocity is speed in a particular direction.
2 2.4 m/s²

⟫ 1.3
1 a The graph would be a straight line with a positive gradient.
   b The graph would be a straight line with a negative gradient.
2 It would be a horizontal (flat) line parallel to the time axis.

⟫ 1.4
1 a An object with an increasing speed.
   b An object with an increasing acceleration.
2 80 m

Answers to end of Chapter 1 questions

1 20 m/s
2 A horizontal (flat) line parallel to the time axis.
3 Acceleration
4 The object is decelerating.
5 The gradient increases.
6 It travels at constant speed in a circular path so its direction and therefore its velocity is continually changing. Because its velocity is changing, it must therefore be accelerating.
7 a 4.0 m/s²
   b Its speed increases steadily from 0 to 40 m/s so the average speed is 20 m/s.
   c 200 m
8 The area under the line.
9 a 2.0 m/s²
   b 100 m
10 a The speed increases from zero at a decreasing rate and becomes constant from about 10 s to 20 s before decreasing to zero at a constant rate.
   b −2.0 m/s²
11 a The acceleration decreases and is zero from about 10 s to 20 s then it becomes negative and constant.
   b i   About 3.5 m/s²
      ii About 2.0 m/s²
12 a 400 m to 420 m
   b About 14 m/s

2 Resultant forces

⟫ 2.1
1 Vertically downwards.
2 The force of the blocks on each running shoe, acting in the direction of motion of the runner.

⟫ 2.2
1 The resultant force is zero.
2 a 7 N
   b 1 N in the direction of the 4 N force.

⟫ 2.3
1 17.3 kN
2 The parallelogram is a square of side length in proportion to 10 kN. The resultant force represented by the diagonal = 14(.1) kN.

⟫ 2.4
1 2000 N

2 Repeat the test with the same force and the same trolley several times and calculate the average acceleration.
3 3.0 N

Answers to end of Chapter 2 questions

1 They exert equal and opposite forces on each other.
2 It is constant.
3 A vector quantity has a direction; a scalar quantity is non-directional.
4 a 2.0 N
   b 10.0 N
5 The parallelogram is a rectangle with adjacent sides of lengths in proportion to 4.0 N and 6.0 N. The resultant force is represented by the diagonal. The resultant force represented by the diagonal = 7.2 N.
6 0.45 m/s²
7 2700 N
8 480 N
9 a −0.8 m/s²
   b 60 N
10 a 1.0 N
   b 2.0 N
11 a −0.50 m/s²
   b 90 N
12 24 s

3 Momentum and force

⟫ 3.1
1 30 000 kg m/s
2 a 5000 kg m/s
   b 1.0 m/s
3 Use your measurements to show that the mass of A × the velocity of A before the collision = the total mass of A and B × their velocity after the collision.

⟫ 3.2
1 It is zero.
2 a They exert equal and opposite forces on each other.
   b X has a smaller mass than Y.
3 a Repeat the test several times. If the ratio from each test varies considerably, the measurements are not precise.
   b Calculate the average value of the distance ratio. Measure the mass of the two trolleys. The distance ratio should be equal to the inverse of the mass ratio. If not, measurements of distance are probably inaccurate.

⟫ 3.3
1 80 000 N
2 The crumple zones at the front and rear increase the impact time and therefore reduce the impact force in a crash.

⟫ 3.4
1 a They continue to move forward when the car stops and will hit the windscreen.
   b The narrow seatbelt would not spread the force across the passenger's body and might cut them.
2 The impact time would be longer and the impact force would be smaller.

Answers to end of Chapter 3 questions

1 kg m/s
2 40 000 kg m/s
3 40 m/s
4 a Zero
   b Zero
5 0.6 m/s
6 0.15 kg m/s
7 0.30 m/s to the right
8 Zero
9 0.06 m/s
10 The change of momentum of the object which the force acts on.
11 72 kg m/s

12 The seat belt prevents the wearer continuing to move forward and hitting the windscreen when the car suddenly stops. It also increases the impact time and spreads the impact force across the wearer's chest.

Answers to Examination-style questions

1 a i The gradient of the line. (1)
   ii 1.2 m/s (3)
   b i The gradient increases with time. (1)
   ii 0.8 m/s^2 (2)
   c Any two: The stopwatch method would involve repeating the timing for different distances whereas the motion sensor method can be done in one run; the timings for short distances would be small and therefore less accurate with a stopwatch; a motion sensor gives continuous timings in one 'run'; reaction time would affect the timings using a stopwatch but not with the motion sensor. (2)
2 a The graph should also include a straight flat line at 20 m/s from 50 s to 200 s then a straight line from 20 m/s at 200 s to zero velocity at 300 s. (2)
   b i 0.40 m/s^2 (2)
   ii Distance travelled = area under line for 1st 50 s = ½ × 20 m/s × 50 s = 500 m (1)
   c i −0.20 m/s^2 (1)
   ii 1000 m (1)
   iii 6000 N (1)
   d i Distance travelled at constant velocity = 20 m/s × 150 m = 3000 m
      Total distance travelled = 500 m + 1000 m + 3000 m = 4500 m (2)
   ii 15 m/s (= total distance travelled / time taken) (1)
3 a i The cable pulls the skier with a force of 125 N so the skier exerts an equal and opposite force on the cable. The tension force in the cable is therefore 125 N so the cable exerts a force of 125 N on the boat. (2)
   ii The resultant force is 246 N. (3)
   b The difference is due to the resistive forces caused by water flowing past the boat and the force due to air resistance. (2)

4 More about forces

4.1
1 The resultant force is no longer zero and it makes the car decelerate.
2 a Stopping distance = thinking distance + braking distance
   b Reaction time increases and the thinking distance = speed × reaction time

4.2
1 600 N
2 a The drag force is zero initially.
   b The initial resultant force is due to its weight. Therefore the initial acceleration is equal to g.
3 The velocity becomes constant.

4.3
1 The spring and the rubber band.
2 9.0 N
3 The extension versus weight line starts to curve.
4 50 N/m

Answers to end of Chapter 4 questions

1 They are equal in magnitude and opposite in direction.
2 The distance travelled by a vehicle in the time it takes the driver to react.
3 The braking distance of a vehicle on a wet road is greater than on a dry road.
4 The stopping distance increases as the speed increases.
5 The velocity an object falling in a fluid reaches when the drag (i.e. resistive) force is equal and opposite to its weight.
6 700 N
7 The object's velocity increases as it falls and the drag force depends on velocity. So the drag force increases.
8 Its acceleration is constant.
9 The difference between its stretched length and its unstretched length.
10 An object that regains its shape when the forces applied to deform it are removed.
11 The extension of a spring is directly proportional to the force applied as long as limit of proportionality is not exceeded.
12 500 N/m

5 Forces and energy

5.1
1 2400 J
2 a 10 N
   b 4.0 m

5.2
1 2.0 × 10^5 J
2 a 1000 W
   b 750 W

5.3
1 a 3200 J
   b 1600 W
2 a 12.5 kg
   b 125 N

5.4
1 a 500 J
   b 10 m/s
2 Some elastic potential energy is transferred by heating.

Answers to end of Chapter 5 questions

1 When a force moves through a distance.
2 Work done = energy transferred
3 The watt (W)
4 A decrease of 540 J.
5 The energy stored in an object when it is stretched or squashed.
6 540 000 J
7 8.0 J
8 5.7 m/s
9 The gravitational potential energy decreases as energy is transferred by the drag force to the surroundings which therefore gain internal energy.
10 2.0 m
11 1.3(3) s
12 500 N

6 Forces in action

6.1
1 The point where the mass can be thought to be concentrated.
2 Repeat the test with the pin at a third position. Use the plumbline to draw a third line on the card. This line should pass through the point where the other two lines meet.
3 a The centre.
   b Where the two diagonals meet.
   c The middle rung.

6.2
1 0.80
2 Length
3 a 0.10 s
   b 0.30 s

6.3
1 12 Nm
2 40 N
3 120 N

6.4
1 The weight of the person acts through the pivot so it has no turning effect about the pivot.
2 a 1.0 m
   b 450 N
3 Repeat the test two more times using the same pivot. Calculate average values for d_o and d_1 and use the average values to calculate W_o.

6.5
1 The weight of the bags has a turning effect about the wheels which will act outside the wheel base if the pushchair is tilted.
2 The line of action of its weight is outside the base of the brick and so has a turning effect about the point of contact with the table which makes the brick topple over.

3 a So they are likely to topple over when they are hit by a ball.

b It is less likely to topple over when someone sitting on it leans sideways as the line of action of the weight will be less likely to be outside the base (lowers the centre of gravity).

6.6

1 a Tension in the string.

b The nut will fly off in a straight line at a tangent to the circle.

2 a Friction between the tyres and the road.

b It slides to the outside of the roundabout as it moves round it.

3 The centripetal force increases.

4 a Their weight and the downward force of the wall provides the necessary centripetal force to keep them moving round.

b As the wheel slows down, the riders would fall out at the highest position.

6.7

1 a 7500 Pa

b 180 MN

2 50 Pa, 75 N

3 a Liquids are virtually incompressible and the pressure in the liquid is transmitted equally in all directions.

b Air can be easily compressed so the force exerted on the system compresses the air instead of the liquid.

Answers to end of Chapter 6 questions

1

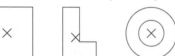

2 Directly below the point of suspension.

3 a i 3.0 Hz

ii 0.33 s

b Larger

4 a It transfers energy doing work against friction at the pivot and air resistance.

b The distance from the equilibrium position to the highest position on either side.

5 a The force × the perpendicular distance from the line of action of the force to the pivot.

b Newton metre (N m)

6 a 7.5 N m

b 25 N

7 A crowbar allows you to apply the same force at a greater distance from the pivot, giving a bigger moment.

8 1500 N

9 The centre of mass will be much higher in this position than when the box is side-on. Less force is needed to tilt it so when it is knocked, it will topple more easily.

10 90°

11 It becomes smaller.

12 50 000 Pa

Answers to Examination-style questions

1 a i The shortest distance travelled by the car from when the driver first reacts to when it stops (thinking distance + braking distance). (1)

ii The braking force must be reduced otherwise the car would skid. So the deceleration is reduced and the car takes longer to stop. (2)

b i 1.0 s (1)

ii 35 m (2)

c i −5.7 m/s² (2)

ii 5200 N (1)

d −6.5 m/s² (3)

2 a i Each piston bears a quarter of the weight of the ramp and the load on it. The pressure in the hydraulic system increases until the oil exerts a force on each piston equal to the total weight it supports. The pistons then move upwards and raise the ramp and the load. (2)

ii Forcing oil into the system would compress the trapped air so the increase of pressure would be less than it should be if no air were present in the system. (1)

b i 6000 N (2)

ii 4200 N (2)

c i $p = \frac{1}{4} (12000 + 1800)/0.012 = 287\,500\,Pa = 290\,kPa$ (to 2 significant figures) (3)

ii 9600 J (2)

iii 1 Work is done to raise the ramp as it gains gravitational potential energy.

2 Work is done to overcome friction between surfaces that slide past each other and/or to overcome resistance to flow in the oil. (2)

7 Properties of waves

7.1

1 Sound waves produced by mechanical waves on a vibrating wire.

2 The particles become closer during a compression then further apart during a rarefaction.

7.2

1 The particles on either side of the centre of a compression are displaced in opposite directions towards the centre. So the centre is at zero displacement. At a rarefaction, the particles either side of the centre are displaced away from the centre where the displacement is zero.

2 a 1800 m/s

b 0.20 m

3 The measurement of *t* is more accurate. Also, an error in counting the number of crossings can easily be identified as it would give an anomalous measurement by comparison with the other timings.

7.3

1 a 30°

b 120°

2 The wavelength doesn't change either.

3 Repeat the test for each angle of incidence several times and calculate an average value for the angle of the incident waves to the barrier and of the reflected waves to the barrier.

4 It is greater as the waves move faster afterwards so they bend towards the boundary.

7.4

1 a Ultrasound waves.

b Light waves, radio waves.

2 a High frequency ultrasound as they have a shorter wavelength.

b Local radio waves.

7.5

1 A small trough is observed.

2 a One set of circles only is seen.

b The wavelength of the waves increases and the points of cancellation and reinforcement move further apart.

3 The detector signal would increase as the microwaves from the other gap would not be cancelled out.

Answers to end of Chapter 7 questions

1 In a transverse wave, the vibrations of the particles are perpendicular to the direction of energy transfer. In a longitudinal wave, the vibrations are parallel to the direction of energy transfer.

2 a Sound

b Any electromagnetic waves (e.g. light).

3 A point on a sound wave where the particles are spaced out most.

4 0.05 m

5 a The height of a peak or the depth of a trough from equilibrium.

b The maximum distance of a vibrating particle from its equilibrium position.

6 0.8 Hz

7 Refraction is where a wave crosses a boundary and its direction changes due to the change of speed at the boundary.

8 The wave refracts and it bends closer to the boundary so its direction is at a larger angle to the boundary.

9 Diffraction is the spreading of a wave as it passes through a gap or round an obstacle. Interference is the cancellation or reinforcement of waves when they pass through each other.

10 TV waves are short wavelength radio waves and do not diffract round obstacles such as hills.

11 The waves from the two slits cancel each other due to interference at certain positions.

12 The observer would hear the sound at any position which was a point of cancellation.

8 Electromagnetic waves

8.1
1 10 000 million hertz (10 000 MHz)
2 a Gamma radiation.
  b Radio waves.
3 Gamma rays, X-rays, ultraviolet radiation, light, infrared radiation, microwaves, radio waves.

8.2
1 Light, infrared radiation, microwaves, radio waves.
2 The intensity of a light beam would decrease due to absorption by the atmosphere and spreading of the beam and the beam would be too faint to be detected.

8.3
1 Light because it has a much higher frequency.
2 Light and infrared radiation.
3 Changing this distance would change the meter reading. If the distance changed the measurements would not be valid.

8.4
1 Suncream absorbs UV.
2 The lead plate.
3 Any of the following: Gamma rays have much more energy than the X-rays used for radiography so would be more harmful; An X-ray tube can be switched on and off whereas a mechanical shutter is needed to block a gamma ray beam; Gamma rays are produced by radioactive substances which would need to be stored securely.

8.5
1 To absorb X-rays so the outline of the organ can be seen on a radiograph.
2 a A charged atom.
  b X-rays are ionising and can kill or damage living cells, causing cancer.
3 The shorter the wavelength, the higher the energy.

Answers to end of Chapter 8 questions

1 Radio waves, microwaves, infrared radiation, light, ultraviolet radiation, X-rays, gamma rays.
2 Gamma radiation.
3 The skin would be overheated and be damaged or destroyed.
4 a Microwaves
  b Radio waves near the microwave region.
5 The rays undergo total internal reflection repeatedly.
6 Advantage: more information can be transferred or greater security;
Disadvantage: Optical fibres cannot be used for very long distances or optical fibres take the signal to one receiver only.
7 The atmosphere absorbs infrared radiation.
8 a The process of producing ions from uncharged atoms.
  b It damages or kills living cells and can cause cell mutation and cancer.
9 Any two from radio waves, microwaves, infrared radiation, light, ultraviolet radiation.
10 Bones absorb X-rays much more than soft tissue does, so bones create a shadow on a radiograph.
11 Killing harmful bacteria in food or sterilising surgical instruments or killing cancer cells.
12 Advantage: A CT scanner distinguishes between different types of soft tissue (or produces a 3-D image)
Disadvantage: The dose of ionising radiation received is much higher.

9 Sound and ultrasound

9.1
1 The furnishings absorb sound waves which would otherwise reflect at the bare surfaces of the room. In an empty room, echoes due to reflected sounds would be present but not in a furnished room.
2 68 m
3 If the spread of the frequency measurements is significantly larger than the precision of the measurements, it can be concluded that the upper frequency limit of the human ear varies from one person to another. If not, the group tested have the same limit but this may not be true generally.

9.2
1 The pitch increases then decreases.
2 a The waves would have a greater amplitude so would be taller and the frequency would be lower so there would be fewer waves stretched out across the same horizontal distance.
  b 860 Hz to 2 significant figures.
3 The measured value of T would be less accurate because the uncertainty in a timing measurement doesn't depend on how many cycles are measured. So the uncertainty in the time period is reduced by measuring across several cycles rather than one cycle.

9.3
1 It would diffract and spread out too much so the reflected pulses would be much weaker and the direction they came from would be unclear.
2 Partial reflection is when a wave is partly reflected and partly transmitted.
3 a 0.18 m
  b 0.09 m

Answers to end of Chapter 9 questions

1 The particles vibrate along the direction of energy transfer. They repeatedly become closer together and then further apart.
2 The wings vibrate in the air creating sound waves that spread out in the surrounding air.
3 The pitch of the sound increases then the sound becomes inaudible once the frequency is above 20 000 Hz.
4 A temperature difference between the layer of air near the ground and higher up would cause the speed of sound waves moving upwards to change so the sound waves would refract towards the horizontal direction so they would be heard much further away.
5 Ultrasound waves have a higher frequency than sound waves so they have a shorter wavelength in air. Therefore sound waves diffract and spread out more.
6 A hard flat even surface.
7 a Increase the frequency.
  b Reduce the amplitude.
8 The air in the flute vibrates as you blow across the mouthpiece.
9 Ultrasound is non-ionising and is therefore relatively harmless compared with X-rays which are ionising.
10 To produce and detect ultrasound pulses.
11 At each tissue boundary, some of the waves must pass through the boundary in order to reach boundaries further away. If the waves were reflected totally at the first boundary, waves could not reach any further boundaries.
12 0.075 m

Answers to Examination-style questions

1 a 26.5 s (1)
  b 0.0166 m/s (2)
  c Reaction time starting and stopping the stopwatch differed each time or the difficulty in deciding where the exact crest of a wave is. (1)
2 a The vibrations of a transverse wave are perpendicular to the direction of propagation of the wave whereas the vibrations of a longitudinal wave are parallel to the direction of propagation. (2)
  b i Infrared radiation, light. (2)
    ii Infrared radiation is absorbed by the Earth's atmosphere; light is refracted and partly absorbed by the Earth's atmosphere. (2)
  c The signals from the terrestrial transmitter pass over the valley as they are not diffracted enough by the hill to reach the valley. The satellite signals travel in a straight line from the satellite to each receiver. (2)
  d i A metallic surface reflects the microwaves so the dish focuses the reflected microwaves onto the aerial. (2)
    ii Diffraction; The signal is weaker at the edge than elsewhere in the reception area. If the dish points directly at the satellite, the received signal is just strong enough to be detected at the edge. A large dish diffracts the microwaves less than a small dish and therefore focuses them to a smaller area. This makes the signal harder to detect if the dish doesn't point directly at the satellite. (2)
3 a Sound waves of frequencies which cannot be heard by the normal human ear (or above about 20 000 Hz). (1)
  b i There is a clear description of partial reflection at boundaries between different tissues and a recognition that there is also a transmitted pulse which may be partially reflected at further boundaries. The answer has very few errors of spelling, punctuation and grammar. It is coherent and in an organised, logical sequence. It contains a range of appropriate or relevant specialist terms used accurately. (5–6)

There is a description of partial reflection at boundaries between different tissues and some recognition that there may be reflections at further boundaries. The answer has some errors of spelling, punctuation and grammar but has some structure and organisation. The use of specialist terms has been attempted but not always accurately. (3–4)

There is little or no reference to reflection at boundaries between different tissues and only limited recognition that a pulse may be reflected from more than one boundary. Spelling, punctuation and grammar are very poor and there is little organisation in the answer. Little or no use has been made of specialist terms. (1–2)

Examples of physics points:
- When a pulse from the transducer reaches a boundary between two different types of soft tissue, the pulse is partially reflected.
- The partially reflected pulse travels back to the transmitter.
- As the pulse is not totally reflected, it is partially transmitted as well as being partially reflected.
- The transmitted pulse may reach further boundaries which cause partial reflection.
- Several reflected pulses may return to the transducer from each pulse it sends out.

  ii The boundary that reflects the pulse is 93 mm inside the body. (2)

  c Ultrasound waves are non-ionising unlike X-rays. Ionising radiation is harmful because it damages cells. (2)

10 Reflection and refraction of light

10.1
1 60°
2 3.0 m
3 Draw a straight line AB on a sheet of paper. Mark a point P on the line and use a protractor to draw the normal at the point. Draw straight lines through P at several different angles to the normal. Number the lines. Place the mirror exactly on the line AB and direct the light ray from the ray box at P along each numbered line so the ray reflects. Mark the path of each reflected ray for each incident ray. Remove the mirror and use the protractor to measure the angle of incidence and the angle of reflection of each of the numbered lines.

10.2
1 The speed of light in water is greater than in glass.
2 Red

10.3
1 200 000 km/s
2 27°
3 50°
4 A systematic error.

10.4
1 a 42°
    b 1.39
2 a X
    b X. X retains more light because its critical angle is greater than Y's critical angle so more light is totally internally reflected in X.

Answers to end of Chapter 10 questions

1 The line perpendicular to the boundary at the point of incidence.
2 a 40°
    b 80°
3 An increase of 2°.
4 1.0 m
5 Virtual
6 1.33
7 13°
8 41°
9 90°
10 The angle of incidence must be greater than the critical angle.
11 red light
12 The speed of light in glass is less than the speed in water.

11 Lenses and the eye

11.1
1 a real
    b inverted
    c diminished
2 a virtual
    b upright
    c diminished
3 Place the lens on the stamp and observe the stamp through the lens. Raise the lens above the stamp and the stamp will be seen magnified.

11.2
1 The first row (Object beyond 2F).
2 The image is real, inverted and magnified.
3 a The image is virtual, upright and smaller in size than the object.
    b The image is on the same side of the lens as the object and is nearer the lens than the object is.

11.3
1 0.3 m
2 a 1.0 m on the same side of the lens as the object.
    b i virtual
      ii upright
      iii larger
3 The location of the image position is less precise than the object position because it is not easy to tell the position of the image where it is in sharpest focus.

11.4
1 a The iris controls the amount of light passing through the eye lens.
    b The ciliary muscles control the thickness of the eye lens.
2 The ciliary muscles relax so the eye lens becomes thinner, enabling it to focus clearly on the distant object.
3 The iris makes the eye pupil become narrower so less light passes through the eye lens.

11.5
1 a +4.0 D
    b −5.0 D
2 a A converging lens.
    b The eyeball may be too long or the eye lens may be unable to become thin enough.

Answers to end of Chapter 11 questions

1 The point where rays parallel to the principal axis converge after passing through the lens.
2 A converging lens focuses the light rays so they converge at the principal focus. A diverging lens makes the light rays diverge as if they appear to originate at the principal focus.
3 4
4 a Nearer
    b Smaller
5 a

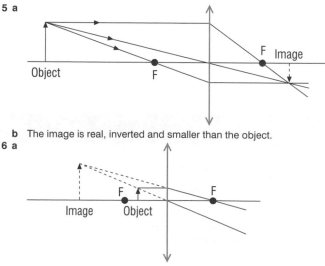

  b The image is real, inverted and smaller than the object.
6 a

  b 3

7 $v = (-)30.0\,\text{cm}$

8 $v = -6.0\,\text{cm}$ so the image is 6.0 cm from the lens on the same side of the lens as the object and is virtual, upright, smaller in size than the object.

9 a The nearest point to the eye of an object that is seen in focus.

  b The furthest point to the eye of an object that is seen in focus.

10 a +2.5 D

  b Long sight.

11 See Table 1 Topic 11.4.

12 a Short sight.

  b The eyeball is too long or the eye lens is too powerful.

  c A diverging lens.

12 Red-shift

▶ 12.1

1 a Its wavelength is increased.

  b Its frequency is increased.

2 a Y

  b Z

3 The further away a distant galaxy is, the greater its red-shift is so the faster it is moving away from us. This means the universe must be expanding.

▶ 12.2

1 The Big Bang, which was a massive explosion in which the universe originated at a very small point.

2 a Gamma radiation.

  b Microwave radiation.

Answers to end of Chapter 12 questions

1 The change of wavelength of waves from a moving source due to the motion of the source.

2 The increase in the wavelength of light from a light source moving away from the observer.

3 The faster a galaxy is moving away from us, the greater its red-shift is.

4 The galaxy is moving towards us and is not a distant galaxy.

5 a Q

  b Q is moving away faster than P is.

6 The further away a distant galaxy is from us, the greater its red-shift is.

7 The further a galaxy is from us, the greater its red-shift is so the faster it is moving away. This is explained by assuming the universe is expanding.

8 The universe originated in a massive explosion and has been expanding ever since.

9 Microwave radiation that can be detected coming from all directions in space.

10 It was created as gamma radiation just after the Big Bang.

11 It is low-energy microwave radiation that comes from all directions in space.

12 The universe originated in a massive explosion.

Answers to Examination-style questions

1 a There is a clear description of how the angles of incidence and refraction are measured using a protractor, including drawing the normal at P and measuring the angles to the normal. Knowledge of how to calculate the refractive index from the measured angles should be present. There should also be a clear recognition that repeating the measurements for different incident angles to obtain several values of the refractive index and hence an average value gives a more accurate value for the refractive index. The answer has very few errors of spelling, punctuation and grammar. It is coherent and in an organised, logical sequence. It contains a range of appropriate or relevant specialist terms used accurately. (5–6)

There is some description of how the angles of incidence and refraction are measured using a protractor, including drawing the normal at P. Knowledge of how to calculate the refractive index from the measured angles should be present. The answer has some errors of spelling, punctuation and grammar but has some structure and organisation. The use of specialist terms has been attempted but not always accurately. (3–4)

There is little or no clarity in the description of how the angles of incidence and refraction are measured using a protractor. Little or no awareness of the need to draw the normal is shown. Knowledge of how to calculate the refractive index from the measured angles may be absent or incorrect. Spelling, punctuation and grammar are very poor and there is little organisation in the answer. Little or no use has been made of specialist terms. (1–2)

Examples of physics points:

- Trace the outline of the block on paper, locate P and draw the normal at P.
- Remove the block and draw a line for the incident ray path at a measured angle to the normal.
- Place the block on the outline and direct the light ray at P as in Figure 1 along the ray path line.
- Mark the direction of the refracted ray where it leaves the block then remove the block and draw the refracted ray. Measure the angle of refraction.
- Use sin i/sin r to calculate the angle of refraction.
- Repeat for other angles of incidence.
- Calculate an average value for the refractive index.

  b i 41° (2)

    ii Total internal reflection is where a light ray in a transparent substance reaches a boundary with a less refractive substance or air at an angle of incidence such that it reflects at the boundary instead of passing through the boundary. (2)

    iii (3)

Incident ray

Reflected ray

2 a i Short sight or myopia. (1)

    ii The minimum power of the eye lens is too great or the eyeball is too long. (1)

  b i +2.5 D (1)

    ii The thinner lens; if it was made of lower refractive index, its focal length would be longer and its optical power would be less so it would be unable to correct the sight defect. (2)

3 a The further away a distant galaxy is, the faster it is moving away from us. (1)

  b The universe is expanding. (1)

  c Electromagnetic radiation that was created soon after the Big Bang (the event that created the universe) and has been stretched to much longer wavelengths by the expansion of the universe. (2)

  d It can only be explained by the Big Bang theory of the universe. (1)

13 Kinetic theory

▶ 13.1

1 In a liquid the particles move about at random; in a solid, they vibrate about fixed positions.

2 The particles in a liquid are in contact with each other whereas the particles in a gas are separated by relatively large distances. Therefore particles in a gas occupy much more space than in a liquid.

▶ 13.2

1 a i 2100 J

    ii 10 500 J

  b 4500 J

2 Measure the temperature of the block every minute for 5 minutes after the heater was switched off. The temperature should not decrease during this time if the insulation is effective. In practice no insulation is perfect so the temperature would decrease very slowly over a longer period of time.

3 42 000 J

▶ 13.3

1 a 0 °C

  b It is below 0 °C.

2 Evaporation takes place from the surface of a liquid below its boiling point. Boiling takes place throughout a liquid at its boiling point.

3 The temperature of the flat section of the graph gives the melting point.

13.4

1 0.23 MJ
2 Energy transfer from the surroundings is the same with the heater on as it is with it off. This is because the temperature difference between the ice and the surroundings in the same. Thus $m_2 - m_1$ is the mass of ice melted due to the energy from heater.
3 340 000 J/kg

Answers to end of Chapter 13 questions

1 The particles in a gas move much faster than in a liquid and they have more kinetic energy.
2 A liquid is much more dense than a gas or a liquid has a surface.
3 a The particles move away from each other and become a gas.
   b The particles form a rigid structure.
4 Water changes to water vapour at the surfaces in your lungs making the air in the lungs moist. Water vapour in the air from your lungs condenses on the cold window and forms a film of liquid on the glass.
5 The process in which a liquid changes to a gas at the surface of the liquid.
6 1.5 MJ (to 2 s.f.)
7 The steel panel.
8 The energy needed to melt 1 kg of the substance at its melting point.
9 920 kJ
10 a 2.52 kJ
    b 2.7 kJ (2.688 kJ)
    c 52 s
11 0.049 kg
12 Y

14 Energy transfer by heating

14.1

1 a Metals are good conductors so they transfer heat energy effectively. Wood is a poor conductor so it does not become as hot as the metal and so the handle can be used to lift the pan without burning the hands.
   b Metals contain free electrons that can transfer energy whereas insulators do not have free electrons so energy transfer is not as good in an insulator as in a metal.
2 a Air is a poor conductor so it cuts down energy transfer by conduction. As the air is trapped, heat cannot be transferred by convection.
   b A duvet contains light, insulating materials that contain trapped air. So it is a poor conductor.
3 The rate of decrease of the water temperature depends on how much water is in the beaker as well as how well insulated the beaker is. The effect of the insulation could not be deduced if the amount of water was not the same each time.

14.2

1 a Convection currents cannot flow in a solid, as particles in a solid are not free to move.
   b The fluid expands when heated so a given mass of the fluid has a greater volume when heated. Hence its density is less.
2 The gases from the fire are less dense than the surrounding air as they expand when heated. So they rise above the fire and go up the chimney.

14.3

1 It would increase.
2 Evaporation from the liquid would increase and the liquid would cool due to evaporation.
3 a Someone in the car would release moisture (water vapour) in the air when breathing out. The water vapour would circulate in the car and condense as a thin film of water on the cold windscreen.
   b Warm air across the windscreen would cause the film of water to evaporate.
4 Molecules escape at a faster rate so the cooling effect would be greater.

14.4

1 The higher the temperature, the greater the energy loss per second due to radiation emitted from its surface.
2 The Moon has no atmosphere so infrared radiation emitted from its surface travels directly into space. The Earth's atmosphere absorbs infrared radiation so it keeps the Earth warmer.
3 Not enough energy would be transferred by the radiation to the thermometer so the temperature change would be too small to detect.

14.5

1 a A white surface is a poor absorber of infrared radiation and it reflects it.
   b Black surfaces are good emitters of infrared radiation.
2 The pipes are designed to transfer energy to the surroundings from inside the radiator. So if they are painted black, they emit more infrared radiation per second than if they were painted any other colour.
3 A shiny surface does not heat up when sunlight is incident on it as it reflects infrared radiation from the Sun much more effectively than a black surface. A black surface would heat up too much and may therefore be damaged by excessive heating. A shiny surface also radiates less infrared radiation at night so stops the building cooling too much at night.
4 The mass of water is a control variable that needs to be the same otherwise the temperature comparison would not be valid.

14.6

1 The fins increase the surface area of the heat sink and hence increase the emission of infrared radiation from the heat sink.
2 A dull black surface is a more effective radiator of infrared radiation than any other surface.
3 Air is a good insulator so in small pockets helps to reduce energy transfer by conduction and by convection.
4 The plastic cap, the container, the cover, the sponge pad, the plastic spring.

14.7

1 It expands.
2 X is on the outside of the bend.
3 The spring makes the valve open when the thermostat cools and close when it is too hot.

Answers to end of Chapter 14 questions

1 The particles vibrate and transfer energy from the hotter parts where the vibrations are more energetic to the cooler parts.
2 Wool itself is a poor conductor and the fibres of wool contain trapped air which also is a poor conductor.
3 A convection current is a flow of liquid or gas caused by heating the liquid or gas making it expand and rise, causing circulation of the liquid or the gas.
4 Evaporation
5 The wind increases evaporation of water from the wet clothing.
6 The vacuum cuts out heat transfer by conduction and by convection.
7 A black surface absorbs infrared radiation, in this case from the Sun, more effectively than a silvered surface.
8 At the end of the race, the runner is likely to be hot and sweaty. The runner would heat the air trapped by the blanket and the air would transfer energy to the blanket. A silvered foil blanket is a poor emitter of infrared radiation. So it would reduce energy loss from the runner. Also, the shiny surface on the inside of the blanket would reflect infrared radiation from the runner's body so further reducing energy transfer to the blanket.
9 a A metal is a good conductor so would conduct energy effectively from a hot component to the surface of the heat sink which would then lose energy to the surroundings.
   b The fins increase the surface area.
10 It reduces energy transfer by infrared radiation so the house would lose less energy.
11 a X
    b Turn the contact screw so it is further from X.
12 The balloon surface emits infrared radiation to the surroundings and it also warms the air it is in contact with, so it also loses energy by convection.

15 Energy transfers and efficiency theory

15.1

1 a Chemical energy in the battery → electrical energy → light energy + energy transferred to the surroundings by heating + energy transferred to the wires by resistance heating.
   b Chemical energy in the fuel → energy transferred to the surroundings by infrared radiation + light energy + sound energy.
2 Descent: gravitational potential energy changes to kinetic energy of the pendulum + energy transferred to the surroundings by air resistance.
   Ascent: kinetic energy changes to gravitational potential energy + energy transferred to the surroundings by air resistance.

15.2

1 Some is usefully transferred to the surroundings as light and the rest is wasted by heating the surroundings.
2 It is transferred to the surroundings, as the frictional forces that prevent the lift accelerating heat the lift brakes.

15.3
1 a 20%
  b 80%
2 a 60 W
  b 20%

15.4
1 a Glass is a poor conductor and glass fibre contains pockets of air which is a good insulator.
  b It has a shiny silvery surface so it is a poor absorber of infrared radiation.
2 20 years.

Answers to end of Chapter 15 questions

1 a Kinetic energy.
  b Elastic potential energy.
2 a A hairdryer changes electrical energy to energy that heats the air and to kinetic energy of the air.
  b Electrical energy changes to light energy and sound energy.
3 Gravitational potential energy changes to kinetic energy and elastic potential energy of the cord.
4 a Energy that is transferred to where it is wanted in the form it is wanted.
  b Energy that is transferred and is not useful energy.
5 Kinetic energy of the machinery.
6 Energy used to heat the food container, sound from the rotating turntable and heating of the moving parts due to friction.
7 Three-quarters (0.75)
8 The fan wastes energy due to the frictional forces between its moving parts. So for a certain amount of energy supplied to the heater, the useful energy transferred and hence the efficiency is less.
9 42 J
10 9600 J
11 a 750 000 J
   b 250 s
12 a 32 000 J
   b 25 200 J
   c 79% (78.75%)
   d Energy is used to heat the beaker and to rotate the turntable.

Answers to Examination-style questions

1 a 840 kJ (1)
  b i 672 kJ (2)
    ii 59 kJ (2)
    iii Energy is transferred to the surrounding by heating as a result of conduction through the kettle walls, convection of air in contact with the hot kettle and infrared radiation emitted from the hot kettle surface. (3)
  c A bimetallic strip consists of two equal lengths of different metals joined together and fixed at one end. When the temperature of the strip is increased, one metal (X) expands more than the other (Y) so the strip bends with X on the outside of the bend. In the kettle, X initially presses against a contact screw to complete the kettle circuit. When the temperature of the strip reaches 100 °C, the strip has bent so much that it is no longer in contact with the contact screw so the current is switched off. (3)
2 a i 1 Evaporation takes place at the surface of the liquid whereas boiling takes place throughout the liquid.
      2 Evaporation takes place from the liquid at any temperature whereas boiling takes place only at the boiling point of the liquid. (2)
    ii Some of the molecules have enough kinetic energy to escape from the surface of the liquid. Some molecules would return to the liquid but the steady wind carries them away. So there is a net loss of the more energetic molecules from the liquid. The average kinetic energy of the liquid molecules decreases so their temperature falls. (3)
  b i Liquid to vapour. (1)
    ii Vapour to liquid. (1)
    iii Conduction (1)
    iv The substance at this stage is hot and may transfer energy through the pipe walls back to the room. (1)
    v The heat exchanger pipes lose energy as they are hot so they emit infrared radiation. The rate of energy transfer by radiation is greater from a black surface than from any other surface. (2)
3 a The energy transfer through the double-glazed window is half the energy transfer through the single-glazed window. (1)
  b There is a clear description of where and why conduction, convection and radiation contribute to the energy transfers through the double-glazed window and a clear recognition of which of these processes are absent in

the vacuum space. Recognition of the effect of wavelength on the absorption by glass of infrared radiation may be present. There should also be a clear recognition of where and which processes are reduced in the double-glazed window in comparison with the single-glazed window. The answer has very few errors of spelling, punctuation and grammar. It is coherent and in an organised, logical sequence. It contains a range of appropriate or relevant specialist terms used accurately. (5–6)

There is some description of where and why conduction, convection and radiation contribute to the energy transfers through the double-glazed window and some recognition of which of these processes are absent in the vacuum space. There should also be some recognition of which processes are reduced in the double-glazed window in comparison with the single-glazed window. The answer has some errors of spelling, punctuation and grammar but has some structure and organisation. The use of specialist terms has been attempted but not always accurately. (3–4)

There is little or no description of where and why conduction, convection and radiation contribute to the energy transfers through the double-glazed window and little or no recognition of which of these processes are absent in the vacuum space. There is little or no recognition of where and which processes are reduced in the double-glazed window in comparison with the single-glazed window. Spelling, punctuation and grammar are very poor and there is little organisation in the answer. Little or no use has been made of specialist terms. (1–2)

Examples of physics points
- Conduction takes place through the glass but not through the vacuum.
- Glass is a poor conductor.
- Convection in the air takes place at and near the outer surface of the window.
- (Short wavelength) Infrared radiation passes through the glass and the vacuum. Long wavelength infrared radiation is absorbed by the glass.
- Conduction through double-glazed unit is less than through the single-glazed window because it has two panes of glass so the total thickness of glass is greater.
- Convection cannot occur in a vacuum.
- Less convection occurs at the outer surface of the double-glazed window because its outer surface is colder than that of the single-glazed window.
- More infrared radiation is absorbed by the glass in the double-glazed unit because the total thickness of glass is greater.

16 Electric circuits

16.1
1 The cloth.
2 a They repel each other.
  b They attract each other.

16.2
1 60 C
2 a

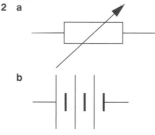

  b

16.3
1 The same current passes through the ammeter and the component when they are in series.
2 48 J
3 a 1.5 Ω
  b 0.75 V

16.4
1 More than 1.0 A.
2 Repeat the measurement for that current and use the new measurement to plot a new point.
3 It emits light when it is forward biased (or when current passes through it).
4 a Its resistance increases.
  b An equal current passes through it in the opposite direction.

16.5

1 The current in the circuit is zero.

2 a

6.0V

4Ω 8Ω

   b i 12Ω
      ii 0.5A

16.6

1 No current passes through that component. The current passing through each of the other components is unchanged (except for the battery as less current passes through it).

2 a The pd across each component is the same as the supply pd.
   b The supply current is equal to the sum of the currents through each component.

3 a

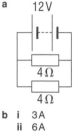

12V

4Ω

4Ω

   b i 3A
      ii 6A

Answers to end of Chapter 16 questions

1 a Negative charge
   b Positively charged

2 Negative

3 3000 C

4 a

   b The diode could be reverse-biased; one of the cells could be the wrong way round.

5 60Ω

6 4.5V

7 The reading decreases because the resistance of the thermistor increases.

8 Its reverse resistance is much much larger than its forward resistance.

9 a The current decreases.
   b The pd across R decreases.

10 0.5A

11

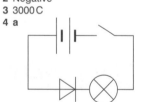

A

V

12 a

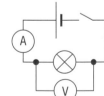

12V

12Ω

4Ω

   b i 3A through the 4Ω resistor; 1A through the 12Ω resistor.
      ii 4A

17 Household electricity

17.1

1 a 0V
   b 650V

2 Each half-cycle wave would be replaced by a flat section and the flat sections would be replaced by 'inverted' half-cycle waves.

17.2

1 Brass is a good conductor that does not oxidise or rust.

2 a two-core
   b three-core

17.3

1 3A

2 a It can be used again.
   b It works faster.

17.4

1 a 3kW
   b 540 000 J

2 a 8.7A
   b 13A

3 2300W

4 Use the joulemeter to measure the energy supplied to the heater in exactly 300s when the heater pd is exactly 12V. Divide the energy measurement by 300s to obtain the power of the heater according to the joulemeter. Compare this with the measurement using the ammeter and the voltmeter.

17.5

1 240C

2 a 46 000 J
   b 72 000 J

17.6

1 a 12kWh
   b 0.72kWh

2 a 1006kWh
   b £140.84

17.7

1 Tap water conducts electricity. If your hands were wet, the electrical resistance would be lowered so a larger current would pass through your body if the appliance case was not at zero potential.

2 It becomes hot and heats the bulb and its holder. It transfers more energy by heating than by emitting light.

17.8

1 They are more easily accessed. They are unaffected when the land floods.

2 a Step-down
   b Step-up

Answers to end of Chapter 17 questions

1 a 50Hz
   b 325V

2 The power transferred to a mains heater from the mains is the same as would be transferred if a 230V dc supply was used instead.

3 a Blue
   b 0V

4 a The earth wire.
   b To prevent the case becoming live; if it were not earthed and it became live, anyone touching the case would receive an electric shock which might be fatal.

5 Cable: insulation worn away, bare wire exposed. Plug: chipped or cracked, cable stay loose, wire broken from a terminal inside the plug.

6 a 5A
   b The 1A and 3A fuses would melt when the oven is switched on. When working normally, the appliance current is 4.3A so the 13A fuse would not melt if due to a fault. The current is significantly above 4.3 A and below 13A.

7 a 3A
   b 900C

8 a The circuit breaker can be reused. It cannot be replaced as readily by a circuit breaker with a different current rating.
   b It cuts the live wire off if the current in the live wire differs from the current in the neutral wire. The ordinary circuit breaker cuts the live wire off if the live current exceeds a certain value.

9 1.8MJ

10 a 0.060 A
   b 0.72 J
11 a Heater 4.6 kWh; lamp 0.24 kWh; microwave oven 0.20 kWh
   b 60.5p
12 For a given amount of electrical power transferred, less energy is wasted due to resistance heating of the cables because the current can be much smaller at high voltage.

18 Motors, generators and transformers

▶ 18.1
1 A south pole
2 a A: south pole, B: north pole
   b It is uniform (or the field lines are parallel).

▶ 18.2
1 Clockwise
2 a When the electromagnet is on, the switch is pulled open and it switches the electromagnet off. When the electromagnet is off, the switch closes and switches the electromagnet on.
   b It is an electrically operated switch. It is used to switch on a device in a separate circuit.
3 The graph should start at the origin and curve up with a decreasing gradient and tending to flatten out. The wire is north of the compass and in this position the magnetic field of the wire is at 90° to the Earth's magnetic field. As the current is increased, the magnetic field of the wire increases so the compass deflects more and more in the direction of the field of the wire.

▶ 18.3
1 a To your left.
   b Nothing, it is unchanged.
2 The forces are equal in magnitude but one force acts upwards and the other one downwards.

▶ 18.4
1 The induced current reverses.
2 a There is no induced current so the meter pointer remains at zero.
   b Using a coil with more turns of wire; using a stronger magnet; moving the magnet faster.

▶ 18.5
1 a There would be fewer waves on the screen and they would be smaller in height.
   b The waves would be inverted.
2 The waveform would be inverted.
3 a Brighter
   b No visible difference.

▶ 18.6
1 A steady direct current would not produce a changing magnetic field so there would be no induced pd in the secondary coil.
2 Iron is magnetised and demagnetised more easily than steel.
3 The 800 turn coil.

▶ 18.7
1 a By stepping up the pd, the same power can be delivered with a lower current through the cables. So the heating effect due to the resistance of the cables would be less.
   b 250
2 a 8 V
   b 0.25 A

Answers to end of Chapter 18 questions

1 a Iron can be magnetised and demagnetised much more easily than steel.
   b An electromagnet can be switched on and off. A permanent magnet cannot be switched off so it would not be able to release iron objects it picked up.
2 They are circles centred on the wire in a plane perpendicular to the wire.
3 a South in a horizontal plane.
   b It would be north in a horizontal plane.
4 It reverses the current in the coil every time the coil moves through half a turn. This ensures the forces on the sides of the coil always act to turn the coil in the same direction as the coil rotates.
5 a The ammeter pointer deflects briefly.
   b The pointer stays at zero until the magnet starts to move then it deflects slightly in the opposite direction to when the magnet was pushed into the coil.

6 a The peak voltage is smaller and the frequency is lower.
   b The peak voltage would be larger and the frequency would be unchanged.
7 The dc generator waveform consists of repeat positive half-cycles whereas the ac waveform has alternate positive and negative half-cycles.
8 a It is much higher.
   b It is lighter and smaller (or it uses less power).
9 a 50
   b 4800 V
10 a 0.05 A
   b 12 W
11 The step-up transformer increases the pd of the grid cables which means the same power can be transferred through them with less current. As the current is less, energy transferred to the cables by the heating effect of the current is less so less power is wasted. The step-down transformer decreases the pd supplied to the mains cables that are connected to the consumer.

Answers to Examination-style questions

1 a There is a clear and correct procedure described including checking the zero readings and repeating the measurements for at least five different values of current. In addition, reference should be made to measuring and recording in a table all the readings of both meters. Awareness is evident of how to change the current and of the maximum current and/or of good practice such as obtaining approximately equally spaced readings. The answer has very few errors of spelling, punctuation and grammar. It is coherent and in an organised, logical sequence. It contains a range of appropriate or relevant specialist terms used accurately. (5–6)

There is a clear procedure described including checking the zero readings and repeating the measurements for at least three different values of current. In addition, reference should be made to measuring and recording in a table all the readings of both meters and there should be an awareness of how to change the current and/or of the maximum current. The answer has some errors of spelling, punctuation and grammar but has some structure and organisation. The use of specialist terms has been attempted but not always accurately. (3–4)

There are few or no appropriate procedures described and only limited recognition of what the variable resistor is used for or that readings at different currents should be obtained. Spelling, punctuation and grammar are very poor and there is little organisation in the answer. Little or no use has been made of specialist terms. (1–2)

Examples of physics points:
Check the meters read zero (by opening the switch).
- Draw a table to record the ammeter and voltmeter readings.
- Adjust the variable resistor until the current is about 0.06 A.
- Measure and record the ammeter and voltmeter readings.
- Repeat the measurements for at least five more values of the current between 0 and 0.06 A at roughly equal spaced intervals. (3)

b i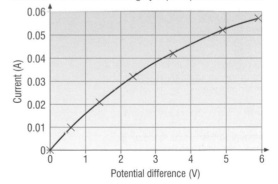
(3)

ii 3.0 V, 79 Ω; 6.0 V, 105 Ω (2)
iii The current is larger at 6 V than at 3 V. The larger the current is, the hotter the lamp. The resistance of the filament increases with increase of temperature. This is because the atoms of the filament vibrate more and make it more difficult for conduction electrons to pass through. (3)
c i 2160 C (2)
ii 13 000 J to 2 significant figures (2)
2 a i A 0.5 A, B 3.0 A (2)
ii 3.5 A (1)
iii The fuse cuts the current off if the current exceeds the fuse rating (1)

iv With both lamps on, the current in the circuit is 3.5 A. If a fault developed and the current increased, the 5 A fuse would melt if the current exceeded 5 A. If a 3 A fuse was used, it would melt every time both lamps were switched on. If a 13 A fuse was used and a fault developed which caused the current to exceed 5 A but not 13 A, the current might cause the wires or the battery to overheat. (3)

b i Both lamps would be either on or off. (1)

ii In the parallel circuit, both lamps would be at normal brightness. Because A's resistance is much higher than B's resistance, when they are in series most of the battery pd would be across A. So A would be almost as bright as normal but B would be much less bright. (3)

19 Radioactivity

19.1

1 a The nucleus.
  b Its nucleus is stable.
2 A process that cannot be predicted.
3 The radiation from a radioactive substance is emitted at random from a nucleus.

19.2

1 92 protons, 146 neutrons
2 a 90
  b 234
3 a 7
  b 14

19.3

1 a Gamma radiation.
  b Beta and gamma radiation.
2 a Alpha radiation.
  b It is uncharged.

19.4

1 It has decreased to a quarter of what it was.
2 37.5 counts per minute

19.5

1 Neither produce sufficient ionisation in air.
2 Too thick.
3 It is absorbed by the body and so cannot be detected outside the body. It would cause damage to living cells if ingested.
4 Wood does not contain uranium.

Answers to end of Chapter 19 questions

1 a 2 protons and 2 neutrons
  b An electron
  c Electromagnetic radiation.
2 a 27 protons and 33 neutrons.
  b i A neutron changes to a proton.
    ii There is no change.
3 a It decreases by 4.
  b It decreases by 2.
4 $^{60}_{27}Co \rightarrow \ ^{0}_{-1}\beta + \ ^{60}_{28}Ni$
5 a Ionising radiation from sources around us all.
  b Radon gas in the air, radioactive substances in the ground or in food and drink, cosmic radiation.
6 a α radiation
  b γ radiation
  c β radiation
7 a It is uncharged so there is no force on it.
  b It carries the opposite type of charge.
8 35 hours
9 a 25 million
  b 7000 years
10 a It is absorbed by metal foil so it would not reach the detector.
  b γ radiation can be detected outside the body; the activity of the tracer sample in the body would decrease quickly.

20 Energy from the nucleus

20.1

1 a Uranium with more uranium-235 than natural uranium, usually 2–3% uranium-235.
  b A fissionable nucleus needs to absorb a neutron.
2 The chain reactions would multiply and the rate of fission events would become uncontrollable.

20.2

1 The temperature outside the core is not high enough.
2 To heat the plasma to a sufficiently high temperature for fusion to occur.

20.3

1 Its nuclei emit alpha particles which would damage or kill cells in the lungs if radon gas was inhaled and so possibly cause cancer.
2 Ionising radiation from the waste is harmful to health; the waste materials may have long half-lives.

20.4

1 It decreased.
2 A collection of billions of stars held together by their own gravitational attraction.

20.5

1 The gravitational force that acts inwards is balanced by the force of the outflow of radiation.
2 a The object that remains after a supernova explosion of a high mass star. It consists only of neutrons.
  b The object that remains after a very high mass star explodes as a supernova. Its gravitational field is strong enough to prevent light escaping.

20.6

1 Iron
2 It was created in the collapse of a high mass star which then exploded as a supernova.

Answers to end of Chapter 20 questions

1 Uranium-235 and plutonium-239
2 a It splits into two smaller nuclei.
  b 2 or 3 neutrons and energy.
3 a A sequence of fission reactions in which one or more fission neutrons go on to cause further fission.
  b 1
4 a They absorb fission neutrons.
  b Uranium-238 and plutonium-239 are removed and stored securely for later use. The remaining material is stored securely for many years.
5 a The fusing together of two nuclei to form a larger nucleus.
  b Protons (or hydrogen nuclei) are fused to form helium nuclei.
6 a The nuclei to be fused repel each other when they are brought close together so higher temperatures are needed.
  b An electric current is passed through it.
7 a Alpha particles damage or kill living cells. The skin absorbs alpha particles so they would not be able to enter the body from outside.
  b Beta and gamma radiation can pass into the body where their ionising effect can damage or kill living cells.
8 Clouds of hydrogen and helium.
9 a The main sequence.
  b It will expand to become a red giant then collapse into a white dwarf then it will fade out and become a black dwarf.
10 a It will expand to become a red supergiant than it will collapse and then explode as a supernova, throwing matter far into space and leaving a core consisting of a neutron star.
  b The core remaining after a supernova explosion of a very high mass star.
11 a The explosion of a supergiant after it collapses on itself.
  b Elements heavier than iron existing on Earth were formed by nuclear fusion in the collapse of a supergiant which then exploded. The scattered matter including these heavy elements formed the protostar which eventually became the Sun.
12 a By nuclear fusion in the core of stars.
  b By nuclear fusion in the collapse of supergiants.

Answers to Examination-style questions

1 a i Isotopes are atoms of the same element with different numbers of neutrons. (1)

  ii 15 protons, 18 neutrons (2)

 b i A β particle is an electron that is created and emitted from an unstable nucleus when a neutron changes into a proton. (2)

  ii $^{33}_{15}P \rightarrow ^{33}_{16}S + ^{\ 0}_{-1}\beta$ (2)

 c i It is the average time taken for the number of unstable nuclei in (or the count rate from) a sample of the isotope to halve. (2)

  ii 25 days (2)

  iii 83 days (2)

2 a There is a clear description of what fission is, with an example of a fissionable isotope, and how fission is brought about and that energy is released in the process. There should also be a clear awareness of what a chain reaction is and how fission is controlled in a nuclear reactor. The answer has very few errors of spelling, punctuation and grammar. It is coherent and in an organised, logical sequence. It contains a range of appropriate or relevant specialist terms used accurately. (5–6)

   There is some description of what fission is, perhaps with an example of a fissionable isotope, and how fission is brought about and that energy is released in the process. There should some awareness of what a chain reaction is although knowledge of how fission is controlled in a nuclear reactor may be patchy. The answer has some errors of spelling, punctuation and grammar but has some structure and organisation. The use of specialist terms has been attempted but not always accurately. (3–4)

   There is little or no description of what fission is or how it occurs in a nuclear reactor although there should be an awareness that energy is released in each fission event. Awareness of what a chain reaction is is limited or absent. Spelling, punctuation and grammar are very poor and there is little organisation in the answer. Little or no use has been made of specialist terms. (1–2)

Examples of physics points:

- Fission is the splitting of a fissionable nucleus in two with the release of neutrons.
- Energy is released in the process.
- Example of a fissionable isotope U-235 or Pu-239.
- Fission occurs when a neutron hits the nucleus.
- Chain reaction is when one or more fission neutrons produce further fission.
- Steady release of energy requires one neutron per fission (on average) to produce further fission.
- Control rods used to ensure number of neutrons stays the same.
- Control rods absorb excess neutrons.

 b i Radiation that ionises substances that it passes through. Ionising radiation damages or kills living cells and can cause cancer. (2)

  ii Alpha radiation is the most ionising; gamma radiation is the least ionising. (2)

 c i 2 protons and 2 neutrons. (1)

  ii Alpha particles emitted from radon gas atoms in the lungs would be absorbed by lung tissue and would damage or kill lung cells and may cause lung cancer. (2)

3 a i A reaction in which two nuclei fuse together to form a larger nucleus. (1)

  ii Hydrogen nuclei are fused to form helium nuclei. (1)

 b i Stars much more massive than the Sun become red supergiants after the main sequence stage. When they can no longer fuse light elements, they collapse and the core is compressed. In this process, nuclei are fused together to form nuclei larger than iron in a very dense core. The layers surrounding the core collapse onto the core forming heavier and heavier nuclei and then rebounding in a supernova explosion, in which the layers surrounding the core rebound and are scattered into space. In this way, nuclei including heavy nuclei are scattered in space. (3)

  ii The Sun and the planets formed from the debris of a supernova. (1)